Letters and Epistolary Culture in Early Medieval China

Letters and Epistolary Culture in Early Medieval China

Antje Richter

A China Program Book
UNIVERSITY OF WASHINGTON PRESS *Seattle and London*

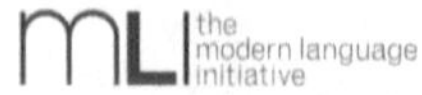

THIS BOOK IS MADE POSSIBLE BY A COLLABORATIVE GRANT FROM THE ANDREW W. MELLON FOUNDATION.

This book was supported in part by the China Studies Program, a division of the Henry M. Jackson School of International Studies at the University of Washington.

17 16 15 14 13 5 4 3 2 1

University of Washington Press
PO Box 50096, Seattle, WA 98145, USA
www.washington.edu/uwpress

Library of Congress Cataloging-in-Publication Data
Richter, Antje.
Letters and epistolary culture in early medieval China / Antje Richter.
pages cm
"A China Program book."
Includes bibliographical references and index.
ISBN 978-0-295-99277-8 (hardback : alk. paper)
ISBN 978-0-295-99278-5 (pbk. : alk. paper)
1. Letter writing, Chinese. 2. Chinese letters—History and criticism. 3. Chinese literature—220–589—History and criticism. I. Title.
PL2400.R53 2013
808.6'0951—dc23 2012046994

The paper used in this publication is acid-free and meets the minimum requirements of American National Standard for Information Sciences—Permanence of Paper for Printed Library Materials, ANSI Z39.48–1984.∞

What's your guess? Can I still get a letter by Sunday? It should be possible. But it's crazy, this passion for letters. Isn't a single one sufficient? Isn't knowing once sufficient? Certainly, it's sufficient, but nevertheless one leans far back and drinks in the letters and is aware of nothing but that one doesn't want to stop drinking.

—FRANZ KAFKA, letter to Milena Jesenská, May 29, 1920

CONTENTS

ACKNOWLEDGMENTS

This book has been in the making for more than a decade, but the debts I have accumulated while reading and writing about personal letters from early medieval China go back even further. My awareness of the genre and its literary and intellectual riches was raised during my studies in Munich (1989–98), where letters first turned up in Wolfgang Bauer's seminars on Chinese autobiographical literature. This teacher remains an enduring inspiration for me, well beyond Chinese Studies and well beyond his untimely death. It was several years later, after I had moved on to Kiel (1998–2006), that I started to focus my own research on Chinese epistolary literature and culture. Since then, I have benefited from countless conversations and correspondences with friends, colleagues, and students during my time in Kiel and Freiburg in Germany, and, after I came to the United States in 2007, in Boulder, Colorado. Among those who provided assistance, inspiration, criticism, and perspective, I would like to mention, in loose chronological order, Thomas Jansen, Franz Xaver Peintinger, Sabine Dabringhaus, Roland Winkler, Christian Soffel, Anja and Christoph Zuncke, Jeffrey Grossman, Gudula Linck, Christoph Harbsmeier, Robert Gassmann, Paul W. Kroll, Terry Kleeman, David R. Knechtges, Martin Kern, R. Joe Cutter, Ronald C. Egan, Robert E. Harrist, Annette Kieser, Nathan Sivin, Ute Engelhardt, Michael Nylan, Y. Edmund Lien, Enno Giele, Lai Guolong, Zhang Junmin, Chen Sougchang, and Joe P. McDermott. I am also truly appreciative of all the valuable comments from colleagues on the many occasions that I presented portions of this book at various conferences since 2002. I regret that I cannot name all of them. I owe special thanks to the two readers for the University of Washington Press, Tian Xiaofei and Cynthia Chennault, as well as to Matthew Wells, Kay Duffy, and Charles

Chace, who read the manuscript in various earlier versions and generously shared their perceptive comments and suggestions with me. Without them, this would be an even more flawed book. Of course, I am responsible for all the imperfections that remain.

I am grateful to the University of Colorado at Boulder for two semesters of leave in 2009 and 2010, which were a great help in bringing this project to completion. I would also like to acknowledge financial support for the preparation of the manuscript from the Center for Asian Studies at the University of Colorado at Boulder. My thanks moreover go to the editors of the *Journal of the American Oriental Society* in which an earlier version of the third part of this book's chapter 2 was published in 2007.

I also want to express my sincere gratitude to the team at the University of Washington Press and the Modern Language Initiative, who guided me gently and most effectively through the process of turning the manuscript into a book, in particular, Lorri Hagman, Tim Zimmermann, Laura Iwasaki, and Tim Roberts.

Finally, I thank Matthias, whose letters and messages I enjoy more than anybody else's—although not as much as his company.

Letters and Epistolary Culture in Early Medieval China

Introduction

Voices a myriad of years old are presented,
responses from a thousand of miles away are incited.
—LIU XIE, *The Literary Mind and the Carving of Dragons* (Wenxin diaolong)

Having grown up in the 1960s and 1970s, in a country where telephones were rare, I learned to consider mail as something that may hold great importance for my life. I vividly recall letters I received—longed for or arriving out of the blue—as well as letters I wrote myself, whether effortlessly or taking great pains. Unlike the e-mails and text messages that have come to replace this form of written communication since the early 1990s, letters are first of all material objects of a distinctive character and with a distinctive transportation history, having passed through many hands. We may fold and unfold them, flatten them and turn them over; we may crumple them or tear them up but also bundle and keep them. Messages that reach us electronically travel with great speed across great distances, although a certain characteristic time lag remains. Easy enough to read and answer, they are cumbersome to collect and store. To search through them in a file after a few years have passed is much less satisfying than to rummage through stacks of envelopes and sheets of rustling paper in different textures, sizes, and colors, bearing different handwritings in all kinds of tints, along with sketches, scrawls, stickers, and stamps. If they are old enough, letters may be faded, smell funny, and easily fall apart, stimulating our memories and imaginations through all the senses. So even if, in a way, we keep on writing "letters" and receiving "mail," probably with greater frequency than ever before in human history, it is not surprising that we prefer to call these electronic and largely dematerialized pieces of writing "texts" and "messages," thus emphasizing a difference between two forms of written communication that we obviously feel to be significant.

This most recent media change and its cultural implications have been studied extensively during the past two decades. Depending on a scholar's general outlook, the appraisals of this transformation differ widely: it may be either characterized dismissively as a cultural decline or embraced as a promising new development.[1] Whatever stand one may take on this issue, it is beyond doubt that the deficits of the new means of written communication—especially the loss of the material and sensual dimension of a letter but also the neglect of traditional epistolary conventions—are counterbalanced by considerable gains. Among these are the enhanced informality and dialogicity of written communication, which appear chiefly to be functions of the greater speed of transmission, as well as the development of a whole new world of words, phrases, complex symbols (such as emoticons), and distinct conventions that are peculiar to e-mails, text messages, and other forms of electronic communication.[2]

This media change is part of a longer process that has led to the almost complete abandonment of letters, one of the earliest-known types of written communication. In the West, the process started in the second half of the nineteenth century, when the typewriter, the telegraph, and the telephone dealt severe blows to the use of handwriting and all written communication.[3] From the beginning, this change triggered not only general concern about the supposed decline of letter writing as a key constituent of any society's communicative practice and literary culture but also scholarly interest of a rather nostalgic turn, often triggered by the particular materiality of traditional letters, which carry a broad spectrum of personal and historical marks, from the individuality of the handwriting to the various traces left by postal transmission. Just as letters themselves live on a handful of topoi—lamenting separation, concern for the recipient, letters as insufficient substitutes for face-to-face conversation, and so forth—so apparently does Western epistolary research, whose most conspicuous common topos is the decline of letter writing. The end of epistolary culture has long been predicted and has been rediscovered and reaffirmed time and again. One of the earliest such voices in Europe was that of Georg Steinhausen who in 1889 already assumed the end of epistolary history. In 1962, Theodor W. Adorno declared, in a preface to a letter collection originally edited by Walter Benjamin in 1936, that history had passed its judgment on letters as a literary form and that those who can still practice it possess "archaic abilities."[4] However, the denial of this variety of cultural pessimism is another common topos of epistolary research. In 1990, when a special edition of the journal *World Literature Today* pursued the question in "The Letter: A Dying Art?" most authors readily admitted to a decline in letter writing but, at the same time, were reluctant to speak of its demise, pointing out that we are witnessing "a magnificent autumnal flowering" of letter writing and suspecting that "perhaps, who knows, one day it may rise again from the tomb."[5] The list of autumn flowers is impressive indeed, given the corpora of letters that came to light during the past century. Some of them are gigantic in size, for instance, the 250,000 preserved letters and postcards by George Bernhard Shaw alone.[6] Others are fascinating because of their literary powers and startling frankness, such as the letters of Franz Kafka, Virginia Woolf, and many other prominent writers. Outside of the literary world, a crucial development in terms of epistolary research was the discovery, exploration, and publication of enormous collections of personal letters that were never meant to be published—such as war letters, immigrants' letters, women's letters—and yet have come to be appreciated as invaluable primary sources of history, language, and the culture of everyday life.[7]

EPISTOLARY RESEARCH IN CHINESE STUDIES AND BEYOND

In the West, research on epistolary cultures of the ancient and medieval world has been a thriving field for more than a century. Comprehensive and detailed studies on letter writing in Mesopotamia, Egypt, Greece, Rome, and medieval Europe have illuminated the fundamental questions of written communication in different societies and have made translations of letters from these cultures available to a wide audience.[8] In addition to these general studies, a great number of works have been published that are dedicated to specialized areas of investigation, from epistolary subgenres, letter-writing manuals, specific formal features of letters, letters written by specific groups of people (such as women or merchants) to letters by individual authors and epistolary fiction.[9] Letter writing in the early modern and modern periods has received even more scholarly attention, resulting in a rich body of secondary literature that provides fascinating insights into a broad range of fields, from history to literature to sociology, to name but a few.[10]

The same cannot be said of Chinese studies. In Sinology, scholars are not only a long way from the abundance and diversity of specialized research, as it is known from the West and Near East, but also lack basic studies. Western secondary literature on personal letter writing for China's entire imperial period (221 BCE—1911 CE) consists of no more than three unpublished dissertations,[11] a textbook on late imperial epistolary language,[12] and about three dozen articles,[13] (much less than has been written on the letters of Cicero or Pliny alone) and is utterly insufficient to do justice to more than two millennia of vibrant Chinese letter writing. Translations of Chinese letters into Western languages are also scarce. One of the most prolific translators of premodern Chinese letters remains Erwin von Zach (1872–1942), whose translations from *Selections of Refined Literature* (Wen xuan) into German include many official and personal letters.[14] So far there is only one publication that presents a sizable selection of Chinese epistolary literature through the ages, the 1994 edition of the Hong Kong journal *Renditions*, a collection of about forty famous letters in excellent English translations along with short commentaries. All in all, Chinese epistolary literature and culture are seriously underrepresented areas in Chinese studies that definitely deserve to be made visible, both within Chinese studies and for a wider audience in the humanities and beyond.

The reason for the lack of critical interest in the epistolary and the marginality of the genre is certainly not that letters were irrelevant in this part of the world. The significance of correspondence in China, whether official or personal, is beyond doubt. Written communication informed administrative processes, social and business networks, family relations, and personal friendships. Thousands of letters of all kinds became part of the transmitted corpus of Chinese literature. The neglect of letters and the epistolary sphere in China is due to a multitude of reasons, among which the absence of two major scholarly motivations appears to be foremost. First, letters play no remarkable role in the Confucian canon, that is to say, there is no Chinese equivalent to the epistles in the New Testament that were so decisive in instigating and sustaining research on letter writing in the West.[15] If the Confucian canon contained texts in letter form comparable to the Epistles of Paul, the genre would have had a very different history in China. Second, scholarly nostalgia for a vanishing mode of communication, a key motivator for research today, is only a recent phenomenon in China. In the West, concern about the supposed decline of letter writing emerged at the end of the nineteenth century. Owing to the peculiarities of the Chinese script (which rendered the typewriter impractical) and to the sparse distribution of the telephone in China for the greater part of the twentieth century, personal letter writing was very much alive and taken for granted until about the mid-1990s, when it abruptly started to be supplanted by new media such as e-mail, cellular phones, and text messaging.

Since the mid-1990s, interest in Chinese letters has been growing steadily, in both China and the West. A look at the prestigious *Cambridge History of China* confirms this rise in interest. While the early volumes of the 1980s do not even list "letters," "postal service," or similar subjects in their indexes, the latest volume, published in 1999, features a substantial chapter on the transportation of official documents and private letters via courier and postal systems.[16] A number of ongoing studies pursue promising approaches that either focus on letters or take epistolary material into account.[17] In China itself, the recent growth in epistolary awareness is not only noticeable on the art market, where handwritten letters can command exorbitant prices; it has also stimulated moderate scholarly interest.[18] The first and so far only book-length survey of Chinese epistolary literature in Chinese came out in 1999,[19] and articles about individual literary letters or correspondences are published occasionally.[20] However, in China, letters are still rarely perceived as a genre that needs and deserves to be treated on its own in order to realize its potential. Letters are utterly marginal, and if they are mentioned in more general literary scholarship at all, they are usually noted only because they constitute part of the literary oeuvre of an author or on account of their subject matter, but there is no reflection on the epistolary character of these texts.[21]

TEXTUAL SOURCES OF EARLY MEDIEVAL CHINESE LETTER WRITING

The majority of ancient and medieval Chinese letters have come down to us because they were considered to be of historical or literary value and were thus incorporated into other works: standard histories, encyclopedias, anthologies, collections of biographies, and so forth. We have little information about the particulars of this process, especially its beginning. It is not known, for instance, how personal letters achieved wider circulation and thus could be included in a standard history or any other received text. Did their authors copy them before they sent them off? Or did their recipients keep and disseminate them? Had these letters been published in any other way before they were incorporated in a received text?

Certainly letters were subjected to editorial interventions, mostly abridgments and embellishments, in order to adapt them to the requirements of their new literary environments.[22] While it is impossible to accurately assess the extent of literary enhancement the editors deemed appropriate, the pruning they effected is clearly evident, since it concerned mainly the largely formulaic frame of a letter. Unfortunately, it is precisely the frame that usually contains the most interesting information about both the particular context of a letter and contemporaneous epistolary practice, as some of the few apparently intact letters demonstrate. In beginning and concluding letters, authors usually mentioned the external and internal circumstances of their writing, sending, receiving, and reading letters and made reference to the tangible and emotional importance that these pieces of personal communication held for them. However, most editors obviously regarded the frame to be of little significance compared to the main text that all too often bears no trace of originally having been part of a letter but reads like a treatise instead. Of the more than two thousand extant letters and letter fragments from early medieval China, only about 10 percent seem to have been received in their entirety, with prescript and postscript intact; about 30 percent retain other parts of the epistolary frame, such as the proem or the epilogue. This means that in the process of reducing them to their perceived relevant core, most early medieval letters were practically "de-epistolarized" and turned into much less genre-specific vignettes. This editorial practice continues even today, despite a general awareness of the importance of genre for the appropriate understanding of a text.[23]

A second route of transmission, particularly relevant for early medieval China, is the collection and subsequent reproduction of letters that were cherished as masterpieces of calligraphy. Since these letters were transmitted not for literary or historical reasons but because of their visual appeal, they usually differ in content and character. Calligraphic letters generally are short, casual, and intimate and seem to represent the more quotidian of written communication. Although calligraphic letters may initially have been transmitted in their entirety and not deliberately modified, many of them eventually also suffered losses, either from material damage of the writing support or from textual damage of various kinds—not to mention the problem of forgery. Textual damage could be caused by misrepresentations during the process of transcription or by copying practices, which occasionally interfered with the original layout of the source document, produced only excerpts of a given letter, or combined originally unrelated texts into one piece.[24]

Finally, personal letters were and continue to be archaeologically recovered, albeit on a smaller scale than official communication, which is clearly prevalent among the manuscripts from early and early medieval China.[25] However, the amount and content of these manuscripts are hard to assess, as only the smallest portion of them has been published or is otherwise accessible.[26]

So even if an ample number of early medieval Chinese letters are available for scholarly investigation today, we need to be aware of the problematic nature of this corpus. A minor problem lies in the form this corpus takes, consisting mostly of fragmentary texts scattered all over medieval literature.[27] Not only must we accept that many of the transmitted texts are products of editing, but the composition of this corpus is also unlikely to be representative of letter writing at the time, which must have been much more extensive and diverse than what is known today. Although similar caveats need to be considered for other literary genres as well, the discrepancy in quantity and quality between the letters that were written at the time and those that have survived until today is much larger than in the case of other literary genres, such as poetry. The main reason for this difference is that no other genre was practiced by such a large part of society, including authors who were untrained amateurs, lacked any kind of literary talent, and often enough were not even literate.

The philological difficulties involved in reading and understanding early medieval letters pose further challenges. These difficulties, although shared by other genres of the period, are magnified in epistolary writings by the problem of contextualization that complicates the study of any letter. This problem often remains unresolved, because it is impossible to reconstruct the original communicative framework along with the specific knowledge that allowed the intended reader, be it the addressee or a wider audience, to understand a letter with all its implications.[28] Some of the most eminent Chinese scholars have remarked upon the complex difficulties of reading early medieval letters, among them Luo Zhenyu (1866–1940) with reference to archaeologically retrieved letters[29] and Qian Zhongshu (1910–1999), who, writing about the letters of Wang Xizhi, pointed out that the correspondents shared a "universe of discourse" (*yuyan tiandi*), which easily eludes and excludes the noninitiated reader: "Trivial family matters, scattered words between relatives and friends, casual jottings, rough and careless, but the recipients understood."[30] The oldest personal letter that was transmitted as a calligraphy, today kept in the Palace Museum in Beijing, illustrates the difficulties of deciphering early medieval letters very well. Although "Letter on recovering from illness" (Pingfu tie) by Lu Ji (261–303) received a fair amount of scholarly attention, not only as a revered example of early medieval calligraphy, but also because it was written by one of the greatest poets of Chinese history, there is little agreement about the content of this brief and humble letter (fig. I.1). Even transcriptions differ considerably, by more than a third of the characters, let alone interpretations.[31] The challenges posed by letters such as Lu Ji's "Letter on recovering from illness" undeniably complicate the exploration of early medieval epistolary literature and culture, but these challenges are more than compensated by the potential of this rich and promising field.

THE ORGANIZATION OF THIS BOOK

Given these problems and the limited general knowledge about the conventions of letter writing in early medieval China, it is not surprising that only a tiny fraction of the extant personal letters from this period have been translated or studied so far.[32] This is a great loss, because we have an abundance of transmitted sources that promise fascinating insights into personal communicative culture and the historical, literary, and intellectual developments related to or expressed in letters. This book addresses this unsatisfactory situation by providing an introduction to the epistolary literature and culture of early medieval China. It aims to make the social practice and the existing textual specimens of personal Chinese letter writing from this period fully visible for the first time, both for the various branches of Chinese studies and for the already well-established epistolary research in other ancient and modern cultures—which has, by the way, provided decisive methodological inspirations for this project. This study also intends to provide an impetus for further research and publications on letter writing in other periods of Chinese history and, in the long

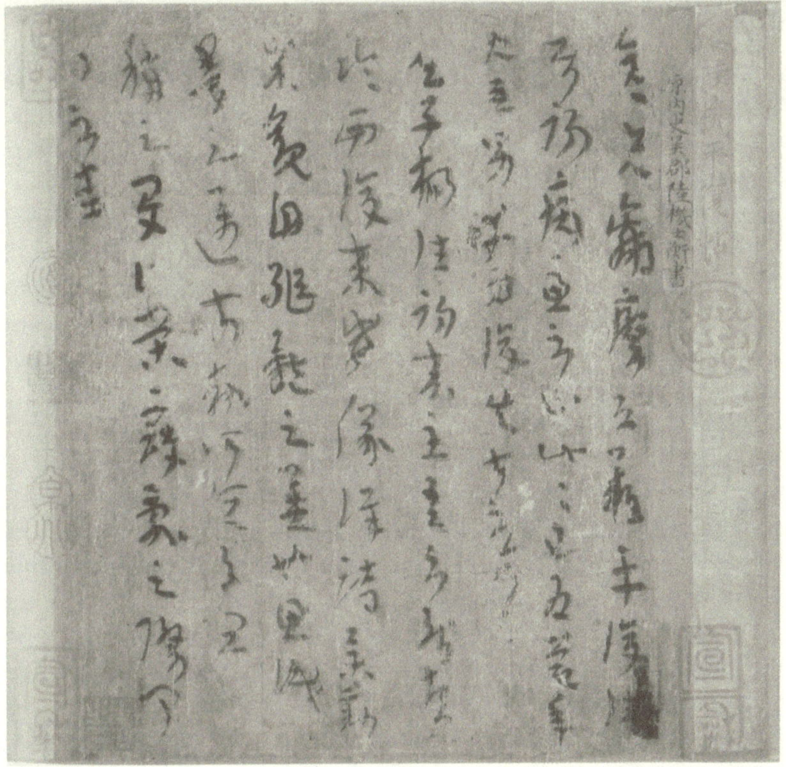

Figure I.1. Lu Ji (261–303), "Letter on recovering from illness" (Pingfu tie), written in ink on paper, 23.7 x 20.6 cm, Palace Museum Beijing.

run, to encourage a more confident and consistent use of letters as historical and literary sources.

While the earliest evidence of diplomatic correspondence in China dates from the seventh century BCE and personal letter writing appears in the third century BCE, it was only in the Han dynasty (206 BCE—220 CE) that letters began to be viewed as constituting a literary genre. Especially the letters written during the last decades of the Han foreshadow the impressive flourishing of letter writing in the four centuries that followed. The early medieval period (ca. 200–ca. 600), with its heightened sense of the individuality of authors, artists, and members of the elite in general, features a mature epistolary literature and thus lends itself particularly well to an introduction of Chinese letter writing. My exploration of the field, which includes translations, analyses, and appraisals of a large number of representative letters, covers the following areas.

Part I, "Materials and Concepts of Letter Writing," explores basic circumstances that defined epistolary culture in early medieval China. Chapter 1, "Materiality and Terminology," is dedicated to aspects of material culture that shaped letter writing and letter terminology, concluding with a definition of the personal letter in early medieval China, the main subject matter of this book. Chapter 2, "Letters and Literary Thought," discusses the critical and theoretical approach to letters in Chinese literary history as expressed in a broad spectrum of early medieval texts about literary thought, including letters that contain self-reflective statements about the genre.

Part II, "Epistolary Conventions and Literary Individuality," describes the peculiar language of letters with respect to vocabulary and textual patterns as well as the correlation between topicality and creativity. Chapter 3, "Structures and Phrases," introduces the most common elements of the letter formula as well as specific forms of address and self-designation used in letter writing. Chapter 4, "Topoi," expands the exploration of the epistolary language and communicative intentions of personal letters by investigating principal topoi. Chapter 5, "Normativity and Authenticity," continues this line of inquiry, exploring the relationship between epistolary normativity and cliché, on the one hand, and authenticity and literary originality, on the other, which provides an occasion to recapitulate the major topics addressed earlier in the book.

REMARKS ON TRANSLATION

All translations are my own, unless otherwise noted. Letters and other source materials translated in this book are usually followed by their Chinese text. If a text is composed in parallel prose, it is presented in tabular form, occasionally with added spaces, to emphasize the parallel structure. Letters are usually referred to by the titles found in Yan Kejun's *Complete Collection of Prose Literature from the Three Dynasties of Remote Antiquity, the Qin, Han, Three Kingdoms, and Six Dynasties* (Quan shanggu Sandai Qin Han Sanguo Liuchao wen). In my translations of these titles, recipients generally appear with their family names and personal names, even if the traditional letter titles use other designations such as official positions (which may be anachronistic). Since the Chinese titles of letters preserved primarily for their calligraphic value rather than for their text are often taken randomly from the first line of a letter, these titles (most of which are of letters by Wang Xizhi) will be left untranslated. Early medieval literature is teeming with allusions, although it is often difficult to decide whether a phrase is intended as a specific allusion to or even a quotation from earlier literature or whether it has already become part of the general vocabulary of educated writers at the time. In order to reveal as many intertextual references as possible in the translations, potential allusions are indicated by quotation marks, even when it is probable that they were just part of the common stock of literary phrases. I highlight the vast variety of words that are translated as "letter" by adding transcriptions of the respective Chinese words—almost two dozen in this book alone—in square brackets (e.g., *shu* or *bizha*), sometimes along with a further explanation (e.g., "*gao*, note" or "*ming*, directive").

PART ONE

Materials and Concepts of Letter Writing

CHAPTER ONE

Materiality and Terminology

Here is a letter, lady;
The paper as the body of my friend,
And every word in it a gaping wound
Issuing life-blood.

—WILLIAM SHAKESPEARE, *Merchant of Venice*

The materiality of letters is more pronounced than that of many other genres. Not only do letters depend on a specific, highly conventional, and immediately recognizable tangible form—usually a piece of writing in a sealed envelope; they also need to undergo the often cumbersome procedure of transmission from writer to addressee. All these material facets of epistolary culture shape the composition and reception of a letter's message and thus need to be taken into consideration in order to understand a letter as fully as possible. The same is true for the complex epistolary terminology, since the materiality of letters often determined what they were called in ancient China. Last but not least, reflections on materiality and terminology are necessary for a preliminary genre definition and delineation of the corpus of personal letters in early medieval China.

THE SPREAD OF PAPER

Not only do we today explore the Chinese epistolary tradition in a day and age of media change, but early medieval China experienced its own media change as well: the gradual replacement of the earlier writing supports of bamboo, wood, and silk by the recent Chinese invention, paper. This means that letters from this period differ considerably in their material form, depending on when they were written and probably also on the region in which they originated and their function.

While the oldest archaeological finds of writings on bamboo, wood, and silk date from the fifth century BCE, the history of these writing supports is no doubt much longer.[1] They were fine and time-tested materials, each produced with a particular finishing technology and coming with their own set of advantages and drawbacks. Bamboo and wood were light and inexpensive and, after being processed and finished, easy to write on with brush and ink, the most common writing implements since at least the Shang dynasty (16th–11th centuries BCE).[2] Writing done on the hard and smooth surfaces of finished bamboo and wood could easily be scraped off with a so-called writing knife (*shudao*), allowing for the correction of mistakes or the reuse of the writing support.[3] Formats differed, but the long and narrow bamboo slips were usually just wide enough for one vertical line of text, written on one side of a finished bamboo slip from top to bottom.[4] Bamboo slips bound together with cords accommodated longer texts; this method, however, seems not to have been employed in the case of personal letters—at least no evidence of such a practice has so far been discovered. A material that seems to have been much more common than bamboo in personal correspondence is wood. Wooden tablets were typically wider than bamboo slips, resembling thin rectangular boards, and offered two writing surfaces, the front and back sides of the board, so that they could carry longer texts and even drawings or diagrams. It would appear that this made them more convenient than bamboo slips for the purposes of personal correspondence, but again, we need to be aware that the vagaries of archaeological discovery do not necessarily yield a representative impression of cultural practices during a time period so far removed. Perhaps it is no coincidence that the two earliest extant personal Chinese letters, dating from around 224 BCE and found in a tomb at Shuihudi, Hubei, were written on wooden tablets.[5] They are family letters, written by two Qin conscripts, obviously brothers on a military campaign in the south, to a relative, probably another brother who was still at home (fig. 1.1). The letters are no literary masterpieces, but they do convey—apart from urgent requests for money and clothes—the strong affection of the writers for their relatives and possibly also friends and neighbors. Even if the letters do not speak of any imminent danger for the writers, they exude the air of vulnerability that is so characteristic of war letters. After all, messages written in a time of war are especially unreliable signs of life, since there is a higher probability that

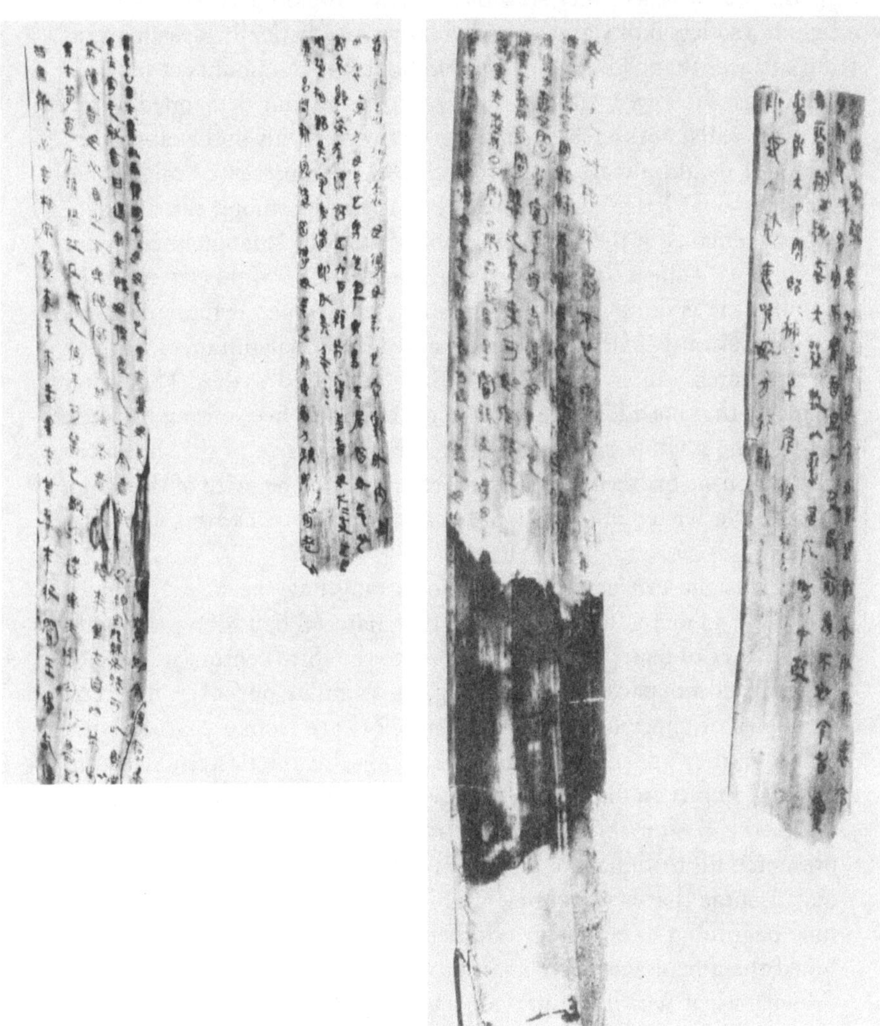

Figure 1.1. Letters written on wooden tablets, excavated from tomb no. 4 in Yunmeng, Shuihudi, Hubei.

the writers did not survive the time that it took for letters to reach their addressees.

Silk was a much finer stationery than bamboo and wood. It was lighter and less bulky and provided larger, aesthetically pleasing writing surfaces that could easily accommodate great amounts of text and drawings. However, silk was more expensive and demanded better writing skills, not the least since corrections on this highly absorbent material would always be discernible.[6] A well-preserved and rather long personal letter written on silk was found among the archaeological remains of the Xuanquan postal station (Xuanquan *zhi*) near Dunhuang, Gansu.[7] Despite its exquisite stationery, this letter, dated 37–32 BCE, is quite mundane in its message, which is more or less a mail order on behalf of the writer and a few acquaintances, framed and repeatedly interrupted by greetings and good wishes. The writer requests that his addressee send a pair of shoes, five writing brushes, a seal, and a whip, specifying the material and size of the shoes, the quality of the brushes, the seal inscription, and the price of the whip, which, the writer noted, should make a good cracking sound (fig. 1.2).

Fine as the earlier writing supports may have been, they turned out to be no match for paper, once this material had been perfected.[8] The history of paper goes back at least to the third century BCE, when it was used for packaging, padding, and similar purposes. The first examples of paper used as writing support are from a century later, although they are still very rare.[9] Traditionally, the Eastern Han official Cai Lun is credited with the invention of writing paper. According to the *History of the Eastern Han Dynasty* (Hou Han shu), he presented his formula in a memorial to the throne in 105 CE,[10] and we may assume that it was a new and improved kind of paper that was now beginning to be widely adopted as writing support. Paper combined the advantages of the earlier materials without retaining their drawbacks: it was light, provided large and bright writing surfaces that allowed for fluent writing and easy folding, and was inexpensive.[11] Both transmitted literature and archaeological finds indicate that the gradual replacement of bamboo, wood, and silk with paper started in the early second century. For about two centuries, these materials coexisted until paper became the standard writing support in the fourth century. The Xuanquan find also included fragments of letters written on paper, both from the Han dynasty and from early medieval China (fig. 1.3).[12] As early as in the third century, special

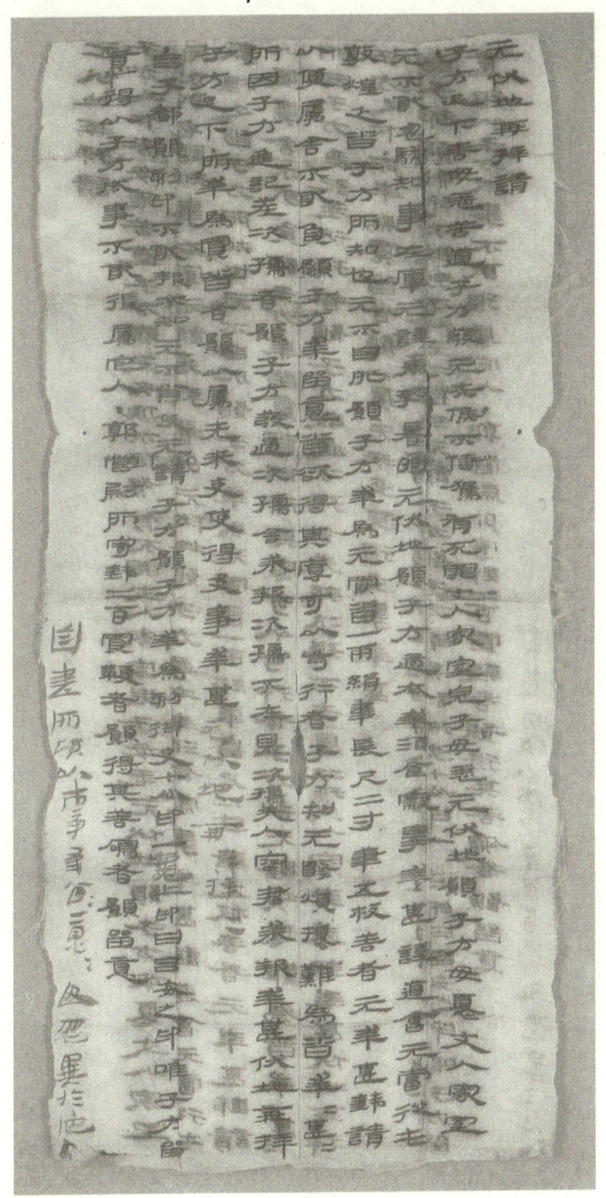

Figure 1.2. Letter written on silk, 37–32 BCE, 23.2 x 10.7 cm, found in Xuanquan, Dunhuang, Gansu. Courtesy of the Gansu Provincial Institute of Cultural Relics and Archaeology.

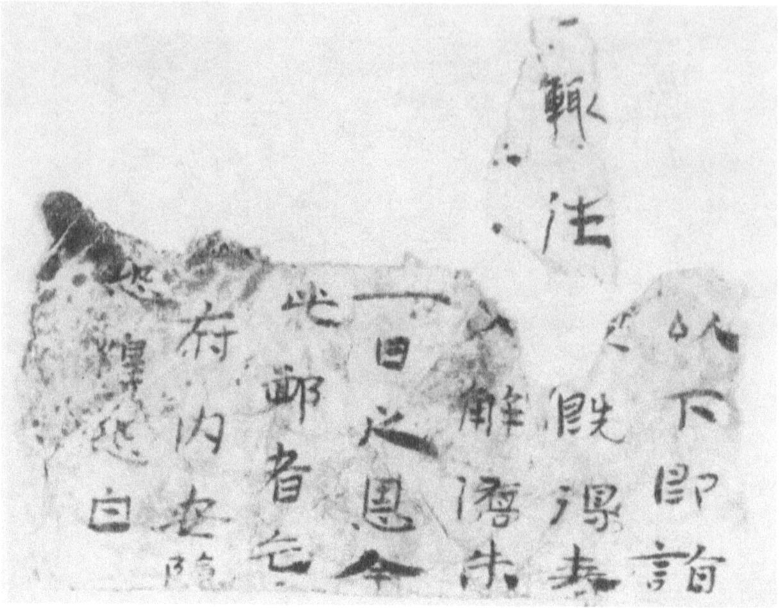

Figure 1.3. Fragment of a letter written on paper, 3rd– 4th century, 7.4 x 14 cm, found in Xuanquan, Dunhuang, Gansu. Courtesy of the Gansu Provincial Institute of Cultural Relics and Archaeology.

letter paper was produced, sometimes dyed or otherwise decorated, and even scented.[13]

In letters transmitted from early medieval China, paper is mentioned throughout the period, often as a reference to the letter itself or to other texts written on paper. Wu Zhi (177–230), at the beginning of his "Letter in reply to Cao Zhi [192–232]," writes:

> [Wu] Zhi lets you know:
>
> The messenger arrived and presented me with your kind letter [*kuang*, bestowal]. I opened the envelope and unfolded the paper. Of what immense literary beauty and comforting affection [your letter] is! . . .
>
> 質白。信到。奉所惠貺。發函伸紙。是何文采之巨麗而慰喻之綢繆乎。 . . .[14]

The phrase "opened the envelope and unfolded the paper" is repeated verbatim in letters of later writers, in particular by three Liang dynasty (502–57) authors, among them the crown prince Xiao Tong (501–531).[15] Since little is known about the circulation and collection of personal letters in early medieval China, it is usually impossible to tell whether the writer alluded to an earlier letter or merely employed a common epistolary phrase. In this case we can be fairly sure that the phrase was actually an intra-epistolary allusion (i.e., an allusion used in a letter that goes back to another letter), because there is sufficient proof that Wu Zhi's letter was well known among Liang literati, since Xiao Tong selected it for inclusion in his anthology *Selections of Refined Literature*. There are, however, also conventional epistolary phrases that incorporate a reference to paper, such as "leaning over the paper, I keep on sighing."[16]

CALLIGRAPHY AND LETTER WRITING

The social and cultural implications of the spread of paper can hardly be overestimated. By facilitating writing as well as the storage and transportation of documents, paper enabled the more effective and extensive spread of knowledge throughout society. Personal letter writing without doubt profited enormously from this development, not the least because it had become more affordable.[17] New types of cursive script that had emerged in the Han dynasty, especially running cursive (*xingshu*) and draft cursive (*caoshu*), which were first practiced on bamboo and wood,[18] later flourished on paper and in turn became the objects of a culture of calligraphic appreciation. In the first century, anecdotes dedicated to the admiration of handwriting appear, although they do not yet expressly mention paper. One of them portrays Chen Zun as an excellent calligrapher, since "whenever he sent someone a letter [*chidu*], the recipients would collect it for appreciation."[19] Liu Mu, a relative of Emperor Ming of the Han dynasty (r. 28–75), was so admired for his handwriting that when he was sick and on the verge of dying, "the emperor sent a courier on horseback, ordering Liu Mu to write ten letters [*chidu*] in draft cursive script" in order to secure some more pieces of his precious calligraphy before it was too late.[20]

By the Eastern Jin dynasty (317–420), calligraphy had become a full-fledged art form that through sophisticated connoisseurship and critical evaluation was an essential part of elite culture. The iconic figure of this calligraphic turn in Chinese cultural history is the Eastern Jin statesman Wang Xizhi (303–361), who was already admired for his handwriting during his lifetime (fig. 1.4). After his death, a series of imperial recognitions led to his quasi-canonization in the early Tang dynasty

(618–907), so that his reputation soared to the heights of being called "sage of calligraphy" (*shu sheng*), a position that has remained largely unchallenged.[21] Wang Xizhi's transmitted calligraphic oeuvre consists mostly of short personal letters and is thus exemplary for the close connection between calligraphic and epistolary culture that emerged during the Eastern Han dynasty.[22] As Robert Harrist has observed, this connection is not coincidental but necessary, since many of the most coveted features of Wang Xizhi's handwriting and that of elite calligraphers who were his contemporaries, such as "sudden changes of speed and brush direction that vividly recorded the impulses of the writer's hand . . . would have been unacceptable in more formal types of writing or in the work of professional scribes."[23]

The increasing focus on the aesthetic dimension of handwritten letters led to a general disregard of their content by later connoisseurs of calligraphy, for whom, as Bai Qianshen put it so succinctly, "reading was subordinated to viewing."[24] This functional shift of a letter—from being predominantly the carrier of a personal message to being a piece of fine art—may also be detected in early medieval letters. Replying to an unidentified relative, the famous Liang dynasty poet Xu Ling (507–583) depicted the great aesthetic pleasure that his addressee's handwriting afforded him without even mentioning the content of the other's letter.

> . . . The two Attendants-in-ordinary[26] Liu and Fu have returned and again brought me a letter [*shuzha*] from you. The silver hooks [of your handwriting] are utterly beautiful, and your jade script is still the same as it used to be. As soon as I had opened the envelope and unfolded the paper, my worries were shattered and turned into smiles. White autumn has just arrived, and the sweltering heat has abated a little. How is your health? Take good care of your excellent fortune! . . .
>
> . . . 劉、傅 (三) 〔二〕常侍還, 又承書札。銀鉤甚麗, 玉疏依然。開封伸紙, 破愁為笑。素秋方屆, 溽暑稍闌。體中何如。善保元吉。 . . .[26]

Xiao Ziliang (460–494) in a letter to Wang Sengqian (426–485), a descendant of Wang Xizhi's, also describes the pleasures of viewing the other's handwriting in powerful terms. It is difficult to decide whether his remarks refer to Wang Sengqian's letter itself or to an accompanying calligraphic gift—the "five sheets of paper" mentioned at the beginning of his letter—but this detail is of little consequence.

> I was honored to receive your letter [*gao*, note] along with five sheets of paper. The whole layout shows a rich essence and a profound

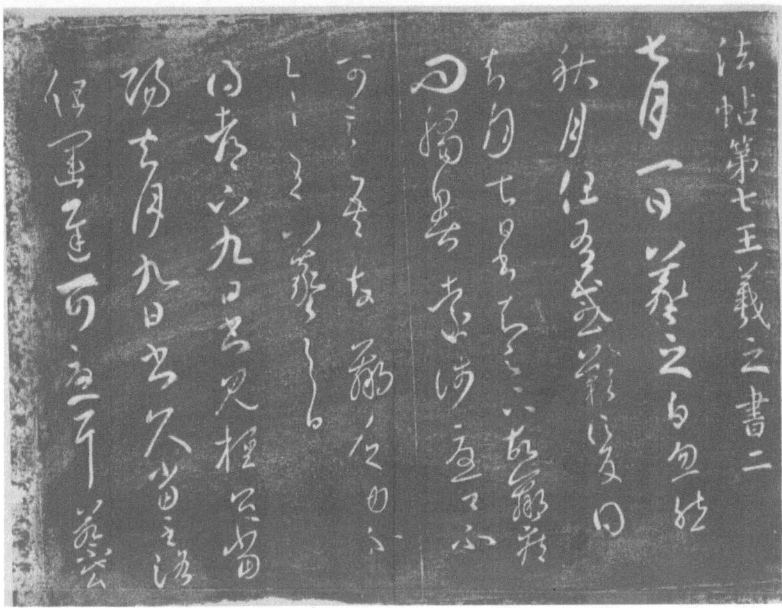

Figure 1.4. Wang Xizhi (303–361), "Qiuyue tie" (aka "Qiyue tie"), ink imprint of a 1646 stele of *Model Letters in the Imperial Archives in the Chunhua Era* (Chunhua ge fatie), H 26.5 cm. Harvard Fine Arts Library.

> numinosity.[27] Again and again I held [your writings] to cherish them; I would not let them out of my hands. . . .
>
> 辱告, 幷五紙。舉體精雋靈奧, 執玩反覆, 不能釋手。 . . .[28]

These first few words of Xiao Ziliang's letter reveal much about the notion of calligraphy that had developed during the early medieval period. Through the phrase "a rich essence and a profound numinosity," Xiao seems to spell out the cosmological integration of the calligrapher's body and work, since it ascribes to a piece of handwriting two aspects of vital energy, or *qi*, that are closely associated with the human body and the universe: *jing*, referring to the many layers of individual creative power,[29] and *ling*, the human ability to communicate with the numinous. *Qi* signifies the breath or vital energies that are seen as running through animate and inanimate nature. It is an omnipresent concept in Chinese thought, be it in literature, medicine or meteorology, that became essential in Chinese calligraphic theories as well.[30] Handwriting was considered to be an outer manifestation of the writer's vital energies, "a line of energy, materializing through the brush into the ink-trace,"[31] an idea that recalls the forceful Shakespearean image of the letter "issuing life-blood." This approach not only dissolves the boundaries between the calligrapher's body and his handwriting but also assumes that the artist is connected with the universe, which allows the individual to participate in the numinous. Implicitly, Xiao Ziliang further asserts that the continuum created by the artist is open and accessible. It may thus be shared by the perceptive connoisseur who, discerning the presence of "a rich essence and a profound numinosity" in someone's handwriting, feels compelled to grasp and cherish (*wan*) this piece of writing and thus becomes a part of an artistic continuum, which includes and transcends the body of the writer. This approach to calligraphy and handwriting in general has tremendous implications for the notion of letter writing in early medieval China, especially concerning the question of personal authenticity (discussed in more detail in chapters 4 and 5).[32]

WRITERS AND TRANSPORTERS OF LETTERS

The letter writers we have encountered so far are quite diverse and include ordinary soldiers and high officials, poets, and heirs to the throne; however, it is difficult to assess the actual social distribution of letter writing in early medieval China. On the one hand, the extant literature suggests that correspondence was mainly an elite activity, an impression that is probably due to the selective process of transmission. Archaeological discoveries, on the other hand, prove that rather lowly people wrote personal letters, too. The existence of epistolary guides, to be discussed in chapter 5, seems to support this finding, because they indicate that letter writing was not exclusively an elite activity but was practiced in lower social strata as well, among less educated people who were in need of guidance in its conventions.

The first differentiation that is necessary in this context is that between the writer of a letter and its sender. Usually they are the same person, but in some cases, for various reasons, the sender would employ a scribe. The most obvious motive for seeking scribal help was insufficient literacy on the part of the sender. According to different notions of full or partial literacy,[33] this covers a broad spectrum of situations, from the illiterate laborer who never learned to read and write and would thus always need help, to the educated scholar who, in a particularly delicate case of correspondence, would engage a professional scribe or even a poet.[34] The corpus of transmitted letters includes many pieces by famous authors that were written on behalf of someone else, usually a ruler, but there are also letters written on behalf of a husband addressing his wife.[35]

Unfortunately, too little is known about the spread of writing and reading abilities in early and early medieval China to assess, for instance, whether the two Qin conscripts mentioned in "The Spread of Paper" section wrote the letters themselves or if, and to what extent, they had to rely on a scribe or professional letter writer.[36] It goes without saying that the same kind of uncertainty arises with regard to reading, because the addressee of a letter may not necessarily have been able to actually read it; he or she may well have needed help in deciphering it or even had to rely on someone to read it aloud. There are indications in transmitted literature that epistolary communication did not depend on literacy, as in the case of clearly illiterate authors, such as Shen Qingzhi (386–465), who is reported to have dictated his poems and will thus have dictated his letters as well.[37] At the same time, dictation seems to have been common among highly literate authors, too. We may infer this from the occasional emphasis on letters in the author's own handwriting, as in the biography of Tao Kan (259–334), which states that "to every one of the letters [*shushu*] from near and far he replied in his own hand."[38] In a letter to Wu Zhi, Cao Zhi expressly mentions dictation, albeit in the topical phrase "my dictation cannot express all."[39] Finally, there are rare cases such as the purchase order written on silk from Xuanquan mentioned in "The Spread of Paper" section, which carries an autograph subscript in a distinctly different hand that says,

> Written by myself: I wish [*yuan*] that you may take good care of these purchases, take very good care of them! Do not be lax about them like other people are!
>
> 自書: 所願以市事幸留意留意。毋忽異於它人。[40]

Taking into account this letter's place of discovery and its materiality, it seems very likely that it was the product of an undoubtedly literate official taking—possibly illicit—advantage of the resources that the Xuanquan postal station provided: an easy supply of expensive stationery as well as skilled scribes and official couriers.

The transportation of a letter from writer to addressee is a process that has always been fraught with hazards, especially so before the establishment of a reliable postal service for general use, which is much more recent than is usually assumed, in both China and the West. A letter could be delayed, misdirected, or intercepted; its message could be misused or altered; or it could get lost forever. Even today, with efficient postal services installed all over the developed world, we may now and then feel some trepidation if we have written an important letter, put it in an envelope, addressed and franked it, and finally dropped it into a mailbox, surrendering it to a largely anonymous institution, whose enormous complexity escapes most of us.

The initial step in this process—to put a letter in an envelope—is an integral part of epistolary communication, since it is dedicated to the twofold protection of the letter's integrity. While envelopes first of all keep a letter from physical damage that might spoil the message by making it undecipherable, they also protect it from unauthorized eyes, thus drawing attention to the fact that a letter is normally not meant to be read by anyone but its specified addressee.[41] The idea of the confidentiality, privacy, and inviolability of correspondence is further emphasized by the use of various sealing techniques. How crucial these are for the notion of the letter becomes evident in early modern and modern Western fine art, in which the seal features prominently in the iconography of letters.[42] In early and early medieval China, the material of the envelope corresponded roughly to the writing support of the letter. This means that bamboo or wooden letters from the Han dynasty were covered with wooden "sealing boards" (*jian*) that were fastened with cords. The cords were passed through the "sealing tooth" (*yinchi*), an indentation in the sealing board that was then filled with moist "sealing clay" (*fengni*) and stamped with a seal carrying an inscription (fig. 1.5). Once dried, the clay served to both fasten the cords and display the imprint of a seal for identification, authentication, and proof of inviolacy.[43] Letters written on silk or paper were sent in envelopes of the corresponding material,[44] which were sealed by stamping them in black or, starting in the fifth to sixth centuries, vermilion ink. Apart from the name of the recipient, sealing boards and envelopes often also carried a few words characterizing the content of the letter, especially in official communication.[45]

That even putting a letter into an envelope can turn out to jeopardize the success of a message is illustrated by an anecdote about the Eastern Jin official Yin Hao (306–356), who was famous for his intellectual superiority and his skill in "pure conversation" (*qingtan*). The story is recorded in his biography in the *History of the Jin Dynasty* (Jin shu).

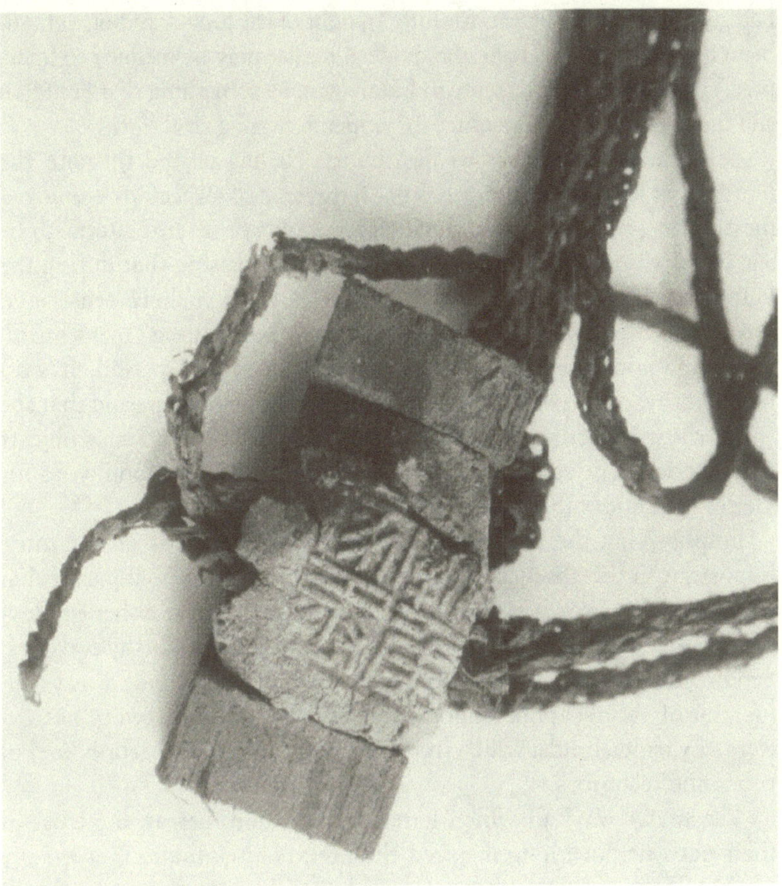

Figure 1.5. Sealing board with clay-filled sealing tooth, 4.4 x 2.7 x 1.2 cm, excavated from tomb no. 1 in Mawangdui, Changsha, Hunan. Courtesy of the Hunan Provincial Museum, Changsha.

> Later, when Huan Wen[46] planned to appoint Yin Hao to the position of Director of the Imperial Secretariat, he sent him a letter [*shu*] to notify him. Yin Hao was only too pleased to accept. But when he set out to write his letter of reply [*shu*], he kept worrying about making mistakes and opened and closed the letter dozens of times. When it finally arrived, the envelope was empty. This greatly annoyed Huan Wen, so that he broke with him. Yin Hao died in the twelfth year of the Yonghe period [356].[47]

This tale about the excessive importance that one may attribute to a single letter is strangely moving, not the least because Yin Hao's trepidations had such dire consequences for him. In light of the long-standing antagonism between the two men, the modern reader may be inclined to interpret Yin Hao's failure to reply to Huan Wen as something of a Freudian slip that betrayed his reluctance to cooperate with a rival.[48]

Before a letter reaches its destination, it has passed through the hands of at least one other person—in the case of a specially employed messenger—but more often through the hands of several intermediaries, usually unknown people. It is thus not surprising that during the Han dynasty, the word *xin*, originally meaning "to believe, trust" and "to be trustworthy, reliable," assumed the new meaning "messenger," which it maintained throughout the early medieval period. It was, incidentally, only toward the end of the early medieval period that the word *xin* was used to designate not messengers but letters as objects they carried. The same holds for *shuxin*, the most common word for "letter" in modern Chinese.[49]

Emphasizing the trustworthiness of messengers was all the more important in the absence of a public postal system, which meant that most letters were delivered by private envoys, who were either employees of the sender's family or, it was to be hoped, trustworthy travelers. Sending a letter hence entailed further costs in the form of direct payment or of social capital embodied in a stable private network of travelers of various kinds, which indirectly also involved a certain level of economic resources.[50]

The many ways in which letter carriers may betray the trust of their patrons have long inspired the literary imagination, especially in those cases when letters were intentionally misused: intercepted, misdirected, or forged.[51] A famous early medieval Chinese anecdote illustrates the hazards of sending letters via a coincidental traveler, implying the whole range of mail-related imponderabilities that had already become a literary topos by the Eastern Han. The unreliable messenger featured in this anecdote is Yin Xian (late third–early fourth century), father of the anxious letter writer Yin Hao. In Richard Mather's translation in *A New Account of Tales of the World* (Shishuo xinyu), the story reads as follows:

> When Yin Xian was appointed Governor of Yuzhang Commandery [Jiangxi], on the eve of his departure to take up his post the people of the capital [Jiankang] took the occasion to entrust him with a hundred or more letters [*han shu*] to deliver. After he reached Shitou [in Jiangxi] he threw them all into the water [of the river Gan]. As he did so he muttered the following incantation:

> "Let those that sink sink,
> And those that float float,
> But Yin Xian never can
> Become a mailman."[52]

If we ask why the idea of being a mailman would be so abhorrent to Yin Xian, we may find an explanation in a passage in the Western Han *Discourses Weighed in the Balance* (Lunheng), in which scholars studying the Confucian canon are compared to couriers and doormen who, after all, merely transmit, faithful as the transmission may be.[53] As on many other occasions throughout *Discourses Weighed in the Balance*, the approach of its author, Wang Chong (27–ca. 100), directly challenges Confucius (551–479 BCE), who, in the *Analects* (Lunyu), famously described himself as a faithful transmitter of ancient ideas.[54] In another epistolary anecdote in *A New Account of Tales of the World*, Yin Xian emerges as equally willful, although he seems to have faith in the delivery of letters, as he is described writing to general Yu Yi (305–345). Enclosed in his letter to the general, who happened to be on a precarious military mission, was the cruelly teasing gift of a broken "as-you-wish" scepter (*ruyi*), a most blatant violation of epistolary conventions, which revolve around wishing the addressee well.[55]

In the Eastern Han, at about the same time that the unreliability of messengers had become a literary topos, the complementary topos of the reliable transmission of letters via animals emerged. The counterpart to Yin Xian's human fallibility may thus be found in the supposed canine fidelity of a dog belonging to the Western Jin (265–316) poet Lu Ji, Tawney Ears (Huang'er), whose story is told in the *History of the Jin Dynasty*.

> When Lu Ji had had no news [*wen*] from home for a long time, he laughed and said to his dog: "There is simply no messenger in our family. Couldn't you bring them a letter [*shu*] to get me some news [*xiaoxi*]?" The dog wagged his tail and growled. Lu Ji then wrote a letter [*shu*] and put it into a bamboo cane, which he fastened at the dog's neck. The dog found his way south, finally reaching Lu Ji's family. Having collected a reply, it returned to Luoyang. Afterward, this [way of delivering letters] became quite common.[56]

Believable or not, the story of Lu Ji's "dog letters" (*quan shu*) has always been popular in China, much like similar stories about the understanding and loyalty of dogs in other cultures.[57] Again, the underlying assumption is that there is no public postal system and reliable messengers are more of a hope than a reality for most people.

In many civilizations, the first and greatest efforts made to diminish the imponderabilities of transmitting letters were directed at official communication.[58] The same is true for ancient China, where, in the course of the Zhou dynasty (1045–221 BCE), a complex state postal network had developed, consisting of postal roads and relay stations equipped with personnel and horses.[59] The speed of the mounted couriers moving back and forth between the stations must have been impressive, at least if a comparison attributed to Confucius and often quoted in the context of postal history is to be believed: "Virtue spreads faster than an order transmitted by courier."[60] During the Qin dynasty (221–207 BCE), after the unification of China, the basis for a centralized postal relay system (*youyi*) emerged, "a governmental communication and transportation system for the transmission of official documents, the accommodation of envoys and the transportation of goods."[63] It was perfected during the Han dynasty and remained in place throughout the history of imperial China.[62] After the political fragmentation following the decline of the Han, the official courier network suffered losses but was still basically intact within the borders of individual states. Two developments of material culture, the spread of paper beginning in the second century and the introduction of the stirrup in the fourth century, facilitated official and personal communication in early medieval China.[63] While official couriers were not to be used for the transmission of personal letters, at least on record,[64] it is very probable that the illicit use of the state postal network for private purposes was rather common.[65]

Nevertheless, we can be sure that the majority of transmitted personal letters from early medieval China were delivered by private messengers, either employees of the sender or incidental travelers. While the first private post offices were established in the Tang dynasty, it took until the Ming dynasty (1368–1644) before private systems reached a certain level of stability.[66] Although early medieval epistolary literature itself provides only meager information about postal procedures, dependence on messengers is a regular topos. Cao Pi (187–226), Emperor Wen of the Wei dynasty (r. 220–26), in a letter to Wu Zhi complains about the scarcity of their correspondence, which he blames on the awkwardly situated region under Wu Zhi's administration.[67] Knowing about the difficulties of sending letters, other authors even moderate their requests for replies: Liu Chengzhi (354–410) hopes frequently to receive letters, "provided there are messengers,"[68] and Xie Lingyun asks for an immediate reply "should there happen to be a messenger."[69] It was also conventional to justify the brevity or imperfection of one's letter by attributing it to the messenger's impending departure: Sengzhao (384–414) writes in one of his letters that "since the messenger returns south, [my letter] cannot express all,"[70] and Lu Jing (ca. 250–ca. 280) remarks that "because the messenger is here, I forget so many words [that I wanted to write]."[71] There are also indications of specially dispatched carriers who went back and forth between the residences of writers and their addressees. They probably not only delivered letters but also were expected to return with replies, as repeated references to their "return" (*fan*, *huan*) suggest.

> On the first day of the seventh month, [Wang] Xizhi lets you know:
> Suddenly, it is the first month of autumn, and I am full of nothing but sighs. When the messenger returned, I received your letter [*shu*] of the seventh of last month. . . .
>
> 七月一日羲之白。忽然秋月。但有感歎。信反。得去月七日書。 . . .[72] (see fig. 1.4)

Occasional archaeological finds show that the reply was not always written on a new piece of material but could be added to the original letter, which was then returned to the first sender.[73] This practice is also indicated by references in transmitted literature, for instance, a well-known anecdote about Wang Xizhi's youngest son, Xianzhi (344–386/88), who was a notable calligrapher himself. Purportedly he once sent a letter to Xie An (320–385), clearly expecting that the recipient might keep it for its handwriting, share it with others, and perhaps pass it down to posterity. But to Wang Xianzhi's dismay, Xie An wrote his reply on the back of this letter and sent it back, thus demonstrating his disregard for Wang Xianzhi's calligraphy.[74]

Regarding the frequency of letter writing, textual evidence is scanty and diverse. In epistolary literature itself, letters are reported to have been delivered and answered at quite different intervals. The following examples testify to letters received within hours, probably in a city or between two hamlets of a county, after a few days or after several months, possibly across much longer distances; very seldom are places specified or other contextual clues provided.

On the eleventh day of the tenth month, [Wang] Xizhi respectfully inquires:

Having received your letter [*shu*] of this morning, I know that you are in good health, which comforted me. . . .

十月十一日羲之敬問。得旦書。知佳。為慰。 . . .[75]

On the fifteenth day of the seventh month, [Wang] Xizhi lets you know:

In these autumn days, I feel a deep longing for you. Having received your letter [*gao*, note] of the fifth, I feel quite comforted. Recently the heat has been extreme. . . .

七月十五日羲之白。秋日感懷深。得五日告甚慰。晚熱盛。 . . .[76]

On the fourth day of the third month, [Wang] Xun knocks his head on the ground:

At the end of winter, I am visited by a mass of feelings. Having received the letter [*shu*] you wrote in the seventh month, I gratefully acknowledge your consideration. . . .

三月四日珣頓首。末冬衆感。得七月書。知問。 . . .[77]

As correspondences usually consist of a series of replies, we may conclude that some correspondents—obviously people living in each other's vicinity—exchanged letters quite frequently, in some cases, practically daily. Besides these everyday exchanges, they probably kept up a number of less frequent correspondences, either because the relationship was not as intimate or because greater distances had to be bridged, which would have slowed the exchange.

TERMINOLOGY

In Chinese, epistolary terminology is as diverse as the genre itself.[78] Some of the terms for personal letters are motivated by their communicative function, such as "instruction" (*shi*), and others by modes of later reception, as in the case of "calligraphy model" (*tie*), or by poetic images, for instance, "wild goose" (*yan*). The great majority of terms that are used to designate a personal letter reflect aspects of its materiality, from writing itself to the writing supports, envelopes, seals, and the like. However, since many of these material aspects are peculiar not to letters but to writing in general, the terminology may be ambiguous and, in a given context, not always allow for a satisfactory differentiation between letters and other kinds of writings.

This semantic ambiguity is quite evident in the case of the oldest and most common letter designation, *shu* 書. Used as a verb, *shu* means "to write"; as a noun, it denotes the products of this activity, that is, "writing(s)" or indeed anything written, including what we today would call a "book," a "document," and, not least, a "letter."[79] A similarly broad lexical range can be observed in other languages as well, for instance, *litterae* in Latin, "letters" in English, *lettre* in French, and *Schreiben* and *Brief* in German.[80] In pre-imperial China, *shu* could still denote personal and official communication alike, but the word underwent a semantic narrowing in the Han dynasty, when the development of a complex state bureaucracy led to the proliferation and diversification of official communication accompanied by the terminological determination of genre names. During this process, *shu* became a special designation for personal letters addressed to equals or inferiors and continued to be used in this capacity throughout the early medieval period. At the same time, *shu* was maintained as a part of compounds designating subgenres of official communication, such as *shangshu* 上書 (memorial to the throne, to memorialize, lit., "submit a letter to a superior").

Most other terms for letters allude to the older writing supports—bamboo, wood, and silk. As in the case of *shu*, these words are often ambiguous, since they turn out to be specific neither to letters nor to a certain material. The word *jian* 簡 (bamboo writing slip), for instance, can refer to a letter in early medieval China[81] but more often refers to any kind of writing, be it on a bamboo slip or another kind of support. The use of a term indicating a particular writing support usually did not require that the letter or other piece of writing in question actually be written on this material. It is, for example, much more probable that a letter written by Liu Jun (458–521), which he called "*qing jian*" 青簡, was written on paper rather than on green (i.e., unprocessed) bamboo,[82] because by 500, when this letter was composed, paper had almost completely replaced bamboo, wood, and silk. A similar kind of metaphorical use may be observed for the words *du* 牘 and *zha* 札 (wooden writing tablet),[83] which both occur in compounds that can designate a letter. Among them is *chidu* 尺牘, which, although infrequently seen in early medieval literature, became one of the most common words for the literary letter in late imperial and modern China.[84] The word is derived from the measure of length *chi* (foot) and obviously refers to the length of the wooden writing tablet, which, during the Han dynasty, when the term was coined, amounted to approximately twenty-three centimeters.[85] *Chi* is also used in other compounds such as *chishu* 尺書 (a foot of writing) and *chisu* 尺素 (a foot of plain [silk]), denoting letters[86] as well as other kinds of writing.[87] In later compounds, *chi* appears to be used metonymically, referring *pars pro toto* to letters. Examples are *chihan* 尺翰, (lit., "a foot of brush") and even *chili* 尺鯉 (a foot of carp), when the image of the carp as a carrier of letters had become a common metaphor.[88] Silk as a writing support is present not only in compounds with *su* 素 (plain [silk])[89] but probably also in the designation *tie* 帖, which was mostly applied to writings that were appreciated for their calligraphy. According to Lothar Leddderose, "the term denotes primarily handwritten pieces of informal content, a casual type of script, and of relatively small format,"[90]—all criteria that usually pertain to letters. Paper obviously was too late an invention to have an impact on letter terminology. Other tangible aspects that were reflected in terminology include the brush, the envelope, and seals. While *han* 翰 (brush) became a letter designation in early medieval China, used both on its own and in compounds,[91] words denoting envelopes and sealing such as *han* 函 and *feng* 封 were used mostly as measure words for letters.

In addition, there is a group of conventional terms for personal letters that are motivated by their communicative function. Usually, they are used in letters themselves, where they refer to letters of the writer, the addressee, or mutual acquaintances. When referring to the addressee's letter, writers often choose words that amount to honorifics, such as "bestowal" (*kuang* 貺/況), "instruction" (*shi* 示), "note, announcement" (*gao* 告), "teaching" (*hui* 誨), or "directive" (*ming* 命). Other, more neutral terms are "news" (*wen* 問) or "message" (*yin* 音), words that originally implied oral transmission. This usage produces a further kind of ambiguity, since we cannot always be certain whether a word such as *shuwen* 書問 (letter, message) meant a written or an oral communication.[92]

Finally, there are poetic or more distinctly metaphorical letter designations. Since these are often inspired by the hope for a swift and safe delivery, the most common metaphors are fish (*yu* 魚), particularly carp (*li* 鯉), and birds, such as the swallow (*yan* 燕) and the wild goose (*yan* 雁, *hong* 鴻). These words can be combined with many of the above-mentioned terms to form compounds, for instance, *lisu* 鯉素 (carp silk [letter])[93] and *yanshu* 雁書 (wild goose letter).[94]

In sum, the range of terms that may denote a letter is broad. Most of the terms are ambiguous in meaning and do not allow conclusions as to the materiality of a letter or its function. Both issues complicate understanding and translation. Generally, the term "letter" is used in translations only if there is sufficient evidence that the piece of writing in question actually was a letter; otherwise, the ambiguity of a term is retained in translations such as "message" or "news." While it is possible to translate certain designations terminologically (such as "memorandum"), the majority of Chinese letter designations are rendered "letter" in English. In order to still convey the underlying lexical diversity, transcriptions of the respective words are provided in square brackets (such as *shu* or *bizha*), sometimes along with a further explanation (such as "*gao*, note" and "*kuang*, bestowal").

THE GENRE OF PERSONAL LETTERS

Letters of thanks, letters from banks,
Letters of joy from girl and boy,
Receipted bills and invitations
To inspect new stock or to visit relations,
And applications for situations,
And timid lovers' declarations,
And gossip, gossip from all the nations.
News circumstantial, news financial,
Letters with holiday snaps to enlarge in,
Letters with faces scrawled on the margin,
Letters from uncles, cousins and aunts,
Letters to Scotland from the South of France,
Letters of condolence to Highlands and Lowlands,
Written on paper of every hue,
The pink, the violet, the white and the blue,
The chatty, the catty, the boring and the adoring,
The cold and official and the heart's outpouring,
Clever, stupid, short and long,
The typed and the printed and the spelt all wrong.

—W. H. AUDEN, "Night Mail III" (1935)[95]

A letter is easy enough to recognize. It is a communication written on a tangible medium by one historical person and addressed to another (or, as the case may be, by one narrowly circumscribed group to another), which, in order to reach its spatially removed addressee, undergoes some form of physical transmission involving a third party and is, more often than not, part of an exchange.[96] Several features are derived from this basic epistolary situation, some of them textual, others extralinguistic. The most consequential of the extralinguistic features is the time lag, due to transmission, between writing, reading, and responding to a letter. It creates a distinct, staggered type of communication that determines a number of textual characteristics. Another important extralinguistic feature is the fact that letters are transmitted in envelopes, which marks the particular directedness and exclusiveness of epistolary communication, both of which are also expressed on the textual level.

The most significant textual features of a letter are its inherent dialogicity and self-referentiality. While dialogicity denotes a range of textual features that prove a writer's sustained efforts to engage a specific addressee,[97] self-referentiality describes a letter's peculiar self-referential capacity. Patrizia Violi in her study of the genre spoke of the letter's illocutionary force as being bound up with its "capacity to refer to itself and to its own communicative function independently of any propositional content it may express."[98] Claudio Guillén made a similar observation when he described the letter as "writing proclaiming itself as writing in the process of correspondence."[99] Both dialogicity and self-referentiality are expressed through recurring and manifold references to the time, place, and other circumstances of its writing and expected reading, including references to the addressee and his or her world, to the spatial distance between writer and addressee, to the time lag between writing, reading, and responding, and so forth.

It is, nevertheless, a commonplace in epistolary research throughout cultures that letters pose a challenge for genre typology.[100] Despite its apparent lucidity, the word "letter," on closer examination, turns out to be so difficult to define that even the question "What, after all, is not a letter?" no longer seems exaggerated.[101] The textual indeterminacy of the letter even appears to be one of its defining features, and not only because of its ability to assimilate other genres.[102] Letters from early medieval China also manifest this genre-specific openness, which extends to subject matter,[103] occasion for writing, literary style, level of formality (depending mostly on the hierarchical relationship between the correspondents but also on the occasion), and communicative function. At one end of the spectrum are short, casual, intimate notes that convey affection and little else, while at the other end, long, elaborate, scholarly treatises on religious and philosophical questions or highly adorned declarations of friendship display a rigorous parallel style verging on poetry. The diversity between these extremes of epistolary communication is practically infinite—from letters of friendship and the ending of friendships, to letters of condolence or farewell, itinerary letters from travelers, admonitory letters from fathers, letters of recommendation addressed to prospective masters, and so forth.

What is more, the ends of the spectrum are far from being marked by clear-cut borders. Rather, they are areas of transition connecting letters to other literary genres that avail themselves of the epistolary mode without actually being letters. Epistolary poetry, for instance, is widespread in many cultures, in early medieval China taking the form of the poetic subgenre presentation and response (*zeng da*) and in the West appearing well before the celebrated *Heroides* of Ovid (43 BCE–17/18 CE).[104] Epistolary narratives have played a remarkable role in Western literature since antiquity as well, most notably in the genre of the novel, some of the greatest examples of which are written in epistolary modes.[105] These are largely absent from premodern Chinese literature, the general understanding being that Chinese epistolary fiction was brought about by exposure to Western examples, in particular, translations of *The Sorrows of Young Werther* by Johann Wolfgang Goethe (1749–1832).[106] However, if we define epistolary fiction broadly to include the "imitation of the letter by the letter" in all its forms,[107] we could take fictitious correspondences into account, such as the letters between Li Ling and Su Wu, clearly an early medieval fabrication,[108] or the love letters between Qin Jia (fl. ca. 147) and his wife Xu Shu, another correspondence of uncertain authenticity.[109] This avenue of inquiry could be expanded by taking a closer look at letters that are embedded in semi-historical or fictitious narratives, such as "accounts of the strange" (*zhi guai*) or "tales of the marvelous" (*chuan qi*), or by investigating the motif of the letter in poetry, to point out just two promising areas.

Within the body of texts that are usually regarded as letters, additional typological questions arise. One derives from the mode of transmission of early medieval Chinese literature, which has left texts that are called letters but are no longer recognizable as such because they were stripped of many or all genre-specific features before they were included in an anthology or encyclopedia. An example is the case of a short text by Dongfang Shuo (154–93 BCE) that modern anthologies claim as a letter. In the early Tang encyclopedia *A Collection of Literature Arranged by Categories* (Yiwen leiju) and in Yan Kejun's *Complete Collection of Prose Literature from the Han Dynasty* (Quan Han wen), this text is titled "Admonishing his Son"

(Jie zi) and classified as a piece of prose writing, while Zhang Pu (1602–1641) labels the text "Poem admonishing his son" (Jie zi shi) in his *Collected Writings of 103 Famous Writers of the Han, Wei, and Six Dynasties* (Han Wei Liuchao baisan mingjia ji).[110]

Another question, particularly pertinent for this book, regards the distinction between personal and official letters. If we ask what criteria allow us to call a transmitted text from early medieval China a personal letter, it seems expedient to approach this question through a process of elimination.

First, that a text is a personal letter cannot be ascertained by relying on its genre label alone.[111] Although in early medieval China, the label *shu* is a very good indication that a text is a personal letter, this criterion is not comprehensive enough, because *shu* covers only letters written to equals or inferiors. Personal letters addressed to superiors were often labeled *jian* 箋/牋 (memorandum), a word used to designate a subgenre of official communication, which, however, was not applied consistently. This terminological problem is manifest in the letters that were exchanged between Cao Pi, Cao Zhi, and their mutual friend but obvious inferior, Wu Zhi. While the Cao brothers' letters were all labeled *shu*, Wu Zhi's replies are labeled differently: his letter to the elder brother Cao Pi as *jian*, his letter to Cao Zhi as *shu*. Perhaps *jian* was chosen in the case of Cao Pi because of his status as heir apparent of the Wei dynasty (220–65), but this assumption turns out to be precipitate, since letters to the younger brother were labeled *jian* as well.[112] The eventual discovery that letters not only to superiors but also to inferiors could be labeled *jian* finally proves the unreliability of genre labels.[113] A large number of personal letters are moreover found among the texts labeled *tie*, mostly short, casual notes that were transmitted as calligraphies. Finally, there are a few personal letters that, without any apparent reason, carry sundry other labels, such as *shu* 疏 (petition), which was originally used for official communications but had already become a synonym for *shu* 書 in the Han dynasty.[114]

We may thus conclude that a certain hierarchical relationship between writer and addressee is not a sufficient criterion for deciding whether a letter is personal either. Personal letters are not limited to correspondences between equals but are perfectly possible between inferiors and superiors, even if epistolary conventions entailing a higher degree of politeness had to be observed.

A third criterion that is not reliable in deciding whether a letter is official or personal is a text's personal content or flavor. As transmitted examples demonstrate, official communication can be more revealing as to the writer's personal circumstances or his relationship with the addressee than many a treatise on politics or literary thought in the guise of a letter of friendship. Zhuge Liang (181–234) in his "Memorial about the troops marching out" (Chu shi biao) adopts a distinctly personal, almost fatherly tone toward Liu Chan (207–271), son of the late Liu Bei (161–223), Emperor Zhaolie of the Shu-Han dynasty (r. 221–223).[115] Li Mi (227–287), in his "Memorial expressing his feelings" (Chen qing shi biao), addressed to Sima Yan (236–290), Emperor Wu of the Jin dynasty (r. 265–90), writes movingly about his relationship to his grandmother, whom he needs to care for, in asking that his rejection of office be accepted.[116] Bao Zhao's "Communication asking for leave of absence" (Qing jia qi) gives a touching description of the deplorable condition of his house.[117]

Finally, the fourth inadequate criterion is the form of a letter. Because holding an office usually implied literacy and vice versa, many letter writers were officials. It is only to be expected that they employed the features of official writing with which they were familiar in their personal letters as well, perhaps even in a playful manner, so that linguistic characteristics of official communication are present in personal letter writing, too.

The only conclusive criterion for a definition of personal letters is derived from linguistic pragmatics and asks for the writers' motives and the intended function of the texts they produced. On the one hand, official communication is exchanged between functionaries in service who are exercising their offices (or, as the case may be, with one of the correspondents acting in such a capacity). Personal letters, on the other hand, are written because of personal motives and intentions that are largely independent of the writer's official standing. Letters exchanged between officials of whatever rank can hence still be personal, as long as the correspondents do not write to each other as officials.[118] These two fundamentally different types of written communication were differentiated in early medieval literary thought, since books such as *The Literary Mind and the Carving of Dragons* and anthologies such as *Selections of Refined Literature* treat or collect them in separate chapters. Once again, however, there is no clear-cut definition, so that we need to accept a certain hybridity as belonging to the genre.[119] Notwithstanding these difficulties of definition, this book focuses on personal letters, meaning those that, in contrast to forms of communication such as edicts (*zhao*), commands (*ling*), and memorials (*biao*), are motivated chiefly not by the official role of their writer and addressee but by a personal relationship between them.

Singling out the personal relationship between writer and addressee as a criterion for the differentiation of letters raises the question of the personal "authenticity" or "truthfulness" of the transmitted epistolary texts that are known from early medieval China. As with other genres, transmitted letters may be assumed to have been considered worth preserving for certain reasons, usually because of their writer, their textual characteristics (such as content, historical significance, intellectual value, literary qualities), or their calligraphy. This results in roughly two groups of transmitted letters that differ considerably as to their content and form (although there is, of course, overlap). Very generally speaking, the first group is content-oriented, formal, and literary, while the second group is relationship-oriented, informal, and quotidian. Despite these differences, both groups of letters were written by authors who were probably aware that their writings were potentially relevant for audiences beyond their immediate addressees. That they anticipated or even intended the wider circulation or publication of their letters seems to be evident in the case of politicians, famous writers, eminent scholars, or other public figures, whose letters often contained expositions on a particular topic and resemble essays or treatises about politics, literature, religion, and the like. Anecdotes about the appreciation and collection of calligraphy also suggest that celebrated calligraphers expected that their writings would be seen by more eyes than those of the addressees.

Many of the transmitted letters thus seem to have been part of a discourse that was more public than personal, and the exchange of ideas among a greater number of people was most likely one of the main functions of letter writing in early medieval China. An outstanding case are the sixty-odd letters of various authors addressed to Shi Fayun (ca. 467–529) concerning a Buddhist doctrinal question that was raised by Fan Zhen's (ca. 450–ca. 510) "Disquisition on the Destructibility of the Spirit" (Shenmie lun) and initiated by Xiao Yan (464–549), Emperor Wu of the Liang dynasty (r. 502–49).[120] Another example is the correspondence between Shi Huiyuan (334–416/417) and Kumārajīva (ca. 343–413), published as *On the General Meaning of Mahāyāna* (Dacheng dayi zhang).[121] Letters such as these apparently served a function that made them to some extent comparable to today's mass media, enabling the spread and exchange of ideas and opinions on socially and culturally relevant matters.[122]

As we may safely assume that most received personal letters were written in view of a wider audience and probably designed to this end, we could easily disqualify them as pretentious and fakes as far as personal authenticity is concerned and refuse to consider them as personal letters at all.[123] However, that a letter is written with its eventual publication in mind does not necessarily undermine its personal character. As Gérard Genette has suggested, the "first addressee interposed between the author and the possible public" should not be dismissed "as just an intermediary or functionally transparent relay, a media 'nonperson'," but instead regarded "as a full-fledged addressee, one whom the author addresses for that person's sake even if the author's ulterior motive is to let the public subsequently stand witness to his interlocution."[124] This means that the first addressee acts like a "catalyzer" whose personality shapes the content as well as the form of a communication.[125] Not the least because literariness itself can never be a constant, the borderline between everyday letters and literary letters remains blurred, so that there is a certain hybridity to reckon with in this respect, too. Again, indeterminacy should not be deemed a flaw but recognized as a defining feature of the genre. This is true of early medieval Chinese letters no less than of letters written in Western antiquity or the Middle Ages, for which studies have long abandoned the earlier, strict differentiation between the nonliterary letter and the literary epistle.[126]

CHAPTER TWO

Letters and Literary Thought

The others think, this time [the letter writer] has entered the stage stark naked. But in fact he is still wearing a flesh-colored, tight-fitting dress and even a brassiere, something he normally should never put on.

別人以為他這回是赤條條的上場了罷，他其實還是穿著肉色緊身小衫褲，甚至於用了平常决不應用的奶罩。

—LU XUN, "Preface to Kong Lingjing's *Letters of Contemporary Poets*" (Kong Lingjing bian *Dangdai wenren chidu chao* xu)

The origins of Chinese letter writing are unknown, and one may only speculate whether letters in China are the first type of text put into writing, as has been claimed for other parts of the world.[1] There are Chinese scholars who maintain that the earliest known Chinese writings, Shang dynasty oracle bone inscriptions, since they are messages to deified ancestors, essentially are letters.[2] While this is certainly a too inclusive view, it proves how open and indeterminate the epistolary genre is often perceived to be. The first transmitted examples of written communication in a narrower sense date from the Spring and Autumn period (722–481 BCE), one of the oldest being a diplomatic letter from 610 BCE quoted in *Zuo Tradition* (Zuo zhuan).[3] The few other letters transmitted from pre-imperial China are politically or rhetorically motivated as well, which is probably not representative of letter writing during these times but due to the vagaries of transmission. It well could be that personal letters, similar to the ones found in Shuihudi mentioned in chapter 1 and dating from the late third century BCE, were written during this period, too.

As a literary genre, the letter was established in the Han dynasty, a development that was furthered by the increase in and diversification of official communication at this time. Some nonofficial, very personal letters from this period acquired the highest literary fame and developed paradigmatic power for centuries to come. The most celebrated among them is the magnificent letter of Sima Qian (ca. 145–ca. 86 BCE) to Ren An (d. ca. 91 BCE), in which the author explains why he preferred to live with the shame of castration rather than die and leave the *Records of the Historian* (*Shi ji*) unfinished.[4] This letter was written at about the same time that Cicero elevated letter writing to an art form in the West. Next to this first and now classical autobiographical letter by Sima Qian, which "set the pattern for more intimate and personal autobiographical writing" in China,[5] there are smaller pieces that are still appreciated today, such as the letter from Ma Yuan (13 BCE—49 CE) to his nephews, which became the prototype of the familial admonitory letter.[6] Many famous letters dating from the Jian'an period (196–220) at the end of the Han dynasty herald the flourishing of Chinese epistolary literature in the early medieval period, such as the polished, satirical letter of Kong Rong (153–208) to Cao Cao (155–220), in which he criticizes his addressee's move to prohibit wine,[7] and Ruan Yu's (d. 212) exemplary political argumentations on behalf of Cao Cao.[8] It is thus hardly surprising that the Jian'an period also produced, along with more comprehensive writings on literary criticism and genre theory, the first reflections on letters as a literary genre.

CAO PI'S "DISQUISITIONS ON LITERATURE" ON LETTERS AS A GENRE

While the origins of Chinese literary thought in early and early imperial China lie in the concern for the moral and didactic value of literature, mainly for the state and society,[9] the Jian'an period and the following Wei dynasty have been apostrophized as "the age when literature became aware of itself."[10] This period saw the rise of an approach to literature that laid more stress on aesthetic criteria, or, as Donald Holzman put it, "we find men discussing literature as a thing in itself for the first time."[11] A superb example of this tendency, if not its archetype, is the essay "Disquisitions on Literature" (Lun wen) by Cao Pi (187–226), a fragment of his work *Classical Disquisitions* (Dian lun) and probably written in 217 or 218, after he had been made heir apparent.[12]

Starting with the famous words "literary men disparage each other; this has been so since antiquity," Cao Pi first turns to the "ill of lacking self-awareness" among critics before developing his ideas about the fundamentals of literature.[13] A concise characterization of eight literary genres serves as the starting point of his discussion of the connection between an author's innate personality and literary style.

夫文本同而末異	As for literature, its root is the same, but its branches are different.
蓋	Hence:
奏議宜雅	presentations and appeals [*zou yi*] should be decorous;
書論宜理	letters and disquisitions [*shu lun*] should be structured;
銘誄尚實	inscriptions and dirges [*ming lei*] value truthfulness;
詩賦欲麗	poems and rhapsodies [*shi fu*] require beauty.
此四科不同	Because these four classes are not the same,
故能之者偏也	a skilled writer leans [towards one of them].
唯通才能備其體	Only a universal talent can master their entire body.
文以氣為主	Literature is dominated by one's vital energies [*qi*].
氣之清濁有體	The clarity or turbidity of these vital energies are of a certain type
不可力強而致	that cannot be brought about forcibly.[14]

The attempt to discern four classes (*ke*), or, implicitly, eight genres of literature, and to define the purpose of each class by only one quality may seem oversimplified, but it is illuminating as to Cao Pi's extensive notion of *wen*, here meaning "literature." It includes none of the three genres (comedy, tragedy, and epic) that are traditionally traced back to ancient Greek literary thought and only one of the three Goethean "natural forms" of literature (epic, poetry, drama), which seems only reasonable since neither epic nor drama occur in ancient or early medieval China.[15] Of the Western core genres, Cao Pi mentions only poetry, represented by poems (*shi*) and rhapsodies (*fu*). The remaining genres in his catalog refer to literary types, which in modern Western typology would be classified as utilitarian texts[16] and thus determined chiefly by external pragmatic functions. The dirge, for instance, is governed primarily by the desire to pay homage to a deceased person's life and merits and not by the wish to produce a work of literature. It goes without saying that this crude differentiation cannot do justice to the diversity of literary production—be it in China or the West, past or present—because a poem may very well be determined by external pragmatic functions and a dirge by the wish to produce a piece of literature. Even if the differentiation between utilitarian texts and belles lettres is complex, it is helpful to keep the literary diversity in mind.

Unlike poetry, which is covered quite well by the two genres Cao Pi mentions, prose appears to be unevenly represented in his list. Obviously, his catalog was meant to be selective rather than comprehensive.

Given this selectiveness, it is all the more striking that three of Cao Pi's six prose genres indicate types of written communication. The two that are examples of official communication, presentations (*zou*) and appeals (*yi*), fall into one group, for which decorousness or elegance (*ya*) is prescribed,[17] while letters (*shu*) and disquisitions (*lun*) are expected to be structured or well-organized (*li*).[18] This grouping of letters with disquisitions suggests that Cao Pi perceived letters as nonofficial, personal letters that follow genre expectations that are different from those for official communication. Both Cao Pi's demand for structure and his association of letters with disquisitions or essays may also be found in Western epistolary theory.[19] Despite the fact that Cao Pi presents his ideas of genre not in a descriptive but in a prescriptive mode, his point of departure ensures an essentially nondogmatic understanding. Since he emphasizes *qi*, the breath or vital energies that shape an individual's personality and character, and, in the case of authors, their writings or other creations,[20] the distinctive individuality of everybody's blend of vital energies will inevitably lead to genre variety as well: no letter will be like another, even if they are all "structured."

Elsewhere in his "Disquisitions on Literature," Cao Pi remarks upon two writers of official and personal communication, his abovementioned contemporaries Chen Lin and Ruan Yu.

琳瑀之章表書記	Chen Lin's and Ruan Yu's memorials and letters [*shuji*]
今之雋也	are currently the most outstanding.[21]

The identification of excellent writers or texts is a crucial part of Chinese literary criticism, often more important than or even replacing abstract elaborations. Especially if they were effected by an influential personage, these accentuations usually amounted to a canonization of the selected authors or texts. Although in this case Cao Pi's praise is unspecific and does not even offer a pithy phrase as in his probably somewhat later "Further letter to Wu Zhi" (You yu Wu Zhi shu), no. 1 (see the "Letters about Literary Thought" section), it is not surprising to find both Chen Lin and Ruan Yu mentioned frequently in later works of literary thought and in connection with written communication.

THE ABSENCE OF LETTERS IN LU JI'S "RHAPSODY ON LITERATURE"

When the great Western Jin poet Lu Ji (261–303), almost a century later, wrote his "Rhapsody on Literature" (Wen fu), he accomplished a significant advancement of literary thought.[22] Compared to Cao Pi's short essay, Lu Ji's rhapsody is longer and treats a broader spectrum of literary questions in a much more sophisticated way. For the first time, literary creation itself was described in great detail and, moreover, in the form of a rhapsody, one of the most demanding literary genres of ancient China, famous for its intricacy and profundity. Lu Ji's "Rhapsody on Literature" also includes a slightly expanded literary typology, which lacks two of Cao Pi's eight genres and adds four others, so that his list now comprises poems, rhapsodies, epitaphs (*bei*), dirges (*lei*), inscriptions (*ming*), admonitions (*zhen*), eulogies (*song*), disquisitions, presentations, and persuasions (*shui*). At five words each, the descriptions of each genre are also more complex. However, not only are letters missing from Lu Ji's list, but also appeals, so that only one genre of official communication remains, presentations. Retaining Cao Pi's genre requirement, Lu Ji characterizes presentations as "calm and thorough as well as refined and decorous."[23] His list of genres makes clear that he, like his predecessor Cao Pi, was attempting not to comprehensively cover the whole spectrum of literary works but to give a representative choice of genres he deemed important.[24]

Although Lu Ji does not mention letters anywhere in "Rhapsody on Literature," there is one passage that is occasionally quoted in the context of letter writing, albeit erroneously. It is found within the following almost ecstatic description of the creative process:

課虛無以責有	The writer examines nothingness, requesting being,
叩寂寞而求音	and knocks on silence, seeking sound.
函綿邈於尺素	He encloses infinite distances within a foot of plain [silk] [*chisu*]
吐滂霈乎寸心	and spits out torrential rains from his inch of heart [*cunxin*].[25]

Neither the passage itself nor its context of literary creativity provides any indication that *chisu* is to be understood as a reference to letters, and most scholars have read or translated it accordingly.[26] The misattributions[27] are based mainly on the semantic ambiguity of the term *chisu*, which is a well-known letter designation but may also refer to just a sheet of writing silk intended for any purpose. Misinterpretations could moreover have been encouraged by Li Shan's (ca. 630–689) commentary on "Rhapsody on Literature" in *Selections of Refined Literature*, which refers to a verse of the Han dynasty poem "Song about Watering the Horses in a Cave at the Great Wall," which mentions a "letter on a foot of plain [silk]," although in this phrase, *chisu* serves only as an attribute modifying *shu* (letter).[28] A similar reason for misunderstanding could have been that Liu Xie in chapter 25 of *The Literary Mind and the Carving of Dragons* alludes to Lu Ji's passage, now in fact in the context of letter writing.

LIU XIE'S *THE LITERARY MIND AND THE CARVING OF DRAGONS* ON LETTERS

If neither Cao Pi nor Lu Ji aspired to comprehensiveness in their descriptions of literary genres, Liu Xie (ca. 475–ca. 520) certainly did. In the preface to his magnum opus *The Literary Mind and the Carving of Dragons* (ca. 515),[29] Liu Xie dismissed the attempts of his predecessors, among them Cao Pi and Lu Ji, because "they all illuminated nooks and gaps but rarely kept an eye on the main avenues." Unlike them, Liu Xie boldly claimed to have been "almost comprehensive" in his own work, and he certainly was.[30] *The Literary Mind* is the most outstanding work of literary thought in China, distinguished by an uncommonly systematic approach and a wealth of detail on an unprecedented scale of literary issues. The literary form of Liu Xie's work is magnificent as well, not only in its overall layout, but also in the lines of its mostly parallel prose and their almost organic interconnectedness.[31] Liu's coverage of genres by far supersedes former attempts at genre classification in China, spanning the whole field of literature from poetry to philosophy to doctors' prescriptions. Chapter 25, "Shu ji" 書記, contains the first detailed characterization of personal letters in Chinese literary history.

Disregarding the preface in chapter 50, the arrangement of *The Literary Mind* is tripartite. In the first five chapters, Liu Xie gives an exposition of his basic literary concepts, the subsequent twenty chapters introduce a broad range of literary genres,[32] and part 3 is dedicated to a variety of questions concerning the creative process, rhetoric, reception theory, and so forth.[33] Traditionally, the twenty chapters on genre are further divided into *wen* and *bi*—variously understood as rhymed and unrhymed, patterned and unpatterned, or refined literature and utilitarian texts. Although this division is commonly attributed to Liu Xie, *The Literary Mind* itself does not provide conclusive information on this point, so that interpretations abound.[34] After the *wen-bi* division had become obsolete in the course of the Tang dynasty, the discussion seems to have been revived only in the nineteenth century, first by Ruan Yuan (1764–1849) and his followers[35] and a century later in the wake of the rediscovery in Japan of *Disquisitions from the Secret Repository of the Literary Mirror* (Bunkyō hifuron) by Kūkai (774–835), which contains the only transmitted medieval list of *wen* and *bi* genres.[36] Among the most influential modern scholars who discussed *wen* and *bi* are Liu Shipei (1884–1919) and several commentators on *The Literary Mind* such as Huang Kan (1886–1935) and Fan Wenlan (1891–1969). Most of them disagreed about the understanding of the two concepts, as well as about the question of where in the typological part of *The Literary Mind* to draw the dividing line between chapters dealing with *wen* and chapters dealing with *bi* genres. Assuming that *wen* refers to refined literature and *bi* to utilitarian texts, and that both kinds of writing are differentiated by pragmatic and aesthetic features alike,[37] this division is located between chapters 14 and 15, which results in two ten-chapter sections: chapters 6–14 covering *wen* and chapters 15–25 covering *bi* genres. The higher degree of "literariness" of the genres categorized as *wen* would thus result from a mixture of pragmatic and formal characteristics, including prosodic features. The last chapter of both the *wen* and the *bi* section (i.e., chapters 14 and 25) appears to be designated to gather the odds and ends not covered in the preceding chapters of each section. As regards chapter 14, this interpretation is supported by the title "Miscellaneous Kinds of Refined Literature" (Za wen) and by the large number of genres it introduces.[38] Chapter 25, which concludes the *bi* section, seems to have been designed in a similar vein, as it presents twenty-nine genres, again many more than any of the preceding chapters in the *bi* section.

Chapter 25 is an appropriate conclusion to the *bi* section and the genre block as a whole in another respect, too, because it treats writing as a distinctive element of genre classification. Generally, the genres described in *The Literary Mind* are defined by textual, not material qualities. The other exception, in addition to chapter 25, is chapter 11, "Inscriptions and Admonitions" (Ming zhen), which similarly introduces a genre, the inscription, that is defined mainly by its materiality. Texts of this genre are engraved (*ming*) into the surface of everyday utensils or ceremonial objects, which means that they are mostly cut (*ke*) into metal, stone, wood, or other hard materials. These objects are of a certain durability and often immobile. Among Liu Xie's examples are inscriptions on doors, walls, bronze vessels, statues, and the like.[39] Writing in the sense of the term *shu* denotes a quite different procedure: the application of a liquid, usually ink, on the surface of various absorbent materials that are mostly light and easy to transport, such as bamboo, silk, or paper. In *The Literary Mind*, *shu* thus designates texts that are distinguished primarily not by textual features but by a material quality, namely, by the fact that they are essentially written texts, which, given the notorious indeterminacy of letters as regards form, content, and function, is a very prudent decision on the part of Liu Xie. Other genres may and frequently do appear in written form as well, but for them, writing is not a necessary condition. This calls to mind the above-mentioned peculiar self-referentiality of letters, the fact that they "present themselves as writing," singled out as a decisive genre feature by modern scholars of Western epistolary literature as well.[40]

As has been established by scholars studying many ancient cultures in the past decades, the production and reception of literary texts were originally not visual but acoustic phenomena. Texts were composed, recited, performed, appreciated, and memorized without necessarily fixing them in writing. Liu Xie himself was well aware that whether texts existed in written or oral form is a significant issue and repeatedly refers to the transition from oral to written modes of communication. In chapter 22, for instance, he maintains that at the court of the legendary Emperor Yao, "memorials were presented by word of mouth" and that "words were spread without resort to the writing brush." He dates the emergence of written documents at court to the Shang dynasty (16th–11th century BCE).[41] This argument is repeated, in part even verbatim, in chapter 23, which is also dedicated to types of official communication.[42] Literacy as opposed to orality is emphasized elsewhere in *The Literary Mind* as well. When Liu Xie characterizes strategies of the persuasions, he expressly points out that persuasions "need not always be effected in speech but can equally well be accomplished in writing [lit., "by knife and brush"],"[43] which implies the preeminence of orality. This means that Liu Xie was clearly aware of the difference between textual and material criteria in his classification of genres.[44] While the greater part of *The Literary Mind* deals with texts and textual properties, chapter 25 collects genres that are distinguished not so much by textual properties as by the fact that they necessarily exist in written form.[45]

This understanding suggests that "Written Records" is the most appropriate rendering of the title of the chapter, rather than "Epistolary Writings" or "Letters and Records" as it is often translated. *Shu ji* 書記 are "written records" in the broadest sense, a term that not only embraces all the textual genres mentioned in chapter 25 but also is the most common meaning of the compound in early medieval Chinese.[46] Although *shu ji* may indeed refer to "epistolary writings," it is only infrequently used in this capacity, for instance, in Cao Pi's "Disquisitions on Literature."[47] The title of chapter 25 adheres to the two-syllable format that is uniformly employed throughout *The Literary Mind*, although the syntactic relation between the two syllables is not the same in all titles.[48] Translating the phrase *shu ji*, we have thus to decide first whether the two words form a subordination or a coordination. The latter would imply that this chapter introduces two genres, *shu* and *ji*, which are dealt with in the first and the second part of the chapter, respectively. However, while *shu* is a common genre designation in *The Literary Mind* and elsewhere in early medieval literature, *ji* is not.[49] In *The Literary Mind*, it occurs only as the second part of two compounds designating types of official documents: *zouji* and *jianji*, the subgenres of presentation.[50] Moreover, while *shu* could well cover the chapter's first part (which, incidentally, includes the introduction of *zouji* and *jianji*), *ji* could definitely not do the same for the second part of the chapter, since none of the many clearly non-epistolary genres presented here is ever called *ji*. All this strongly suggests the reading of the chapter title as a subordination.[51] Second, we have to decide on the interpretation of the title words. The core meaning of *ji* is "record, to record, to commit to memory."[52] As already mentioned, *shu* means "to write, writing(s)." The interpretation of *shu* as "letter" would be too limited, since the titles "Epistolary Writing" and "Letter Records" fail to describe the genres introduced in the second and greater part of this chapter.[53] "Written records" thus remains as the only adequate translation. It furthermore highlights the parallels between the titles of the last chapters in the *wen* and *bi* sections, respectively, since they are both collective designations of a general nature: "Miscellaneous Kinds of Refined Literature" and "Written Records."

Approaching chapter 25 from this perspective (i.e., with the expectation of learning about written records), the text makes for very smooth reading that resolves many of the qualms earlier interpreters expressed.[54] Its composition follows the pattern Liu Xie himself set forth for the genre chapters in his preface. He first traces the genre back to its origin and the Confucian canon and provides an explanation of the genre designation. After that, he outlines the historical development of the genre, mainly by means of a series of exemplary pieces, striving to arrive at a comprehensive genre characterization.[55] Accordingly, the first part of the chapter is dedicated to displaying the canonical ancestry of written records.[56] The introduction is framed by two references to the canonical texts that are conventionally quoted in connection with the topic of writing.

大舜云	The Great Shun said:
書用識哉	"Writing is used to remember."[57]
所以記時事也	By writing, the events of the times are recorded.
蓋聖賢言辭	Hence the words of the sages and the worthies
總為之書	were all put into writing.
書之為體	In the formation of writing,
主言者也	the emphasis is on words.[58]
揚雄曰	Yang Xiong said:
言心聲也	"Words are the voices of the mind;
書心畫也	Writings are the images of the mind."[59]
聲畫形	When voices and images take shape,
君子小人見矣	it becomes apparent who is a gentleman and who a petty man.
故書者舒也	Therefore, to write is to unfold.
舒布其言	Unfolding and spreading one's words,
陳之簡牘	Arraying them on [bamboo] slips and [wooden] tablets,
取象於夬	one takes the hexagram *guai* as a model,[60]
貴在明決而已	which means nothing but to esteem clarity and decisiveness. (lines 1–17)

Most perplexities about chapter 25 arise from the expectation that Liu Xie deals mainly with letters. Read like this, the introduction appears too broad and pointless. But read with the expectation that chapter 25 addresses genres that are defined not primarily in terms of textual properties but by the criterion of existing in written form, it does not appear surprising at all that Liu Xie first discusses the emergence of writing and the production of written records in general. The initial reference to the canonical *Book of Documents* (Shujing or Shangshu) is taken from its chapter "Yi and Ji" (Yi ji), which mentions two methods of committing transgressions to memory: while the scourge may be adequate to fix something in individual memory, writing is necessary to secure an incident in collective or cultural memory over time—*verba volant, scripta manent.* The initial quote also refers back to a topic mentioned in chapter 3 of *The Literary Mind*, "The Canon as the Ancestor" (Zong jing), in which Liu Xie maintains that "the *Book of Documents* recorded words reliably."[61] Liu Xie's second reference to the canon—the connection of writing to "clarity and decisiveness" via hexagram 43 of the canonical *Book of Changes* (Yijing or Zhou yi)—returns to a topic mentioned in the first, pivotal part of *The Literary Mind* as well. In chapter 2, "Evidence from the Sage" (Zheng sheng), hexagram 43 is distinguished by its association with Confucius.[62] In accordance with the established interpretation of this hexagram, which as early as in the "Commentary on the Appended Words" (Xici zhuan) was associated with the replacement of knotted cords by written documents,[63] Liu presents writing as a powerful political and administrative instrument. The two references to the Confucian canon would appear far-fetched if applied to personal letter writing, but they are clearly pertinent to official communication as described in *The Literary Mind.* Liu Xie not only sets out clarity and decisiveness as desirable qualities of official documents[64] but also in chapter 3 identifies the *Book of Documents* as the ancestor to several genres of official communication.[65] Letters are not mentioned on this occasion, nor are they listed among the "descendants" of any other canonical book. Yan Zhitui (b. 531), who established a different genre genealogy in his *Family Instructions* (Yanshi jiaxun), does include letters and locates their origin in the *Spring and Autumn Annals* (Chunqiu).[66]

Although he brings up the *Book of Changes*, Liu Xie does not go on to cite the famous statement, transmitted in the "Commentary on the Appended Words," that "writing does not fully capture words, words do not fully capture meaning" (*shu bu jin yan, yan bu jin yi* 書不盡言, 言不盡意).[67] This skeptical dictum, ascribed to Confucius and immensely popular in early medieval philosophical and literary thought, became an omnipresent topos in Chinese letter writing as well, in which it was used to lament the insufficiency of letters or even language and writing.[68] Instead of citing Confucius, Liu Xie quotes Yang Xiong (53 BCE–18 CE), who, in his *Model Words* (Fayan), asserts that words are the voices and writings the images of the mind. This choice indicates Liu Xie's optimistic attitude toward the mimetic powers of writing and, conversely, his confidence that writing—comprising the aural as well as the visual qualities of a text, which is made explicit elsewhere in

The Literary Mind[69]—is an efficacious means of evaluating someone's moral character. This is the same notion of writing as the "externalization of the writer's mind and personality"[70] expressed in the discussion of calligraphy and letter writing. For the Western scholar of epistolary literature, the ancient Greek idea that "everyone writes a letter in the virtual image of his own soul" comes to mind.[71] This topos, whose locus classicus is the earliest treatise on letters in ancient Greek literature, an excursus in *On Style* (De elocutione) (1st century BCE?) falsely attributed to Demetrius of Phalerum (ca. 350–280 BCE), has remained one of the key elements of Western epistolary theory up to the present day.[72]

Liu Xie's optimistic attitude toward the powers of writing may be related to the fact that he locates the origins of written records not so much in the religious or philosophical realm as in more pragmatic contexts. Literary texts, which are in a more elevated and abstract sense manifestations of the Dao, are discussed in the earlier chapters about genres defined by textual qualities. Liu sees the origins of written records, however, in recording "the events of the times" and "the words of the sages and the worthies" and accordingly stresses reliability (*Book of Documents*) and clarity (*Book of Changes*) rather than more recondite qualities. He insists that "in the formation of writing, the emphasis is on words," that is, on the reliable and clear rendition of spoken words into writing. This is an essential point, because written texts have to do without the abundance of performative means, such as intonation, facial expression, and gesture, that are available in oral communication to assist or subtly modify a message according to the actual circumstances of its perception.[73]

Following this general introduction, Liu Xie turns to those among the "written records" that apparently are of the greatest literary appeal to him—letters, a genre whose very name emphasizes its necessarily written form, as is also true in English. He delineates the development of letter writing from its emergence through its first millennium, mostly along the lines of letters mentioned in transmitted texts. Consequently, in these parts of chapter 25, the term *shu* usually needs to be translated not just as "writing" in general but as "letter." For the sake of stylistic variability, Liu Xie also uses other words that, similar to *shu*, can either refer to writings in general or denote letters in particular (lines 19, 24, 34, 51, and 61), or he refers to writings that, as their historical context shows, are letters without explicitly calling them such (lines 25, 46–47, and 53–58).

三代政暇	During the Three Dynasties, government was leisurely
文翰頗疎	and writings [*wenhan*] were scarce.
春秋聘繁	When in the Spring and Autumn period diplomatic visits became frequent,
書介彌盛	writings and messengers [*shu jie*] became more abundant.
繞朝贈士會以策	Raochao presented Shihui with bamboo slips [*ce*];[74]
子家與趙宣以書	Zheng Zijia gave Zhao Xuanzi a letter [*shu*].
巫臣之遺子反	There was Wuchen's bestowal to Zifan
子產之諫范宣	and Zichan's remonstration with Fan Xuanzi.[75]
詳觀四書	Reading these four letters [*shu*] carefully [reveals that]
辭若對面	their words resemble those spoken face-to-face.
又子服敬叔	There is also Zifu Jingshu,
進弔書于滕君	who submitted a letter of condolence [*diao shu*] to Lord Teng.[76]
固知行人挈辭	We therefore know that the words carried by envoys
多被翰墨矣	were now often recorded by brush and ink.
及七國獻書	The letters [*shu*] later presented in the Seven States
詭麗輻輳	were exceptionally beautiful and very numerous. (lines 18–33)

Liu Xie ascribes the emergence of letter writing to the political situation of the Spring and Autumn period, which required a more extensive exchange of messages, implying a gradual shift from the archetypical transmission of oral messages to the transportation of written documents. While the initial quote from the *Book of Documents* emphasizes the transmission of writings across time, Liu Xie now brings up transmission across spatial distances—the second reason for the production of written records and, with regard to letter writing, the more significant one.

Liu Xie lists five specific letters from the Spring and Autumn period, all of them mentioned or partly transmitted in canonical literature, and summarily treats the letters from the "Seven States," that is, the Warring States period (453/403–221 BCE). He commends two textual features of these early letters. The first, pragmatic one is the resemblance of the written words of a letter to those spoken face-to-face, which amounts to the perception of letters as substitutes for conversation—a universal epistolary topos that appears about the same time in ancient Greece and Han dynasty China. Artemon (late 2nd century BCE?), the editor of Aristotle's *Letters*, is quoted as saying "that a letter should be written in the same manner as a dialogue" and famously compared it to "one of the two sides of a dialogue."[77]

The second textual feature Liu Xie introduces is beauty (*li*) as an aesthetic criterion for the evaluation of letters. This demonstrates his high esteem for the literary potential of the genre, since beauty is a criterion widely employed in the pivotal chapters of *The Literary Mind* and in the chapters dealing with *wen* genres.

In the following lines, Liu Xie further pursues the historical development of letter writing in the Western Han dynasty (206–9 BCE):

漢來筆札	As to letters [*bizha*] from the [Western] Han,
辭氣紛紜	their words and thrust [*qi*] are of dazzling diversity.
觀史遷之報任安	Contemplating scribe Sima Qian's answer to Ren An,
東方之難公孫	Dongfang Shuo's censure of Gongsun [Hong?],[78]
楊惲之酬會宗	Yang Yun's response to Sun Huizong,[79]
子雲之答劉歆	Ziyun's [i.e., Yang Xiong's] reply to Liu Xin,[80]
志氣槃桓	we find their intent and thrust exalted,
各含殊采	and that every one of them has its particular hue.
幷杼軸乎尺素	All of them have woven into a foot of plain [silk] [*chisu*]
抑揚乎寸心	what may weigh down or elate an inch of heart [*cunxin*]. (lines 34–43)

Characterizing the Western Han, Liu Xie again lists individual letters, some of which have been transmitted to the present day. Among the qualities he praises are their diversity and the literary uniqueness of every letter. His emphasis on variety within a literary genre resembles the approach of Cao Pi, but while "Disquisitions on Literature" discusses mainly the differences in vital energy, or *qi*, on the part of the authors, Liu Xie additionally highlights the varying vital energies of the literary texts themselves, obviously referring to their aesthetic and affective thrust. This idea is also expressed in the last two lines, in which Liu Xie doubly alludes to Lu Ji's "Rhapsody on Literature." Taking up his predecessor's image of the literary text as a woven fabric,[81] he ingeniously relates it to the texture of silk, which was a common writing support for letters. The association of "a foot of silk" with "an inch of heart," also owed to Lu Ji, is significantly modified according to Liu Xie's priorities in chapter 25. Drawing attention to the dialogic nature of correspondence, Liu not only talks of the creative mind of the author but equally implies the intellectually and emotionally perceptive mind of the reader.

A sketch of the development of letter writing in the Eastern Han (24–220) and Wei (220–65) dynasties concludes Liu Xie's historical overview.

逮後漢書記	Of Eastern Han letters [*shuji*],
則崔瑗尤善	those of Cui Yuan were especially good.[82]
魏之元瑜	The letters of Yuanyu [i.e., Ruan Yu] of the Wei
號稱翩翩	have been called "full of verve."[83]
文舉屬章	Collecting the works of Wenju [i.e., Kong Rong],
半簡必錄	every fragment was surely registered.[84]
休璉好事	Xiulian [i.e., Ying Qu] was assiduous
留意詞翰	and dedicated to letters [*cihan*],
抑其次也	but he is not as good as [Kong Rong].[85]
嵇康絕交	Xi Kang's severances of relationships
實志高而文偉矣	truly display lofty intentions and literary might.[86]
趙至敘離	Zhao Zhi's description of a separation
迺少年之激切也	expresses the ardor of youth.[87]
至如陳遵占辭	As for Chen Zun's dictations,
百封各意	every one of a hundred makes perfect sense.[88]
禰衡代書	Mi Heng's commissioned letters [*shu*]
親疎得宜	to addressees close and distant achieved propriety.[89]
斯又尺牘之偏才也	These authors were extraordinary epistolary talents. (lines 44–61)

In his appraisal of the masterpieces of Eastern Han and Wei letter writing, Liu Xie continues to demonstrate the great variety in which letters occur and how much appreciated their finest examples have been. Toward the end of this passage, he emphasizes epistolary propriety—that is, the necessary adjustment of letters according to the social status of the recipients and the writer's relationship to them—an aspect that was to become one of the key elements of later epistolary guides in China. When he then mentions Chen Zun's dictations, Liu Xie implicitly also suggests the potential calligraphic value of letters, since Chen Zun's letters are among the first that were collected for their fine handwriting.

Following this historical overview, Liu Xie presents an oft-quoted general characterization of the epistolary genre.

詳總書體	The genre of letters [*shu*], both in detail and in general,
本在盡言	is rooted in the full capture of words.
言以散鬱陶	Words are meant to dispel pent-up emotions
託風采	and to carry demeanor.

故宜條暢以任氣	Therefore they should be smooth in order to convey the thrust
優柔以懌懷	and gentle in order to delight the heart.
文明從容	If a text is clear and unfettered
亦心聲之獻酬也	it truly corresponds to the voices of the mind. (lines 62–69)

In this passage, Liu Xie returns to an issue discussed at the outset of the chapter—the importance of the appropriate rendering of spoken words in written form. By declaring letters to be rooted in the full capture of words (*jin yan*), an allusion to the above-mentioned dictum of Confucius, Liu Xie reiterates his confidence in the fundamental possibility of such an endeavor. However, he also emphasizes, just as Yang Xiong had done, that a text needs to fulfill certain requirements so that it "truly corresponds to the voices of the mind," which also means being true "images of the mind." For Liu Xie, letters had to be "clear and unfettered" if they were to achieve this aim, which can be read as an extension of Cao Pi's demand that letters be structured or well-organized (*li*). While clarity (*ming*) reflects Cao Pi's approach directly, since structure usually results in clarity, Liu Xie's second requirement provides a decisive modification. By requiring that letters also be "unfettered"—*congrong* connotes easy movement, leisure, and spontaneity—Liu Xie seems to moderate Cao Pi's demand for structure and allow them a certain freedom. Again, there are parallels in ancient Greek epistolary theory, which called for the sentences of a letter to be "fairly loosely structured," as opposed to those of a formal speech.[90]

Lines 64 and 65 are often interpreted as Liu Xie's key statement about the function of letters. He first declares that their words are supposed to dispel "pent-up emotions" (*yutao*), which could indicate an outlet for the writer as well as for the reader of a letter. Although *yutao* usually refers to states of unhappiness and worry, it may also characterize joy that has not found expression.[91] That Liu Xie had a more inclusive understanding of *yutao* than just melancholy or sadness is also suggested elsewhere in *The Literary Mind*, in which the word describes a state of emotional fullness as a desirable precondition of literary creativity.[92] The second function that Liu Xie ascribes to the words of a letter is that they should be able to carry *fengcai*, rendered as "demeanor" in order to emphasize that it refers not only to the literary qualities of a text but also to the personality of the writer and thus alludes to the topos of the letter as a substitute for face-to-face conversation.

So far, in lines 18–69, Liu Xie's characterization of the epistolary genre is of a rather comprehensive nature, including personal as well as official correspondence, en route touching upon various subgenres, such as condolences or admonitions. In the following forty lines of the chapter (70–110), Liu Xie takes a closer look at official communication, especially at the diversification of subgenres and names. He mentions memorials and presentations, which he treats fully in chapters 22 and 23, and introduces subgenres of presentation (*zouji*, *zoujian*, *jianji*), which do not appear anywhere else in the book but are treated here in the usual manner, including terminological and historical explanations as well as exemplary pieces. Concerning these types of official communication, Liu Xie generally employs the same aesthetic criteria he uses in the preceding part of the chapter. Drawing attention to the presentations of Liu Zhen (d. 217), for instance, which he believes to be underestimated, Liu Xie describes them as more beautiful (*mei*) than even Liu Zhen's poems, which amounts to a distinct literary valorization of these genres of utilitarian texts.[93]

The following part of chapter 25 is dedicated to the description of twenty-four minor genres of written records, which are first listed in six groups of four, each assigned to a different area of social life:

夫書記廣大	As for written records [*shu ji*], their scope is vast;
衣被事體	they cover a variety of subjects and forms.
筆劄雜名	Written documents [*bizha*] of miscellaneous names
古今多品	are thus manifold in past and present.
是以	Hence:
總領黎庶	In order to integrate and lead the common people
則有譜籍簿錄	there are chronicles, directories, warrants, registers.
醫歷星筮	In medicine, hemerology, astrology, and divination
則有方術占試	there are prescriptions, calculations, prophecies, formulas.
申憲述兵	For spreading laws and transmitting military orders
則有律令法制	there are rules, acts, regulations, ordinances.
朝市徵信	For securing trustworthiness at court and on markets
則有符契券疏	there are tallies, contracts, bonds, sales slips.
百官詢事	For facilitating the diverse official inquiries
則有關刺解牒	there are credentials, criticisms, explanations, certificates.
萬民達志	Allowing the people to express their intentions,
則有狀列辭諺	there are notices, accounts, testimonies, dicta.[94]
并述理於心	All of these perpetuate the order to the mind

著言於翰	through words written down by the brush.
雖藝文之末品	Although they may be marginal specimens of artistic literature,
而政事之先務也	with regard to administrative matters they are of foremost relevance. (lines 111–31)

After insisting on the practical significance of these types of text, Liu Xie goes on to characterize every one of them separately. This takes up the greatest part of the whole chapter (lines 132–289), which is another indication of his high esteem for these apparently petty kinds of utilitarian texts. This may be surprising, but only if we disregard the fact that Liu Xie, like most other literary scholars, was, after all, an official and administrator who knew of the importance of the efficacy of utilitarian texts. However, unlike personal or official letters, these genres are described only in terms of technicalities but never associated with literary brilliance.

In his final summary, Liu Xie again widens his perspective to include all kinds of "written records" he has mentioned so far.

觀此 (四)〔數〕條	Contemplating all these categories, [we find that]
并書記所總	they may all be covered by the term written records [*shu ji*].
或事本相通	Some are principally analogous in subject
而文意各異	but differ in their literary content.
或全任質素	Some entirely rely on substance and plainness,
或雜用文綺	while others variously employ patterning and embroidery.
隨事立體	Form is established according to subject matter,
貴乎精要	giving priority to the essentials.
意少一字則義闕	If there is one character missing of the content, the meaning is deficient,
句長一言則辭妨	and if a sentence is too long by one word, the statement is obstructed.
并有司之實務	All written records are the true responsibility of officials
而浮藻之所忽也	but are neglected because they strive for excessive brilliance.
然才冠鴻筆 多疎尺牘	This being so, when great literary talents generally disregard letters [*chidu*],
譬九方堙之識駿足	they are like Jiufang Yin, who recognized a fine horse
而不知毛色牝牡也	but was unaware of the color of its coat or its sex.[95]
言既身文	When words are the adornment of the person,
信亦邦瑞	they are certainly also auspicious for the state.
翰林之士	All scholars of the literary world

思理實焉	should aspire to structure and truthfulness in [writing]. (lines 290–309)

Liu Xie's insistence on the significance of the apparently minor "written records" is reinforced by his allusion to the legendary equine expert Jiufang Yin, who famously overlooked the exterior features of a horse. Just as the coloration or the sex of an animal may seem irrelevant to its essential value as a racehorse but are nonetheless inalienable elements of a particular horse's physique, the minor genres of utilitarian texts are indispensable parts of the literary domain and their mastery is a condition for being considered a true literatus.

As in every chapter of *The Literary Mind*, an encomium concludes chapter 25.

贊曰	The encomium says:
文藻條流	The brilliance of literature and the thriving of the diverse genres
託在筆札	are entrusted to written records [*bizha*].
既馳金相	They may gallop in golden splendor,
亦運木訥	but also carry wooden stammering.
萬古聲薦	Voices a myriad of years old are presented;
千里應拔	responses from a thousand of miles away are incited.
庶務紛綸	The multitudinous responsibilities that form a dazzling clew
因書乃察	by writing they are made discernible. (lines 310–18)

The encomium is again concerned with the overarching theme of this chapter, "written records" in general, a category informed by the nontextual, material criterion of their written form. Liu Xie emphasizes their great literary diversity reaching from "golden splendor" to honest but plain "wooden stammering," their capacity to cross time and space, and their importance for administrative and other practical affairs, elements that are essential for letter writing as well. The fact that for most readers, chapter 25 is associated with personal letters to such a high degree, while the extensive passages on official communication and miscellaneous written records are usually overlooked, is a reflection of Liu Xie's emphasis on the particular literary potential of letters that far exceeds their pragmatic function.

LETTERS IN XIAO TONG'S *SELECTIONS OF REFINED LITERATURE*

The eminent anthology *Selections of Refined Literature*, probably compiled a few years after the completion of *The Literary Mind*, is of equal importance for our knowledge of genre awareness in early medieval China in general and the literary perception of letters in particular, not the least because it is the only transmitted literary anthology from this period. The exact circumstances and the date are uncertain, but it is known that *Selections of Refined Literature* was compiled by Xiao Tong (501–531), Crown Prince Zhaoming of the Liang dynasty, and a group of collaborators.[96] There have been speculations that Liu Xie may have been involved in the compilation process, because among the minor offices he held after the founding of the Liang dynasty in 502 was a secretarial position at the residence of Xiao Tong. Although the standard *History of the Liang Dynasty* (Liang shu) observes that the crown prince profoundly enjoyed Liu Xie's company,[97] there is no way of knowing whether Liu Xie had any influence on the formation of Xiao Tong's anthology. Starting with the Tang dynasty, the 761 literary works by 130 authors from pre-imperial times up to the Liang that are collected in *Selections of Refined Literature*, among them many letters and other pieces of written communication, became the "core reading of every literate person" in China.[98]

The famous preface to *Selections of Refined Literature* does not provide any information on letters as a genre.[99] In this text, Xiao Tong elaborates on only a few selected genres, such as the rhapsody and the poem, while others are presented in the form of an annotated list, with each genre characterized by a short sentence. A third group of genres is merely enumerated without further comments, among them all types of written communication. The preface's catalog of genres does not, moreover, accord with the genres that are represented in the anthology's sixty chapters.[100] As David Knechtges has pointed out, "to obtain a more precise understanding of the criteria Xiao Tong applied in the process of selection, one must examine the *Selections of Refined Literature* itself."[101] Such an examination shows that the classification of written communication, which is represented in chapters 35–44, is based mainly on the hierarchical relationship between writer and addressee. Chapters 35 and 36 collect genres of official communication that are addressed to inferiors, such as edicts (*zhao*), patents of enfeoffment (*ce*), commands (*ling*), instructions (*jiao*), and examination questions (*cewen*). Chapters 37–40 assemble genres of official communication addressed to superiors, such as memorials, letters of submission (*shangshu*), communications (*qi*), accusations (*tanshi*), memorandums (*jian*), and notes of presentation (*zouji*). Although chapters 41–44, which include the genres letters and proclamations (*xi*), are usually taken to represent communication between equals, they turn out to be hierarchically diverse.[102] While all of the proclamations and the two irregular dispatches (*yishu*, *yiwen*) at the end of chapter 44 are addressed to inferiors, about a third of the twenty-two letters are addressed to superiors.[103] Among the examples of written communication anthologized in *Selections of Refined Literature* examined with regard to their personal or official character, there are personal letters in only two categories: memorandums and letters. While more than half of the nine memorandums in chapter 40 are personal,[104] written communication labeled *shu* is always personal; this includes the twenty-two letters in chapters 41–43[105] as well as two more letters attached to poems of the type "presentation and response" in chapter 25.[106]

The greatest achievement of *Selections of Refined Literature* for epistolary studies lies in its collection itself, that is, the preservation of a substantial number of literary letters, many of which achieved canonical status because of their inclusion in this prestigious anthology. The personal letters anthologized here are so diverse that they allow only limited conclusions about Xiao Tong's notion of epistolary literature. The most remarkable fact is undoubtedly that personal letters were included at all and did not fall victim to Xiao Tong's rigorous "culling of the weeds."[107] It is not surprising that the letters he selected, just like those that Liu Xie mentions in *The Literary Mind*, are exceptional literary pieces that are not at all representative of the more mundane form of the genre as it was practiced in the everyday lives of countless contemporaries.

LETTERS ABOUT LITERARY THOUGHT

The texts discussed so far exemplify the spread of Chinese reflections on literature over many different genres, from disquisitions to rhapsodies and prefaces. Another genre that has always been a popular medium for contemplating literature is, of course, that of letters, not only in China, but in other cultures as well. Two of the most famous

European examples are the letter of Dante Alighieri (1265–1321) to Cangrande della Scala about his *Divine Comedy* and Hugo von Hofmannsthal's (1874–1929) fictitious, semiautobiographical Lord Chandos letter whose striking description of a young writer's intellectual crisis became an important document of the deep modernist unease about cultural and aesthetic developments in Europe around 1900.[108] There are many more and more ancient examples.[109] The letter is especially suited to discussing literary thought because of its genre-specific openness and textual indeterminacy, which allow the assimilation of any material, and because of its dialogicity, which greatly facilitates the development of arguments based on individual convictions and concerns. In premodern times, before the advent of mass media such as journals and newspapers, letters were moreover an important means of exchange among members of the social and cultural elite as well as an instrument of political and intellectual participation for those on the margins of these circles. This is certainly true for early medieval China, where exchanges about crucial intellectual and aesthetic questions were taking place in aristocratic salons not only in the form of conversations but also in correspondences, such as the already mentioned letters about Buddhist doctrinal matters initiated by Liang Wudi, but there are other examples as well. This chapter, while introducing select letters about literary thought and examining how their epistolarity shapes their arguments, also explores what these texts had to say about letters in particular. Although one might expect literati to habitually reflect on the medium they are using, there are only a few among the many letters dedicated to literary questions that mention or discuss the epistolary genre.[110]

One of the most famous early letters about literature is Cao Pi's "Further letter to Wu Zhi," no. 1, written in 218, in which Cao Pi appraises the literary qualities of mutual friends, many of whom had passed away a year before during an epidemic, among them poets who came to be known as the "Seven Masters of the Jian'an period."[111] The following passage is an excerpt from the body of this much longer letter, whose beginning and closing will be introduced in chapters 3 and 4.

> . . . I have just compiled the writings our friends left behind and gathered them in one collection, where their names look like a register of the dead. When I think back to our past excursions, I can still see all these masters in

my mind's eye, but they have already become dung and soil. Is there anything more I can say?

Considering writers past and present, we find that most of them did not guard their behavior in trivial matters and thus could rarely establish themselves through having a reputation of moral integrity. Weichang [i.e., Xu Gan] alone not only cherished literary refinement but also possessed substance. Tranquil and "of few desires,"[112] he had the intentions of Mount Ji[113] and could truly be called a "well-balanced gentleman."[114] He wrote the more-than-twenty-chapters-long *Balanced Disquisitions* (Zhong lun), "words that founded a school."[115] His works are of a classical elegance in both style and message that makes them worth transmitting for posterity. This master is perennial. Delian [i.e., Ying Yang] was always "brilliant"[116] and intent on writing. He had talent and learning enough to write a great book.[117] That he could not fulfill his fine ambition is really excruciatingly regrettable. When I glanced through the writings of these masters, I had to "wipe my tears" in front of their texts.[118] Grieving for the departed, we turn our thoughts to our own death. Kongzhang's [i.e., Chen Lin's] memorials are particularly strong but slightly grandiloquent. Gonggan [i.e., Liu Zhen] was high-minded but not yet forceful enough. The best of his five-word poems are matchless in subtlety among his contemporaries. Yuanyu's [i.e., Ruan Yu's] letters [*shuji*] are full of verve [*pianpian*] and produce ample enjoyment. Zhongxuan [i.e., Wang Can] continued to improve his rhapsodies. It is sad that their bodies were too weak to support their literary adornments. As far as his best rhapsodies are concerned, there are none among the ancients who far surpassed him. . . .

. . . 頃撰其遺文。都為一集。觀其姓名。已為鬼錄。追思昔遊。猶在心目。而此諸子。化為糞壤。可復道哉。觀古今文人。類不護細行。鮮能以名節自立。而偉長獨懷文抱質。恬淡寡欲。有箕山之志。可謂彬彬君子者矣。著中論二十餘篇。成一家之言。辭義典雅。足傳於後。此子為不朽矣。德槤常斐然有述作之意。其才學足以著書。美志不遂。良可痛惜。間者歷覽諸子之文。對之抆淚。既痛逝者。行自念也。孔璋章表殊健。微為繁富。公幹有逸氣。但未遒耳。其五言詩之善者。妙絕時人。元瑜書記翩翩。致足樂也。仲宣續自善於辭賦。惜其體弱。不足起其文。至於所善。古人無以遠過。 . . .[119]

Cao Pi's approach is representative of the early medieval interest in the classifying assessment of personalities and talents.[120] Unspecific or even arbitrary as such assessments may strike later readers, they often became part of the orthodox evaluation of an author. Cao Pi's depiction of Ruan Yu's letters as *pianpian*, for instance, was taken up twice in Liu Xie's *The Literary Mind* as well as by other writers.[121] Cao Pi seems to have been the first author to use *pianpian* in the description of literary qualities; in earlier texts, starting with the canonical *Book of Odes* (Shijing or Mao shi),[122] the word is used to describe the swift and easy movement of birds, clouds, leaves, dragons, and the like in the air and, starting with the Han dynasty, also other effortless movements, of a horse, a boat in the water, or a curtain fluttering in the wind. Also starting in the Han, *pianpian* is used to describe a person's integrity and elegance.[123] Texts characterized as *pianpian* were obviously perceived as exuding ease and swiftness, rendered here as "full of verve." In the case of Ruan Yu, *pianpian* could also have been an allusion to the process of composition, because Ruan Yu was famous for the speed and ease of his writing. According to one anecdote, he once amazed Cao Cao by composing a letter on his behalf while on horseback. When Ruan Yu had finished writing and presented the draft, Cao Cao, an eminent writer himself, reportedly grasped a brush in order to make corrections but, to his surprise, could not find a single word that needed to be changed.[124]

However, Cao Pi's letter yields much more with regard to epistolary thought in early medieval China than just the one sentence about Ruan Yu's epistolary qualities and the epithet *pianpian*, authoritative as it may have been. It also offers the rare opportunity to measure a letter of literary criticism against a literary essay written by the same author. Comparing Cao Pi's "Further letter to Wu Zhi," no. 1, with his "Disquisitions on Literature" reveals similarities, but the differences are more pronounced, especially in tone. While Cao Pi the letter writer appears to be striving for objective and relevant observations about his subject matter just as the essayist does, in the letter, he frequently interrupts his reflections about the literary accomplishments of his friends to make room for very subjective and personal words that not only effectively evoke the dialogicity of correspondence but also achieve an amalgamation of more general interpersonal concerns (confirming his friendship with Wu Zhi) with particular communicative intentions (a review of the contemporary literary scene).

This epistolary flavor is most striking in the passage dedicated to Ying Yang, because it suggests that the author, led astray by his agitated feelings and associations, spontaneously suspended his inventory of literary talent. Thinking of Ying Yang's prematurely crushed literary ambitions, Cao Pi is moved to painful sorrow and eventually to tears, at the same time turning his thoughts and those of his correspondent to their own mortality. Despite the informal character of this letter, it is improbable that this passage directly reflects stream of consciousness or inner monologue. The harmonious structure of the letter and its stylistic elaboration suggest that it was penned not impulsively but with considerable attention to detail. Cao Pi was exploiting the genre-typical potential of the inherent dialogicity of the letter, which allows the loose succession or even juxtaposition of different subjects and a relaxed train of thought resembling the back-and-forth of a conversation.[125] The image of himself that Cao Pi has created in this letter—shedding tears in front of the compositions of his friends—comes across as authentic enough to lend additional credibility to his catalog of literary fortes and weaknesses, which means that he is immensely successful with respect to rhetorical, aesthetic, and personal communication. For modern readers, or, for that matter, any reader apart from the original addressee, the criterion of literary effectiveness is dominant compared with that of the authenticity of the expressed sentiments.[126]

One example that shows how influential Cao Pi's letter to Wu Zhi would turn out to be is a letter in which Xiao Ziliang offers a critical opinion on another epistolary text. Xiao refers to an "epistolary campaign" he had instigated by asking members of his literary salon to write to the Buddhist recluse Liu Qiu (fl. ca. 490) in order to persuade him to join the salon as well.[127] Addressing Liu Yin, who had written to Liu Qiu and obviously received a reply, which he had shared with the members of the salon, Xiao Ziliang writes:

> After you, sir, wrote a letter [*shu*] to the recluse Liu last winter, you have now, in the spring, received a reply. It is "full of verve" [*pianpian*] and enough [to prove Liu Qiu's] ample literary talent. It is truly on a par with Ziyun's [i.e., Yang Xiong's] letters [*bizha*] and Yuanyu's [i.e., Ruan Yu's] letters [*shuji*]. . . .
>
> (冬去)〔去冬〕因君與劉居士書, 今春得其返 (价)〔文〕。辭趣翩翩, 足有才藻。實子雲之筆札, 元瑜之書記。 . . .[128]

Xiao Ziliang's praise of Liu Qiu's letter is in accord with tradition as discussed so far. He summarizes Liu's epistolary accomplishments by using Cao Pi's epithet *pianpian* and compares Liu with Ruan Yu and Yang Xiong, two letter writers whose talents were highlighted by Cao Pi and Liu Xie.[129] Although not exactly an inspired tribute, this must have been the highest praise one could bestow on a letter writer in early medieval China.

The letter of Wang Sengru (465–522) to He Jiong does not mention *pianpian* but contains references to Ruan Yu and Yang Xiong, along with a wealth of other intra-epistolary allusions. Wang Sengru employs them to support the description of his state of mind at the time when he was parting from his correspondent a year earlier, when he had been dismissed from office and was threatened with imprisonment.[130]

近別之後	Since we parted last time,
將隔暄寒	a year has passed.
思子為勞	"Longing for you, I have become weary";[131]
未能忘弭	I cannot forget or stop it.
昔李叟入秦	Formerly, when Old Li [i.e., Laozi] entered Qin
梁生適越	and Young Liang [i.e., Liang Hong] went to Yue,
猶懷悵恨	one was filled with dejection
且或吟謠	and the other chanted a ballad.[132]
況岐路之日	What is more, when the day of parting ways had come,
將離嚴網	I was caught in a tight net;[133]
辭無可憐	there was no word of pity,
罪有不測	and my crime was unfathomable.
蓋畫地刻木	Hence there were "drawings [of a prison] on the ground" and "carvings [of a warden] in wood,"[134]
昔人所惡	which were hated by the ancients.
叢棘既累	A "thicket of thorns" had already grown [around me].[135]
於何可聞	When would we hear from each other again?
所以握手戀戀	That is why I passionately clasped your hands
離別珍重	and urged you to take good care of yourself after taking leave.
弟愛同鄒季	Your affection was like that of Zou Wen and Ji Jie,[136]
淫淫承睫	tears unrestrainedly brimming over your lashes,
吾猶復抗手分背	while I just raised my hands in salute when we parted,[137]
羞學婦人	ashamed to imitate a woman.
素鍾肇節	Plain bells open the season [of autumn];
金飆戒序	metal gales warn about its start.[138]
起居無恙	May you be unharmed at all times
動靜履宜	and may everything you do turn out to be right.
子雲筆札	Ziyun's [i.e., Yang Xiong's] letters [*bizha*]
元瑜書記	and Yuanyu's [i.e., Ruan Yu's] letters [*shuji*]
信用既然	are not only trustworthy and useful
可樂為甚	but also extremely enjoyable.
且使目明	Moreover, they can make our eyes clear-sighted
能祛首疾	and dispel the pain of parting;[139]
甚善甚善	they are very good indeed [*shen shan shen shan*].[140]
吾無昔人之才	I do not have the talents of the ancients,
而有其病. . . .	but I do have their weaknesses [*bing*]. . . . [141]

It is not unusual for texts in parallel prose to be packed with allusions, but this proem in Wang Sengru's much longer letter stands out because so many of its references are intra-epistolary and can thus be read as implicit comments on the literary tradition of letter writing. In the passage quoted above, Wang Sengru alludes to letters written by Cao Zhi, Zhao Zhi, Sima Qian, Yang Xiong, Ruan Yu, and Wang Lang, and refers to at least three more letters—written by Yang Yun, Ren Fang, and Zhao Zhi[142]—in later parts. By evoking these letters and their writers, Wang Sengru not only places himself in a more or less canonical tradition of letters of friendship but also marks the cause of his letter—a plea for support—as perfectly honorable. Examining the way Wang Sengru employs these allusions reveals that they are connected to the standard constituents of the proem. When he laments his separation from He Jiong, he alludes to Cao Zhi and Zhao Zhi; when he describes his state of mind at parting, he refers to Sima Qian's words about the devastating psychological effects of imprisonment. The reference to Yang Xiong's and Ruan Yu's letters, along with an allusion to Wang Lang, takes the customary place of praising the letter one has received from the addressee. Although this convention does not apply here, because Wang Sengru writes on his own initiative, he ingeniously reworks the conventional tribute to the addressee's letter into praise of established epistolary models, a rhetorical strategy that serves two ends. By explicitly setting up these earlier letters as a foil against which his lack of talent must become all the more obvious, Wang first fulfills the expectation of epistolary modesty. His attention to detail shows when he makes use of the ambiguity of *bing*, which can refer not only to illness (the topic of the following part of the letter that is not included here) but also to literary deficits. A second rhetorical aim appears when he mentions the beneficial effects of good letters, because this amounts to an anticipation of the request for a reply that is traditionally placed in the epilogue but is missing in this letter.

As already mentioned, is not unproblematic to assume intra-epistolary or, actually, any kind of allusions, because knowledge about the circulation and collection of personal letters in early medieval China is sparse. It is not known how, when, or to what degree personal letters became public. There is no doubt that any scholar writing in the fifth century would have been familiar with certain Han or Wei dynasty letters, such as Sima Qian's reply to Ren An or Cao Zhi's letter to Yang Xiu, but is there any way of knowing that Wang Sengru knew of Xiao Ziliang's letter, short of him saying so? Not only is the dating of both texts difficult, but even if one assumes that Wang

Sengru wrote his letter later than Xiao Ziliang, perhaps even by a few years, is it certain that he knew of this text? How many people apart from the addressee would read such a letter? Would they have to be members of his salon? How long would it take a letter to become known outside of a small circle? There are no positive answers to these and other questions related to the circulation of letters in early medieval China. It is equally possible that the two identical references to Yang Xiong and Ruan Yu in the letters by Xiao Ziliang and Wang Sengru go back to the common stock of literary phrases scholars typically acquired in the course of their education. This issue becomes even more problematic in considering phrases such as *shen shan shen shan* (very good indeed). Although not at all common in transmitted letters from early medieval China, occurring only half a dozen times, this sentence need not be an allusion at all but could merely be an epistolary phrase.[143] While we may not always be able to decide why a particular phrase was used in a letter, we must certainly reckon with the power of the conventional letter formula and of the common stock of epistolary phrases and topoi.

PART TWO

Epistolary Conventions and Literary Individuality

CHAPTER THREE

Structures and Phrases

There, I flatter myself I have constructed you a Smartish Letter, considering my want of Materials. But, like my dear Dr. Johnson, I beleive I have dealt more in Notions than Facts.

—JANE AUSTEN, letter to Cassandra Austen, February 8, 1807

The particular tripartite composition that emerges in letters all over the world has often been compared to the similar structure of a conversation or an oration, which both also start with a salutation and an introductory part, then turn to the relevant core information and finally to closing words.[1] Further subdividing the opening and closing, European medieval rhetoric since the twelfth century largely agreed on a five-part letter formula,[2] which has been found to be productive in the analysis of non-Western letters as well.[3] Since early medieval Chinese epistolary theory did not elaborate on the structure of letters or develop a distinct indigenous terminology,[4] this chapter's introduction of the main components of early medieval Chinese letters will follow the established three- or, respectively, five-part Western model, which differentiates the letter opening (consisting of prescript and proem), main body, and closing (consisting of epilogue and postscript).[5]

Investigation of the letter formula is complicated by the fact that most of the known early medieval letters were transmitted in edited form, which makes it impossible to decide whether they are complete or not. While some letters appear to be unabridged—that is, they consist of a complete frame and a letter body—others lack certain parts, such as the opening and closing or other epistolary markers. Although we can generally assume that the absence of these parts is the result of editing, which often meant "de-epistolarizing," we should keep in mind the possibility that certain elements may have been dispensable under certain conditions, especially in personal letter writing that was probably not as strictly governed by conventions as official communication. This means that letters that appear to be lacking a part of the frame, for instance, the prescript, may originally never have featured this part.

LETTER OPENING

Prescript

Prescripts and postscripts are the most formalized parts of a personal letter in early medieval China. A complete prescript consists of the date of writing, the writer's self-designation or *superscriptio* (most commonly the given name, *ming*), and a predicate, as the following examples show:

> On the third day of the second month, [Cao] Pi lets you know: . . .
>
> 二月三日丕白。 . . .[6]
>
> On the twenty-fourth day of the twelfth month, [Wang] Xizhi reports: . . .
>
> 十二月二十四日羲之報。 . . .[7]
>
> On the eighth day of the second month [the day with the cyclical sign], *gengyin*, your vassal [Wu] Zhi says: . . .
>
> 二月八日庚寅臣質言。 . . .[8]
>
> On the ninth day of the eighth month, [Sima] Rui knocks his head on the ground: . . .
>
> 八月九日睿頓首。 . . .[9]
>
> On the twenty-second day of the eighth month, [Liu] Zhilin obeisantly salutes you: . . .
>
> 八月二十日之遴和南。 . . .[10]

In personal letters, the *date* usually specifies only the month and the day without indicating the year. In some cases, the month is missing as well, probably because letters were exchanged frequently enough to rule out misunderstandings. The addition of cyclical signs in order to further identify the day, which is common in official communication, is rare in personal letters.[11] Variations of the date include references to seasonal festivals and the phases of the moon, which, because of their rich connotations, also serve as expressions of affection and longing for the addressee.

> The years go, the months come, and suddenly it is the ninth day of the ninth month again. . . .
>
> 歲往月來。忽復九月九日。 . . . [12]
>
> It is mid-month and I am thinking of you. . . .
>
> 月半。念足下。 . . . [13]

Both the Double Ninth, or Double Yang (Chongyang), festival on the ninth day of the ninth month as well as the full moon at mid-month were favorite occasions for writing to friends and family members. The Double Ninth festival was an occasion for getting together with friends, climbing hills, and drinking chrysanthemum wine, while the full moon at mid-month was associated with togetherness and, at the same time, separation, and longing.

Only a handful of verbs could be used in the *predicate* of a prescript. They indicate either the communicative function of writing or the writer's reverence for the addressee, although there are combinations of both. Concerning the function of writing, the most common choice by far is *bai* 白 (to let someone know). Other verbs include *yan* 言 (to speak, say), *bao* 報 (to report, reply), *wen* 問 (to inquire), *shu* 疏 (to write), *yue* 曰 (to say), *shu* 書 (to write), and *xie* 謝 (to thank). Expressions of the writer's reverence for the addressee refer either to a physical act of salutation or to a state of mind. They include *zaibai* 再拜 (to bow repeatedly),[15] *dunshou* 頓首 and *koutou* 叩頭 (to knock one's head [on the ground]), *qishou* 稽首 (to bow one's head [to the ground]), *sizui* 死罪 (to deserve death punishment [on account of this letter's insolence]), and *huangkong* 惶恐 (to be terrified). These phrases had been in use in official communication since the Qin and Han dynasties, when they were originally meant to convey what they literally expressed but soon became formulaic, especially after they were adopted in personal letter writing, which happened as early as the Eastern Han dynasty.[15] Verbs indicating the communicative function of writing and reverence for the addressee also occur in diverse combinations and may be modified by additional expressions of respect, such as *jing* 敬 (respectful) and *jin* 謹 (sincerely).

Given the limited corpus of letters transmitted with prescripts, it is difficult to assess the implications of these verbs, be it with regard to hierarchy or epistolary subgenre, so that only a few clear patterns of use emerge. It seems quite certain that *bai* was hierarchically neutral, because it is found in letters to superiors and inferiors alike. Letters of condolence or mourning, however, appear to avoid *bai*, using *bao*, *sizui*, *dunshou*, or *huangkong* instead. *Yan*, on the other hand, was obviously reserved for letters to superiors, because it usually occurs in combination with other markers of respect, such as the self-designation *chen* 臣 (your vassal).[16] Among the conventional expressions of reverence, *zaibai* and *dunshou* sometimes appear to be almost casual, while *koutou*, *sizui*, and *huangkong* apparently retained a higher degree of reverence because they are usually used in semi-personal letters. *Qishou* is mostly paired with the Buddhist greeting *henan* 和南.

Prescripts show a number of variations from this pattern. Often the date is lacking, since there may have been no need for documentation, and less frequently the self-designation or the predicate, for the sake of brevity or because there were other means to reveal the identity of the writer, such as the handwriting or the envelope. One special case deserves mention here: prescripts of letters to younger members of one's family. Their most conspicuous characteristic is that they not only contain a *superscriptio* but also an *adscriptio*, a designation of the recipient, which was extremely rare in early medieval letters but became the epistolary standard during the Tang dynasty. Prescripts of this particular type regularly use the verb *gao* 告 (to tell, announce, notify), which is usually followed by the given name of the addressee.

> [Tao Qian] notifies [his sons] Yan, Si, Fen, Yi, and Tong: . . .
>
> 告儼俟份佚佟。 . . .[17]
>
> On the tenth day of the seventh month, [Xie] Wan notifies [his son Xie] Lang: . . .
>
> 七月十日萬告朗等。 . . .[18]
>
> On the twelfth day, [Wang Xizhi] notifies the nephew of the Li family: . . .
>
> 十二日告李氏甥。 . . .[19]

Proem

I wish I knew always the humour my friends would be in at opening a letter of mine, to suit it to them nearly as possible. I could always find an egg shell for Melancholy—and as for Merriment a Witty humour will turn anything to Account—my head is sometimes in such a whirl in considering the million likings and antipathies of our Moments—that I can get into no settled strain in my Letters.

—JOHN KEATS, letter to John Hamilton Reynolds, July 13, 1818[20]

The introductory passage following the prescript, in Western epistolography called the "proem" or "exordium," is dedicated to the recollection and reaffirmation of the correspondents' preceding relationship and tries to secure the goodwill of the addressee, equivalent to the *captatio benevolentiae* in Latin rhetoric. Correspondents, in order to resume the temporarily interrupted communicative thread between them, address their current situations and thus attempt to connect the different worlds of writer and reader, reckoning with the time lag typical of epistolary communication. In order to "update" the personal relationship between them,[21] they mention the weather or the time of year as well as the reception or non-arrival of letters; they report the state of their health and inquire about the other's well-being; they express good wishes and complain about their continuing separation. The inherent focus on both the moment of writing and that of reading, which Claudio Guillén has called the "fragmentation of time," is an important expression of the self-referentiality and dialogicity of epistolary writing.[22]

While only one in seven of the transmitted letters features a prescript, more than a third contain a proem, which makes the proem the most frequently transmitted part of the epistolary frame. It appears that proems, despite their relative formulaity, have not been cut by editors quite as rigorously because the small talk they consist of sometimes contains information of personal relevance.

On the first day of the first month, [Wang] Xizhi reports:

Suddenly we have moved into a new year. I am overwhelmed by feelings of longing for you that I can hardly endure. What can I do? What can I do? How have you been with all your ailments in this unusual cold? I have not had any news [*wen*] from you for many days and feel worried beyond words. . . .

初月一日羲之報。忽然改年。感思兼傷。不能自勝。奈何奈何。異更寒。諸疾此復何似。不得問多日。懸心不可言。 . . .[23]

[Wang] Yun obeisantly salutes you:

At the winter solstice I excessively long for you. My mourning is so very deep, I can hardly endure my feelings. How is your doctrinal body during this freezing cold? I hope you have recently been quiet and comfortable. Your disciple is frail and weary. . . .

筠和南。至節過念。哀慕深至。情不可任。寒凝。道體何如？想比清豫。弟子羸勞。. . .[24]

Despite the general relevance and often even dominance of the proem, this part of the letter is regularly missing in certain epistolary subgenres, such as letters of familial admonition, recommendation, or condolence. They all have in common a strong and distinct communicative agenda beyond the maintenance of a personal relationship, but the decisive reason for the absence of a proem is different in each case. In admonitory letters to younger members of one's family, the absence of the proem indicates the superior authority of the writer, who can take the relationship to the addressee for granted and can thus come straight to the point, without any detours devoted to securing the goodwill of the addressee. Recommendations dispense with the proem because it would interfere with the semiofficial function of this type of letter, which very probably was intended for an audience beyond the immediate addressee. It goes without saying that the usual kind of small talk would be out of place in letters of condolence.

Although prescripts are immediately recognizable as such, it is sometimes difficult to distinguish between the proem and the letter body proper because the subject matter of these parts may overlap, especially in more personal, quotidian letters. In official and semiofficial writings, in contrast, the dividing line is very clear, as in the opening of the following letter written in 505 by Qiu Chi (464–508), who attempted to persuade Chen Bozhi, a general who had defected to the Northern Wei dynasty (386–534), to return to the Liang:

遲頓首	[Qiu] Chi knocks his head on the ground:
陳將軍足下	May you, General Chen,
無恙	be unharmed;
幸甚幸甚	this would be very fortunate indeed.
將軍勇冠三軍	The General's courage crowns the Three Armies;[25]
才為世出	your talent stands among your contemporaries.[26]
棄燕雀之小志	Having cast aside the small ambitions of swallows and sparrows,
慕鴻鵠以高翔	you aspire to the high flight of wild geese and swans.

昔因機變化 Formerly [*xi*], because of an opportunity for change,
遭遇明主 . . . you joined our enlightened ruler. . . . [27]

The opening of this piece of parallel prose assembles important elements of the proem: good wishes, including that for good health, and a flattering assessment of the other's abilities and ambitions. These compliments, however, are not quite as innocent as they may appear, because they evoke the famous, if fictitious, Han dynasty correspondence between Su Wu (d. 60 BCE), a Han envoy who was held captive by the Xiongnu for many years but eventually returned, and Li Ling (d. 74 BCE), who, after a long collaboration with the Xiongnu, declined to return to the Han and stayed behind.[28] Since the correspondence between Li Ling and Su Wu was regarded as an exemplary exchange about loyalty and treason, Qiu Chi's well chosen intra-epistolary allusions implicitly offer two alternative models of civic behavior right at the beginning of the letter: to prove one's loyalty by returning or to remain a traitor. The signal word *xi* 昔 (former, formerly) then indicates the start of the letter body and, at the same time, a change of topic and argumentation.

In a letter that Xiao Gang wrote in 531 to his younger brother Xiao Yi (508–554), Emperor Yuan of the Liang dynasty (r. 553–54), the proem is also distinctly marked off. The reason in this case is not the letter's official character but the fact that Xiao Gang had a clear agenda, the description of his Buddhist lay ordination, which had taken place in various stages in the week before he wrote this letter toward the end of the ninth lunar month in 531.

> In the evening of the eighteenth, outside of Hualin Pavilion in the Palace, having received your letter [*shu*] of the first day of the ninth month, I feel quite comforted in my worry and longing for you. We are having a cold and clear autumn. Everything is as usual. There are quite a few provincial matters [that keep me busy], but not enough to fatigue me. My [philosophical] disposition of the "Bridge over the Hao" is not different from what it used to be.[29] I am almost completely happy, and often there are occasions for delight. I frequently enjoy discussions with my literary guests that outlast the end of a banquet. How are you these days? In your work on a commentary on the *History of the [Western] Han Dynasty* (Han shu) you have now made progress. I long to set eyes on this book; I excessively hunger after it.
>
> I have taken the bodhisattva vows and am prepared to become a mahāsattva. This was on the twelfth. . . .

十八日晚, 於華林閣外省中。得弟九月一日書, 甚慰懸想。秋節淒清, 比如常也, 州事多少, 無足疲勞。濠梁之氣, 不異恆日。差盡怡悅, 時有樂事。游士文賓, 比得談賞, 終宴追隨。何如近日。注漢功夫, 轉有次第。思見此書, 有甚飢惄。吾蒙受菩薩禁戒, 篋預大士, 此十二日。 . . .[30]

Xiao Gang's letter opens with a fairly conventional but still highly personal proem. He briefly acknowledges the receipt of his brother's letter, unusual in also indicating the place where this happened, mentions the weather and his own well-being, and goes into some detail about his current state of mind and intellectual life. Then he turns to his addressee, inquiring after his brother's well-being and professing a strong interest in his scholarly work. The following beginning of the letter body is distinct to the point of being abrupt, which gives the impression that Xiao Gang could hardly wait to describe to his brother how he experienced the lay ordination he had just gone through.

The first extant Chinese letter discussing literature, written in 216, has a similarly clear structure, which again reveals a strong and specific communicative urge, albeit of a quite different nature. In this letter, Cao Zhi sets out not only his assessment of the literary scene but also his political ambitions, which he famously ranks higher than any literary accomplishment. The reason for this announcement may have been that Cao Zhi, when he wrote this letter, still cherished hopes that his father Cao Cao might designate him to be heir apparent, hopes that were to be crushed a year later when his elder brother Cao Pi prevailed. Among the supporters of Cao Zhi, who were executed after Cao Pi had been made heir apparent, was Yang Xiu, the recipient of this letter.

[Cao] Zhi lets you know:

I have not seen you for several days. "Longing for you I have become weary." I think you must feel the same.

Your servant has had a penchant for literature since I was child, for twenty-five years now. Therefore I can briefly characterize the writers of our time. Formerly (*xi*), Zhongxuan [i.e., Wang Can] strode without par south of the river Han, Kongzhang [i.e., Chen Lin] soared like an eagle north of the Yellow River,[31] Weichang [i.e., Xu Gan] made himself a name in Qingzhou, Gonggan [i.e., Liu Zhen] vitalized literature on the coast, Delian [i.e., Ying Yang] left his marks here in Wei, while you from up high command a view of the capital. . . .

植白。數日不見。思子為勞。想同之也。僕少小好為文章。迄至于今二十有五年矣。然今世作者。可略而言也。昔仲宣獨步於漢南。孔璋鷹揚於河朔。偉長擅名於青土。公幹振藻於海隅。德槤發跡於此魏。足下高視於上京。 . . .[32]

In this letter, the prescript is followed by a very short proem consisting only of a lament of separation. The intensity of longing that Cao Zhi professes seems at odds not only with the shortness of their separation but also with the sudden change of topic in the next sentence. He maintains the tone of overstatement, since he dates his love for literature to his birth—Cao Zhi was only twenty-five when he wrote this letter. He closes on a note of hubris as well, when he asserts his friendship with Yang Xiu in a composite allusion casting himself as a great Warring States philosopher and a powerful Spring and Autumn politician at the same time, "I rely on Huizi who understands me."[33] The comparison with Guan Zhong (d. 645 BCE) arises because the phrase alludes to Guan's friendship with Bao Shuya as it is put in a letter by Zhang Heng (78–139), which is known from an excerpt quoted in the commentary on *Selections of Refined Literature*, "I rely on Baozi who understands me."[34] By replacing "Baozi" with "Huizi," Cao Zhi evokes the famous friendship between Zhuangzi and Huizi and assumes Zhuangzi's place.[35]

In the rest of the main body of this letter, Cao Zhi continues to assess and criticize other writers and declares that he welcomes criticism himself. Since his letter accompanied a gift of his collected works, this last move may well have implied the request that his addressee criticize his writings. It hardly comes as a surprise, however, that, in his response, his correspondent Yang Xiu rejected the mere possibility of improving Cao Zhi's texts and claimed that he would read them "chanting like a blind old man, and nothing else."[36] The only criticism he offered concerned Cao Zhi's idea that a successful political career is superior to or even inconsistent with literary achievements, which is, of course, a flattering remark as well.

All in all, the body of Cao Zhi's letter resembles a loosely structured essay, and little betrays its origins as a personal letter. Considering the brevity of proem and epilogue, which appear almost perfunctory, as do the rare instances of dialogicity within the body, one may wonder if this text was ever a letter at all or is rather an essay in disguise. If it was indeed composed as a letter, the problem may have been that it was a decidedly utilitarian endeavor, because Cao Zhi needed a cover letter to accompany a gift of his collected works. This would also explain why it was written just one day before a meeting.[37] The presence of a clear communicative purpose is often felt to be slightly problematic in personal letters, especially letters of friendship, since the lack of any particular message actually emphasizes its affectionate nature—an observation about letters of friendship that had also been made in the West, as early as in ancient Rome.[38]

Cao Pi's famous "Further letter to Wu Zhi," no. 1, written about two years later, and quoted in chapter 2 as an exemplary case of a letter dedicated to literary thought, is a very different case altogether. Although concerned with topics similar to those addressed by his younger brother, Cao Pi writes a letter that shows a much higher degree of epistolarity. This quality is indicated not least by blurred boundaries between proem and main body, which produce the impression of a staggered start of the letter body proper.

> On the third day of the second month, [Cao] Pi lets you know:
>
> Years and months are easy to come by. It has already been four years since we parted. Not seeing each other for three years is, in the ode "Eastern Mountain," lamented as a long time.[39] How much more so when three years have been exceeded! How can I cope with my longing for you? Although we exchange letters [*shushu*], they do not suffice to relieve the weariness of longing. Last year when the epidemic raged, our relatives and friends were struck hard by this calamity. Xu [Gan], Chen [Lin], Ying [Yang], and Liu [Zhen] all passed away at the same time. Can the pain be expressed in words?
>
> In former [*xi*] days, whether traveling or staying at home, our carriages would be connected when we drove and our mats would touch when we stopped. When did we ever lose sight of each other, if only for a moment? When the goblet went round amid the sound of strings and pipes, when our ears were hot from wine and we looked up to recite rhapsodies and poems,[40] I was too careless to realize my own happiness. I assumed that each of us had been allotted a hundred years and that we could forever be together and take care of each other. Who could have imagined that within a few years almost all of them would be withered and fallen? My heart aches if I so much as talk about it.
>
> I have just compiled the writings that our friends left behind and gathered them in one collection, where their names look like a register of the dead. When I think back to our past excursions, I can still see all these masters in my mind's eye, but they have already become dung and soil. Is there anything more I can say?
>
> Considering writers past and present, we find that most of them did not guard their behavior in trivial matters and thus could rarely establish themselves through having a reputation for moral integrity. . . .

二月三日丕白。歲月易得。別來行復四年。三年不見。東山猶歎其遠。況乃過之。思何可支。雖書疏往返。未足解其勞結。昔年疾疫。親故多離其災。徐陳應劉。一時俱逝。痛可言邪。昔日遊處。行則連輿。止則接席。何曾須臾相失。每至觴酌流行。絲竹並奏。酒酣耳熱。仰而賦詩。當此之時。忽然不自知樂也。謂百年己分。可長共相保。何圖數年之閒。零落略盡。言之傷心。頃撰其遺文。都為一集。觀其姓名。以為鬼錄。追思昔遊。猶在心目。而此諸子。化為糞壤。可復道哉。觀古今文人。類不護細行。鮮能以名節自立。 . . .[41]

In this text, it is difficult to determine the end of the proem and the beginning of the main body. Although both Cao Pi's and Cao Zhi's letters have a distinct literary agenda, Cao Pi's "Further letter to Wu Zhi," no. 1, also was a personal letter of friendship. It is set apart by a higher degree of attention to both the addressee and the epistolary situation, showing a pronounced dialogicity and self-referentiality. This also means that the conventional subjects of the proem—especially the relationship between the correspondents and the lament of separation and of the passing of time—spill over to the letter body, infusing it with a strong epistolary flavor. As mentioned, it is this amalgamation of more general interpersonal concerns (typical of the proem) with particular communicative intentions (usually reserved for the letter body) that produces the rhetorically, aesthetically, and personally most convincing letters.

Wu Zhi's reply, dated a few days later, opens in a similar vein but is tinged with devotion and reverence toward his young friend, the heir apparent.

> On the eighth day of the second month, [the day with the cyclical sign] *gengyin*, your vassal [Wu] Zhi says:
>
> I had the honor of reading your handwritten letter [*ming*, directive], in which you recall the dead and consider the living. The abundance of your kindness and affection has materialized in literature and ink. The days and months "gradually pass by," "the years are not on our side."[42]
>
> Formerly (*xi*), I waited upon you, sitting with many virtuous men. Outside, we traveled incognito, and inside, we enjoyed the sound of pipes and strings. When wine was offered, we enjoyed drinking; we recited rhapsodies and poems and wished each other a long life. I assumed that we could take care of each other from the beginning to the end, joining together our talents and forces in absolute loyalty to our enlightened ruler. Who would have thought that within a few years almost all of them would be dead and buried? What unique virtues does your vassal possess that allowed me to survive?
>
> The talents and erudition of Chen [Lin], Xu [Gan], Liu [Zhen], and Ying [Yang] are truly as you say in your letter [*ming*, directive]. . . .

二月八日庚寅臣質言。奉讀手命。追亡慮存。恩哀之隆。形於文墨。日月冉冉。歲不我與。昔侍左右。廁坐眾賢。出有微行之遊。入有管弦之歡。置酒

> 樂飲。賦詩稱壽。自謂可終始相保。幷騁材力。效節明主。何意數年之閒。死喪略盡。臣獨何德。以堪久長。陳徐劉應。才學所著。誠如來命。 ...[43]

The proem of Wu Zhi's reply is an amazing piece of mirroring. He not only picks up the topics and the overall nostalgic atmosphere of Cao Pi's letter but even echoes his correspondent's wording, now repeating verbatim, now subtly modifying. Only later in the letter body does he occasionally shake off this submissive attitude and demonstrates that he was not only a personal friend but also a political adviser to Cao Pi.

The question of differentiating between proem and letter body becomes meaningless in the many extremely short letters that consist of little else but opening and closing and apparently lack any "real" communicative intention. Conveying nothing but affection, they have no other purpose but to affirm the relationship between the correspondents for its own sake.

> On the sixth day of the seventh month, [Wang] Xizhi lets you know:
>
> I was dejected because I had not had any messages [*zhi wen*] from you for many days. But now I received your letter [*shu*] of the second and gratefully acknowledge your earlier inquiries. I am concerned about you. Are you better already?
>
> 七月六日羲之白。多日不知問。邑邑。得二日書。知足下昨問。耿耿。今已佳也。[44]

The high percentage of letters transmitted with a proem and the large number of such extremely short letters, especially among the calligraphy models, that relate nothing but typical proem information confirm how crucial the proem's interpersonal concerns were for letter writing in general. Although the principle of securing the goodwill of the addressee that is inherent in most proems can also be exploited to calculatingly prepare the ground for the writer's communicative intentions—as in Qiu Chi's letter quoted above—proems can rarely be reduced to just that, especially in the more personal letters.

In the following, the principal elements of the proem are introduced individually, with the exception of the lament of separation, which is covered in chapter 4.

Acknowledging the *receipt of letters* is an important instance of the self-referentiality of letters. References to the correspondent's letters are a very common element of the proem. This is of course a universal phenomenon in letter writing,[45] although the explicit expression of gratitude for the other's letter, which is so familiar to modern readers, is rare in early medieval Chinese letters.[46] Gratitude seems to be implied in phrases that mention that the writer "knows of" or "learned about" (*zhi* 知) the addressee's "inquiries" (*wen* 問), which usually amount to an acknowledgment of the other's letter. What we also find are conventional expressions of comfort (*wei* 慰) or joy produced by a letter, sometimes extending to accompanying gifts, and praise for the literary or calligraphic qualities of the addressee's letter. Elaborating on the receipt of a letter and on one's response to reading it can be very effective in evoking a shared communicative situation for the otherwise separated correspondents.

[Che] Yong lets you know:
I have received your reply today. I opened it and had hardly finished perusing it when I already jumped for joy. Straightaway I saw mother and respectfully read it to her, three times over. Everybody in the family, young and old, suddenly forgot all their troubles. This letter [*shu*] of yours may well be called a classical speech. . . .

永白。即日得報。披省未竟。懽踊躍。輒于母前。伏誦三周。舉家大小。豁然忘愁也。足下此書足為典誥。 . . . [47]

[Lu] Yun lets you know:
I had not yet replied to your last letter [*shu*] when I received another letter [*kuang*, bestowal] from you. . . .

雲白。前書未報重得來況。 . . . [48]

I have received your letter [*shi*, instruction] and gratefully acknowledge your consideration. . . .

得示。知足下問。 . . . [49]

On the twelfth day of the first month, [Wang] Xizhi writes again:
Having received your letter [*shu*] of the twenty-sixth of last month, I felt comforted. Have you been fairly well lately? . . .

初月十二日羲之累書。至得去月二十六日書。為慰。比可不。 . . . [50]

Having opened your letter [*shu*], I could not suppress a happy smile. . . .

披書歡笑。不能自勝。 . . . [51]

Zhang Fonu returned yesterday, bringing your letter [*shu*] of the twenty-ninth of last month. Reading it, I was increasingly moved. . . .

張佛奴昨還。得去月二十九日書。覽以增慨。 . . . [52]

Shi Huiyuan knocks his head on the ground:

Perusing the parting letter [*shi*, instruction] that you, sir, wrote moved me deeply. . . .

釋慧遠頓首。省君別示以為慨然。 . . .[53]

I have read your reply to [Yin] Zhongkan's letter [*shu*]. It profoundly expresses how dear the advancement of propriety is to your heart. . . .

見足下答仲堪書。深具義發之懷。 . . .[54]

The act of reading a letter can be represented by a number of verbs, such as *du* 讀 (to read [aloud]), *jian* 見 (to see), *lan* 覽 (to look at), *yue* 閱 (to read), *xing* 省 (to examine, peruse), *xun* 尋 (to search, scrutinize), *song* 誦 (to read aloud, recite), *yong* 詠 (to recite, chant), and *yin* 吟 (to chant). It is interesting that both reading out loud and silent reading occur, and that reading aloud sometimes took place in front of other listeners, although this is only occasionally made explicit.[55]

Another part of the update to the personal relationship between the correspondents was to mention the receipt of letters or other messages from mutual acquaintances or to inquire after them. This also helped to embed a particular correspondence within a larger personal or social network and to demonstrate one's connectedness.

The letter [*shu*] I received from Inspector Diao says the following: . . .

得刁僕射書曰。如此。 . . .[56]

Suddenly it is midsummer, and I feel a deep longing for you. How are you in this unseasonable cold? I am concerned about you. I am still unwell. Have you received any news [*wen*] from near or far? When does Yu [Anji] arrive? I am waiting for a meeting. Yesterday I read [Xie] Wuyi's letter of the nineteenth. . . .

忽然夏中感懷。冷冷不適。足下復何似。耿耿。吾故不佳。得遠近問不。虞生何當來。遲一集。昨見無奕十九日書。 . . .[57]

Finally, there are also proems that mention that letters have not arrived.

[Che] Yong lets you know:
Recently you have received a letter [*shu*] from me by way of Wang Hongji. I find it strange that you have not replied. . . .

永白。聞因王弘季有書。怪足下無答。 . . .[58]

I have not received news [*wen*] from Linchuan and feel worried beyond words. Zisong's [i.e., Yu Ai's] son has arrived. . . .

不得臨川問。懸心不可言。子嵩之子來。 . . . [59]

Bringing up the current *weather and season* provides concrete details about a situation that the correspondents, because of their spatial separation, usually do not share. It helps to reconnect them by creating a common frame of reference that supports or supplants the temporal data given in the prescript. Mention of certain seasons, seasonal festivals, or phases of the moon not only help to create a communal cosmological, ritual, and communicative situation but also connotes affection and longing, as with the prescript. The following examples are arranged according to the course of a year:

> On the first day of the first month, [Wang] Xizhi lets you know:
> Suddenly we have moved into a new year. Being at this border between new and old makes me sigh very deeply. You, sir, also share these feelings. Recently I had a letter [*gao*, note] saying that you are suffering from a bellyache. I am worried about you. How have you been lately during this torrential rain? . . .
>
> 初月一日羲之白。忽然改年。新故之際。致歎至深。君亦同懷。近過得告。故云腹痛。懸情。災雨比復何似。 . . . [60]
>
> How are you now in this unusual heat? . . .
>
> 異暑復何如。 . . . [61]
>
> On the third day of the sixth month, [Wang] Xizhi lets you know:
> The summer heat begins to abate.[62] This year is already half over. I sigh deeply with emotion. Having received your letter [*shu*] of the twenty-seventh, I know that you are well. . . .
>
> 六月三日羲之白。徂暑。此歲已半。感慨深。得二十七日書。知足下安。 . . . [63]
>
> On the twenty-fourth day of the seventh month, [Wang] Xun repeatedly knocks his head on the ground:
> It is autumn and I feel a deep longing for you. Having received your latest letter [*shi*, instruction], I feel comforted. . . .
>
> 七月廿四日循遮頓首。秋月感思深。得近示為慰。 . . . [64]
>
> On the ninth day of the eighth month, [Sima] Rui knocks his head on the ground:
> Soon it will be Mid-autumn Festival; my heart does nothing but go out to you in the distance. Soon it will become a bit colder. How are you doing usually? . . .
>
> 八月九日睿頓首。忽中秋。但有遠懷。便微冷。恆何如。 . . . [65]

On the twenth-ninth day of the eighth month, [Wang Ningzhi] notifies the daughter of the Yu family:
Tomorrow starts the ninth month.[66] I remember the past with sighs of sadness. Thinking of you increases my longing for you in the distance. . . .

八月廿九日告庾氏女。明便授衣。感逝悲歎。念增遠思。 . . .[67]

On the fourteenth day of the eleventh month, [Du] Yu knocks his head on the ground:
Soon this year will already be over. That we have been separated for so long increases and doubles the weariness of longing. The road is long, and letters [*shuwen*] are scarce.

十一月十四日預頓首。歲忽已終。別久益兼其勞。道遠。書問又簡。[68]

On the twenty-fourth day of the twelfth month, [Wang] Xizhi reports:
At the end of the year, I heave a sigh. Having received your letter [*shu*] of the twelfth, I feel comforted. Have you been fairly well in these days of the Great Cold? . . .

十二月二十四日羲之報。歲盡感歎。得十二日書。為慰。大寒。比可不。 . . .[69]

Health reports and inquiries are another universal part of the epistolary formula across cultures.[70] As many of the quoted proems demonstrate, in early medieval China these were often connected to references to the weather and season, although they are also used independently. While most health reports and inquiries appear utterly conventional, others give the impression that the exchange about health problems was an important part of a particular epistolary conversation and that talking about ailments served the function of not only updating the personal relationship between the correspondents but also emphasizing the affection and personal closeness between them.[71] Since letter writers rarely profess their good health,[72] there may have been reasons to present oneself as frail and sickly, from epistolary conventions to political caution in dangerous times, although such notions are difficult to prove. As with the receipt of letters, health reports and inquiries may extend to family members and mutual acquaintances.

Are you in good health in this cold weather? . . .

寒佳不。 . . .[73]

Are you better? I am quite concerned about you. My throat is no longer so dry. . . .

足下差否。甚耿耿。喉中不復燥耳。 . . . [74]

How are you, sister-in-law? Has your ailment gotten better? I feel worried beyond words. Mother is blessed with good health, and everybody else here is in good health, too. It is going well. We are constantly worried about another outbreak of malaria. . . .

姨何如。汝所患遂差未。懸心不可言。阿母蒙恩。上下悉佳。宜可行。瘧如復斷要取。未斷愁人。 . . . [75]

On the seventh day of the ninth month, [Xi] Yin reports:

I have recently received your letter [*zhang*, composition]. I was absolutely delighted to learn that you are slowly getting better and hope that you have more or less overcome your illness by now. Can you eat again? When one has just recovered, it is difficult to find something to one's taste. . . .

九月七日愔報。比得章。知弟漸佳。至慶。想今漸勝。食進不。新差。難將適。 . . . [76]

You are just seventy this year. To know that you are invariably in good health is a great occasion for celebration. I hope that you keep on doing your best to take good care of yourself. . . .

足下今年政七十耶。知體氣常佳。此大慶也。想復勤加頤養。 . . . [77]

Your vassal [Wang] Xizhi says:

It is severely cold. I am not cognizant of the state of Your Majesty's body and diet. I sincerely ask to be granted the favor of receiving information about your condition. . . .

臣羲之言。寒嚴。不審聖體御膳何如。謹付承動靜。 . . . [78]

[Wang] Xianzhi lets you know:

I am not cognizant of the state of your venerable body now. How much did you sleep last night? . . .

獻之白。不審尊體復何如。昨夜眠多少。 . . . [79]

It is autumnal but still hot. How is your doctrinal body? Might the ritual of meditation harm your virtue? Your disciple is still afflicted with his old diseases, and medicinal decoctions are ineffective. At the same time, I cannot get any leisure time for myself. . . .

秋色尚熱。道體何如。禪禮無乃損德。弟子老病相仍。湯藥無效。兼不得自閑。 . . . [80]

. . . Cool winds announce the season [of autumn]. How have you been recently? This poor monk is troubled by illness and often unwell. . . .

. . . 涼風屆節。頃常如何。貧道勞疾多不佳耳。 . . . [81]

Reading these proems, we notice that health inquiries, sometimes responding to a letter from the addressee, usually precede health reports. However, the urgency of a current affliction could also cause writers to start a letter by mentioning their own health. It further stands out that health inquiries differ according to the status of the addressee, ranging from a casual "Have you been fairly well lately?" to inquiries after a superior's "venerable body," a monk's "doctrinal body," or "Your Majesty's body and diet." Health inquiries are often followed by conventional expressions of concern, such as *genggeng* 耿耿 (I am concerned about you) or compounds starting with *xuan* 懸 (here, "to worry about or miss"), such as *xuanxiang* 懸想, *xuanqing* 懸情, or *xuanxin* 懸心 (to feel worried), that evoke a whole spectrum of emotions, hovering between worry, solicitude, and longing.[82]

Good wishes, mostly for good health and general well-being, are the most conspicuous manifestations of the proem's function of securing the goodwill of the addressee. Wishes occur in great diversity, often directed not only to the immediate addressees but also to their families.

May you all be as usual. . . .

足下各如常。 . . . [83]

I hope that you and your family are all as usual. . . .

想親親悉如常。 . . . [84]

It is cold. I respectfully hope that you enjoy well-being and harmony. May young and old all be in good health. . . .

寒。伏想安和。小大悉佳。 . . . [85]

On the thirteenth day of the twelfth month, [Shen] Jia knocks his head on the ground, once and again:

I feel a longing for you at this time of the year. It is bitterly cold. I sincerely hope that you are all safe and sound. . . .

十二月十三日。嘉頓首頓首。歲有感懷。深寒。切想各平安。 . . . [86]

Shi Huiyuan knocks his head on the ground:

The tenth month is pleasantly warm. I wish [*yuan*] that Your Majesty's diet may be agreeable. . . .

釋慧遠頓首。陽月和暖。願御膳順宜。 . . . [87]

[Lu] Yun knocks his head on the ground, once and again:
Summer has only just started to be hot. I wish [*yuan*] everyone in your house every good luck and that illness may keep far away. . . .

雲頓首頓首。惟夏始暑。願府館萬福。疾病處遠。 . . .[88]

On the eighteenth day of the fifth month, [Cao] Pi lets you know:
May you, Jizhong, be unharmed. . . .

五月十八日丕白。季重無恙。 . . .[89]

How are you? I hope everything at your house is just well. May men and horses be unharmed. . . .

足下何如。想館舍正安。士馬無恙。 . . .[90]

Among the more formulaic expressions are *ruchang* 如常 (as normal, as usual, all right), *jia* 佳 (in good health, fine), *xing shen* 幸甚 (very fortunate),[91] and *wu yang* 無恙 (to be without worry, disease, or calamity, to be unharmed). The latter phrase has been interpreted not only as a health wish but also as a declaration or a question,[92] and thus it seems to share a certain modal polysemy with the *formula valetudinis* in ancient Greek and Roman letters.[93]

LETTER BODY

While the main body of official communications consists of clearly recognizable opening, middle, and closing parts,[94] supported by signal words and phrases, such distinct structures are less common in transmitted personal letters. They are present, however, in some epistolary subgenres, such as letters of familial admonition or recommendation and in other letters of a more formal and less personal character.

As seen above, *xi*, or "formerly," is one of the more common signal words in personal letters. It often indicates the beginning of the letter body, introducing reflections on historical events or the correspondents' shared past and preparing the rhetorical aims of the letter. Often these are supported by a subsequent passage starting with the contrasting *jin* 今 (now, today), as in Cao Pi's famous "Further letter to Wu Zhi," no. 1, which is dedicated mainly to the memory of mutual friends who have passed away too soon. In this letter, the juxtaposition of *xi* and *jin* emphasizes a passage in the middle of the letter body that evokes two famous historical cases of friendship.

> . . . Formerly (*xi*), Bo Ya cut the strings of his zither after Zhong Qi's death, and Zhongni [i.e., Confucius] covered the minced meat after Zilu's death. One was pained because someone "who understands the tone" is hard to find, and the other was distressed because he would never be able to get hold of his disciple again.[95] Even if our [dead] friends do not measure up to the ancients, they were the talents of their age. Those who live today are not able to reach them anymore. "Youth is to be feared" and "future generations" are difficult to disparage.[96] But I am afraid that you and I will not see anyone measuring up to our dead friends. . . .
>
> . . . 昔伯牙絕絃於鍾期。仲尼覆醢於子路。痛知音之難遇。傷門人之莫逮。諸子但為未及古人。自一時之雋也。今之存者。已不逮矣。後生可畏。來者難誣。然恐吾與足下不及見也。 . . .[97]

Wen 聞 (I have heard that . . .) is another signal word that is frequently used in official communication and occasionally appears in personal letters. It may refer to any kind of knowledge, gleaned from a variety of sources ranging from canonical texts to rumors, and usually also prepares the rhetorical aims expressed later on in the letter.

> [Shi] Bao lets you know:
>
> I have heard that [*wen*] acting upon noticing an opportunity is regarded highly in the *Book of Changes* and that a small state that does not serve a large state in good trust is chided in the *Spring and Autumn Annals*.[98] These examples allude to the harbingers of good and bad luck and to the origins of glory and dishonor. . . .
>
> 苞白。蓋聞見機而作。周易所貴。小不事大。春秋所誅。此乃吉凶之萌兆。榮辱之所由興也。 . . .[99]
>
> I have heard that [*wen*] he who is filial does not turn his back on his relatives in order to gain profit, he who is benevolent does not forget his lord in order to strive for personal benefit, he who is noble-minded does not risk chaos in order to seek luck, and he who is wise does not endanger himself by straying from the Way. . . .
>
> 蓋聞孝者不背親以要利。仁者不忘君以徇私。志士不探亂以徼幸。智者不詭道以自危。 . . .[100]
>
> The weather is cool during daytime. How have you been lately? Last month, the monk Fashi arrived. I have heard that [*wen*] you, sir, want to return to your home country, which made me feel disappointed. Earlier I had heard that [*wen*] you, sir, are about to translate sutras on a grand scale and thus did not want to turn to you to ask for your advice. If this report about your impending departure is not false, everyone will be upset beyond words. Now, I would right away like

to briefly question you about a few dozen topics. I hope that you will have the spare time to explain them in detail. . . .

日有涼氣。比復何如。去月法識道人至。聞君欲還本國。情以悵然。先聞君方當大出諸經。故未欲便相諮求。若此傳不虛。衆恨可言。今輒略問數十條事。冀有餘暇。一一為釋。 . . .[101]

Letters of recommendation are among those subgenres that do without the usual elements of the proem. Having a clear-cut agenda, they instead turn to their business immediately, following a strict arrangement of textual components, which hardly allowed for variation. Introduced by the signal word *wen*, letters of recommendation usually start with a pair of specific allusions to ancient Chinese history or literature, followed by a pair of more general conclusions about the significance of those historic precedents. Both pairs concern the selection of officials and are often interrelated on the basis of *singula singulis*. Then comes the actual recommendation, which praises the qualities of the person recommended and points out the good he will certainly do once in office.

璩聞	[Ying] Qu has heard that [*wen*]
唐堯因群士以興治	Emperor Yao of Tang established his rule with the help of all officials and
齊桓假衆能以定業	Duke Huan of Qi assured his achievement by means of many able men.[102]
是故	Hence:
八元進	because the Eight Capables were promoted [by Emperor Yao of Tang],[103]
則太平之化成	the transformation toward Great Harmony was accomplished;
六賢用	because the Six Worthies were employed [by Duke Huan of Qi],
則九合之功立	the achievement of the Nine Assemblies was established.[104]
切見	It is my humble opinion that
同郡和模字慮則	my fellow countryman He Mo, courtesy name Lüze,
質性純粹	has a pure and immaculate character as well as
體度貞正	a constant and upright demeanor.
履仁蹈義 . . .	He walks in benevolence and righteousness. . . . [105]

The following passage of this letter details the prospective achievements of the recommended person, which are again compared to those of an ancient model. The impression of formality and rigidity is enhanced by the prevalence of parallel structures within all the components of the letters.

Being one of the epistolary genres between personal letter and official communication, letters of recommendation in many respects resemble official writings, for instance, in their use of markers of respect, such as *qie* 切 (sincerely, earnestly) in Ying Qu's letter or other such markers as *jing* 敬 (respectful), *fu* 伏 (respectful, lit., "to lie prostrate"), *qie* 竊 (deferential, lit., "to steal, stealthy"), and *yu* 愚 (humble, lit., "stupid"). These words usually qualify *wen* 聞 as well as other verbs that characterize the writer's opinions or perceptions, such as *wei* 惟 and *si* 思 (to think), *jian* 見 (to be of the opinion), and *wei* 謂 (to say). These markers of respect are also used to qualify a writer's wishes, such as *xiang* 想 (to hope) and *yuan* 願 (to wish), as well as other actions such as receiving and reading a letter. There are fewer of these honorifics in personal letters, but they are by no means rare.

Yuan 願 is usually found toward the end of the letter body, expressing a request or demand, often of a political or moral nature. It is frequently used in official letters, just like *yi* 宜 (it would be suitable, should) or *cheng* 誠 (I sincerely [hope]). But while *yi* and *cheng* are hardly ever used in personal letters, *yuan* is rather common, as in the following letter of familial admonition that the eminent general Yang Hu (221–278) wrote to his sons or nephews,[106] probably toward the end of his life:

> As a child, I was instructed by my late father. At the age when I could speak, he introduced me to the standard texts, and when I was nine, he taught me the *Book of Odes* and the *Book of Documents*. But I had no reputation among the men of my hometown yet; I had not made a distinct and outstanding name for myself. My current position was bestowed upon me through incongruous kindness. I could never have achieved it by my own strength. I am by far inferior to my late father, and you are again inferior to me. Great schemes are something that you, brothers, I am afraid, are not able to come up with, and astounding achievements will, as far as I can see, not be your lot.
>
> Respectfulness is the beginning of virtue, caution the basis of conduct. I wish (*yuan*) that you may be faithful and trustworthy in your words, sincere and respectful in your deeds. Do not promise other people riches, do not spread unfounded rumors, do not listen to slander or flattery. When you hear of an offense committed by somebody, your ears can hear it but your mouth must not articulate it.[107] Think before you act. If your words and deeds lack trustworthiness, you will personally suffer disgrace and incur punishment. How distressed I would be if you brought disgrace upon your ancestors! Ponder your

> father's words; connect with your father's instructions! May each of you recite this.
>
> 吾少受先君之教。能言之年。便召以典文。年九歲。便誨以詩書。然尚猶無鄉人之稱。無清異之名。今之職位。謬恩之加耳。非吾力所能致也。吾不如先君遠矣。汝等復不如吾。諮度弘偉。恐汝兄弟未之能也。奇異獨達。察汝等將無分也。恭為德首。慎為行基。願汝等言則忠信。行則篤敬。無口許人以財。無傳不經之談。無聽毀譽之語。聞人之過。耳可得受。口不得宣。思而後動。若言行無信。身受大謗。自入刑論。豈復惜汝。恥及祖考。思乃父言。纂乃父教。各諷誦之。[108]

The admonition is moving in its solicitousness, which is heightened by Yang Hu's disillusioned view of his mediocre sons or nephews. There is not the slightest effort to secure the addressees' goodwill in this letter, and Yang Hu expresses his not exactly favorable opinion of the addressees in a straightforward, almost blunt manner that is hardly alleviated by the letter's parallel style. After a few autobiographical words, an evaluation of the personalities of the addressees, and an instructive maxim, the signal word *yuan* (I wish) indicates the beginning of the actual admonitory passage. The writer's wishes for the young men's behavior are well within the frame of Confucian ethics, not the least because they ultimately appeal to the central Confucian value of filial piety. The letter contains another potential intra-epistolary allusion, because the warning against engaging in slander is put in words that are very similar to those Ma Yuan used in the letter to his nephews written about two hundred years earlier—a letter that was to be canonized another two hundred years later by Liu Xie in his *The Literary Mind* as the prototype of the familial admonitory letter.[109] Another interesting feature of Yang Hu's letter is its last sentence, which calls upon the addressees to recite or even memorize it. This intensification of reading is also occasionally mentioned in non-admonitory letters from friends or family members, in which it is described as a joyful and quite voluntary response to receiving a letter.[110] In a familial admonition such as Yang Hu's letter, it emphasizes the documentary, testamentary character of the letter, whose message is intended to be available after the writer's death.[111]

Another admonitory letter that expresses a distinct wish, albeit not to a younger family member and thus couched in more polite terms, is Wang Xizhi's letter to Xie Wan, written in 358 or 359 when Xie Wan led the northern expedition against the Former Yan dynasty (337–70). Again, only the main body of this letter has been transmitted.

That you, sir, with your detached and dispassionate demeanor would stoop to mingle with men of all stations is really hard to imagine. But those who are called wise go far exactly because their conduct "in and out of office" is in accordance with circumstances.[112] I wish [*yuan*] that you, sir, may always share weal and woe with the lowliest among your soldiers; this would be "thoroughly beneficial."[113] "His meals were not flavorful, his mats were not lined"[114]—what importance does this have? And yet the ancients have transmitted it as a commendable saying. Benefit and misfortune truly arise from the accumulation of small things that become huge. May you, sir, keep this in mind.

以君邁往不屑之韻, 而俯同群辟, 誠難為意也。然所謂通識, 正自當隨事行藏乃為遠耳。願君每與士卒之下者同甘苦, 則盡善矣。「食不二味, 居不重席」, 此復何有? 而古人以為美談。濟否所由, 實在積小以致高大, 君其存之。[115]

Having quoted this letter, the *History of the Jin Dynasty* laconically remarks that "Xie Wan was unable to accept [Wang's advice] and consequently suffered defeat."[116]

Yuan can also be used in less severe contexts, for instance, to introduce good wishes, as toward the end of Liu Chengzhi's letter to Sengzhao.

[Liu] Yimin [i.e., Liu Chengzhi] obeisantly salutes you:

I recently feasted on the excellent news [*wen*] from you. I cherish a longing for you in the distance. How is your health during this severe cold at the end of the year? The transmission of letters [*yin*, messages] was cut off, so I increasingly contained my longing for you. Your disciple is seriously ill here in the wilderness [of Mount Lu]. I am frequently bedridden with sickness. Because Huiming will soon travel north [to Chang'an], I write to you to communicate my feelings. [Relationships among] the ancients did not become weak, even if they were physically separated, because the [common experience of] enlightenment made them close. Therefore, even if we are further separated by rivers and mountains and have not met for a year, I do hope to cherish your presence and to mirror your image and your vestiges in my mind. My expectant joy is great indeed. For a very long time, there will be no opportunity to meet you. Looking at the clouds, I heave a long sigh. In accordance with the seasons, take good care of your honorable health. Provided there are messengers, I hope frequently to receive news [*wen*] from you. I respectfully wish [*fu yuan*] you all health and harmony. . . .

遺民和南。頃餐徽 (聞)〔問〕。有懷遙竚。歲 (未)〔末〕寒嚴。體中如何。音寄壅隔。增用抱蘊。弟子沈痾艸澤。常有獘瘵。遖因慧明道人北游。裁通其情。古人不以形疏致淡。悟涉則親。是以雖復江山悠邈。不面當年。

> 至于企懷風味。鏡心象迹。佇悅之勤。良以深矣。緬然無因。瞻霞永歎。順時愛敬。冀因行李。數有承問。伏願彼大眾康和。 . . . [117]

If a letter is written with a specific communicative intention in mind, especially in the case of a request, the expression of this intention is typically delayed. Unlike letters of admonition or recommendation that usually come to the point right away, requests obviously were regarded as needing extensive rhetorical preparation, a feature that early medieval letters share with those of later periods. Writing about the Tang dynasty, Patricia Ebrey remarks that, "generally speaking, the 'business' of the letter, if there were any, would come before the last paragraph."[118] This feature is conspicuous in the following letter written in 510 by the great historian, poet, and scholar Shen Yue (441–513), who implicitly asks his younger friend and benefactor Xu Mian (466–535) to approach the emperor on his behalf. The letter was transmitted without opening and closing and its body shows few epistolary characteristics.

> In my youth, I was left fatherless and destitute without a close relative to rely on.[119] I was on the point of falling to the ground, toiling and staggering,[120] miserable from morn to night, hobbling along with meager appointments. My aim was not selfish, but I looked forward to receiving some small emolument and, depending on this, to returning east [to my native Wuxing]. More than ten years went by before I undeservedly got an appointment in Xiangyang Prefecture [in modern Hubei]. Public and private planning is not my forte, but in order to keep my body supplied with material needs, I could not avoid taking responsibility for human affairs. At the end of the Yongming era [483–93], when I left the capital to become Grand Warden of Dongyang, my intention consisted in "stopping when I had had enough."[121] But when the Jianwu era (494–98) began its cycle, the human world once more crowded in on me. To leave the court then once and for all, never to return, was not yet easily accomplished. At the beginning of the reign of the Dark Suspicious One,[122] there were many factions within the royal government, and for this reason planning to retire seemed almost attainable. [At the time,] I commissioned you to convey my feelings to Director Xu;[123] I suppose you remember this and have not forgotten it. When the way of the Sages was restored [in 502, when the Liang dynasty was established], quite by mistake I met with good fortune, and my past resolve and former intention once more became sidetracked. At the beginning of this year, with the celebration of the New Year, my request for retirement was denied because of the emperor's kindness. I truly am unable to promote or proclaim morality or good government or to gloriously unfold the politics of the court. But I still would like to search out and explore

texts and documents to find the similarities and differences among contemporary discussions.

However, since the beginning of the year, my illness has increased and my anxieties have become piercing. It is doubtless due to the fact that my vitality is limited and my work has been excessive. Surely this decline and exhaustion is due to my advanced years. Dragging my staff, now walking, now halting, I exert my strength to work as conscientiously as I can. Looking in from outside, watching from the sidelines, I still appear to be a whole man. But the strength and use of my body and bones are not mutually coordinated. I constantly find it necessary to strenuously gather myself before I can put forth any energy. When I take off my clothes to go to bed, my limbs no longer have any relation to the rest of my body. The upper parts are hot, the lower parts are cold; every month it gets worse, every day more intense. If I take something warm, I feel overheated, and if I apply something cool, I invariably suffer from diarrhea. The later recovery never comes up to the earlier recovery, while the later severity is always greater than the earlier. Every hundred days or every few weeks, I have to shift to a new hole in my leather belt. When I grasp my arm with my hand, I figure that every month it is smaller by half a degree.[124] Estimating my prognosis from this, how can I last much longer? If it goes on like this day after day without stopping, I will leave behind for my Sage Lord [i.e., Liang Wudi] an irrevocable regret. I rashly desire to petition, pleading for an official rank for my retirement and old age [and would like to ask you to investigate the prospect of such a petition]. If Heaven lends me the years that I may return to the days of my normal health, when I was able to employ my talents and strength, this is all I would ever want.

吾弱年孤苦, 傍無朞屬, 往者將墜於地, 契闊屯邅, 困於朝夕, 崎嶇薄宦, 事非為已, 望得小祿, 傍此東歸。歲逾十稔, 方忝襄陽縣, 公私情計, 非所了具, 以身資物, 不得不任人事。永明末, 出守東陽, 意在止足; 而建武肇運, 人世膠加, 一去不反, 行之未易。及昏猜之始, 王政多門, 因此謀退, 庶幾可果, 託卿布懷於徐令, 想記未忘。聖道聿興, 謬逢嘉運, 往志宿心, 復成乖爽。今歲開元, 禮年云至, 懸車之請, 事由恩奪, 誠不能弘宣風政, 光闡朝猷, 尚欲討尋文簿, 時議同異。而開年以來, 病增慮切, 當由生靈有限, 勞役過差, 總此凋竭, 歸之暮年, 牽策行止, 努力祇事。外觀傍覽, 尚似全人, 而形骸力用, 不相綜攝。常須過自束持, 方可僶俛。解衣一臥, 支體不復相關。上熱下冷, 月增日篤, 取煖則煩, 加寒必利, 後差不及前差, 後劇必甚前劇。百日數旬, 革帶常應移孔; 以手握臂, 率計月小半分。以此推算, 豈能支久? 若此不休, 日復一日, 將貽聖主不追之恨。冒欲表聞, 乞歸老之秩。若天假其年, 還得平健, 才力所堪, 惟思是策。[125]

Although we can assume that Xu Mian was familiar with Shen Yue's story and the offices he had held in the past, Shen presents his request in the context of his whole biography, looking back on more than half a century and three dynasties. The most impressive part of the letter is certainly Shen Yue's vivid description of his failing health, which leads directly to his request. Although the letter provides a compelling argument for granting the sixty-nine-year-old his wish and Xu Mian indeed interceded on his friend's behalf, asking the emperor to appoint Shen Yue to the office of one of the Three Dignitaries (San Si), this request was eventually denied. Xu Mian's approach to the emperor in this matter is unknown, but since letters were often "forwarded" to other recipients, we might assume that he presented the emperor with Shen Yue's original letter, perhaps in the hope of bringing its persuasive power into play. If this was indeed the case, then a rhetorical flaw may have contributed to the failure of this letter's communicative goal, because the remark that the emperor, should he not grant Shen Yue's request, may soon be left with "irrevocable regret" comes across as presumptuous and almost threatening.

As these examples demonstrate, it is difficult to make generalized statements about the structure of the main body of personal letters, because it is this part that truly reveals the formal diversity of the transmitted epistolary texts from early medieval China. They range from short informal notes that hardly feature a letter body at all and seem to consist of nothing but the frame, to letters of friendship in which the main body is permeated with the same personal concerns that are raised in the frame, to rather formal letters that resemble pieces of official communication or essays.

LETTER CLOSING

Epilogue

In the ideal case of a letter with a complete frame, the letter closing mirrors the opening: the postscript, which corresponds to the prescript, is preceded by an epilogue, corresponding to the proem. The epilogue, not always clearly set apart from the letter body, voices concerns similar to those expressed in the proem, such as wishes for good health and the lament of separation. However, unlike the proem, which is concerned mainly with the past, the epilogue looks to the time ahead, trying to secure the correspondents' future relationship. This intention is also expressed in a number of further elements that typically are reserved for the epilogue, such as the request for letters or for a reunion of the correspondents. Finally there are conventional reflections about the act of writing, especially its limitations compared to a face-to-face meeting. They appear to have been a favored way to conclude a letter, certainly also because they allow for a gentle termination of the letter conversation, which is probably a rhetorically even more delicate matter than starting a letter.[126]

About a third of the early medieval Chinese letters that have been studied were transmitted with an epilogue, which proves that editors appreciated the epilogue as much as the proem. Most elements of a typical epilogue appear at the close of Zhao Zhi's famous letter to his cousin Xi Fan.

> . . . I am gone, Scholar Xi! We have parted forever. Wretched and lonely, I am drifting far from home, close to the desert. Long are the three thousand miles I have covered and difficult the roads I have plodded. The day when we will be able to hold hands again is unreachably distant. My longing ties me ever closer to you. Who says it is already dissolving? Do not make your letters [*yin*, messages] as rare as gold and jade and do not detach your heart from me.[127] Even if our bodies are as far from each other as the northern and the southern borders [lit., "Hu and Yue"], may our regard for each other remain strong enough to split metal.[128] May each of us respect decorum[129] and sincerely tread in deep honesty. The gentleman does not admire extravagance and dissipation. Leaning over my letter [*shu*], I am full of disappointment. I do not know what else I could say.
>
> . . . 去矣嵇生。永離隔矣。煢煢飄寄。臨沙漠矣。悠悠三千。路難涉矣。攜手之期。邈無日矣。思心彌結。誰云釋矣。無金玉爾音。而有遐心。身雖胡越。意存斷金。各敬爾儀。敦履璞沈。繁華流蕩。君子弗欽。臨書悵然。知復何云。[130]

The most conspicuous part of this epilogue is the lament of a separation whose extent is emphasized dramatically, in both spatial and temporal terms. Almost as an antidote, Zhao Zhi offers vows of unswerving friendship, along with amiable admonitions, an important aspect of friendship in China[131] and another common element of an epilogue. At the end of the letter, which has been transmitted without a postscript, Zhao Zhi includes a conventional phrase bemoaning the deficiencies of written communication. Only one element of the epilogue is missing—good wishes for the recipient's health. They are quite prominent in the following letter, written three centuries later by the southern recluse Zhou Hongrang (ca. 498–ca. 571) to his friend Wang Bao, a poet kept in captivity in northern China:[132]

. . . 但願	. . . I only wish [*yuan*] you may
愛玉體珍金相	take care of your jade body and cherish your golden visage,[133]

保期頤享〔壽考〕黃髮	preserve it until you become a centenarian and enjoy your gray hair.[134]
猶冀	I also hope that
蒼雁赬鯉	dark green geese and crimson carps
時傳尺素	may frequently deliver a foot of plain [silk].
清風 (明)〔朗〕月	In a fresh wind, under the bright moon,
俱寄相思	I send you all my longing.[135]
子淵子淵	Ziyuan, Ziyuan,[136]
長為別矣	our separation has lasted long!
搦管操觚	Clutching my brush and holding the writing tablet,
聲淚俱咽	my words are muffled by loud weeping.[137]

Elegant parallel constructions, dense intertextual references, and original images result in the strong poetic intensity of Zhou Hongrang's "Letter in reply to Wang Bao." The author's literally colorful request for letters—living "dark green geese" and cooked "crimson carps" acting as carriers of "feet of plain [silk]"—combines at least three complex allusions to Han dynasty literature. In the context of letter writing, the wild goose, a powerful and multifaceted image, alludes not only to Su Wu, who is said to have fastened his letters to the feet of wild geese migrating south to his homeland (which in this letter makes for a particularly apt geographical consonance) but also, more broadly, to separation as such.[138] The association of fish and in particular carp with letter writing was probably derived from the rebel Chen Sheng's (d. 208 BCE) attempt to use fish as carriers for letters.[139] It has been a common poetic image since the Han dynasty, just like the "foot of plain [silk]."

In the epilogue of Xiao Yi's letter to the Buddhist monk Liu Zhizang (458–522), the transmission of letters is likewise entrusted to a nonhuman poetic carrier.

. . . 白雲間之	. . . White clouds are separating us;
蒼江不極	the dark green river never ends.[140]
未因抵掌	There is no opportunity to hold hands;
我勞如何	"How can I describe the weariness of longing that I feel?"[141]
想無金玉	I hope that news from you may not be as rare as gold and jade
數在郵示	and that the messenger may often bring me a letter [*shi*, instruction].
弱水難航	Because the Weak River is hard to navigate,[142]
猶致書於青鳥	I would rather have my letters [*shu*] delivered by the blue birds;
流川弗遠	because the rivers do not move far,

佇芳音於赤玉	I wait for your fragrant letters [*yin*, messages] written in scarlet jade.
鶴望還信	Craning my neck, I watch out for the return of the messenger,
以代萱蘇	in order to replace the drugs *xuan* and *su* [with a letter].
得志忘言	Catch on to the idea and forget about the words[143]—
此寧多述	this is better than relating too much.
法車叩頭叩頭	[Xiao] Fache knocks his head on the ground, once and again.[144]

The concluding passage of Xiao Yi's letter starts by evoking the spatial distance between the correspondents, which soon assumes a temporal dimension as well. Since there are no prospects for a meeting, the request for letters is intensified by involving the "three blue birds" (*san qing niao*), legendary messengers of the mythical Queen Mother of the West (Xiwangmu), promising ease, speed, and reliability of transmission.[145] The hope to receive letters written in scarlet jade (*chi yu*) has supramundane connotations as well, because this material is associated with a transcendent, master An Qi.[146] Comparing the effects of receiving a letter with that of the plants *xuan(cao)* and *(gao) su*, which purportedly could dispel sorrow and weariness, is an established epistolary convention.[147] An allusion to the *Zhuangzi*, which serves as a reminder of the limitations of not only epistolary communication but words in general, concludes the letter.

Of the various greetings and good wishes expressed in the proem, only *wishes for good health*, valedictions in the truest sense of the word, are repeated in the epilogue, albeit in different form. According to the general purpose of the epilogue, writers at this point in a letter refer to the future well-being of the recipients, asking them to take good care of themselves, using phrases such as *zi ai* 自愛 (to take care of oneself),[148] *bao ai* 保愛 (to protect and love), or *zhen zhong* 珍重 (to treasure).

How deeply I regret that I cannot hold your hand! May you all take good care of yourselves. Let there be many kind letters [*gao*, note]! Leaning over my letter [*shu*], I am full of disappointment.

不得執手。此恨何深。足下各自愛。數惠告。臨書悵然。[149]

. . . That I could not bid you farewell in person made me sad and resentful. Take very good care of yourself. Leaning over my letter [*shu*] increases my longing for you.

Wang Xianzhi

. . . 不得面別。悵恨。深保愛。臨書增懷。王獻之。[150]

. . . Who is your servant to endure this for much longer? Once pines and cypresses cover the ground and tomb mounds pierce the sky, when will we ever be able to have a cup of wine together again? I am restless, as if insane. I wish [*yuan*] that you may take good care of yourself.

. . . 僕亦何人, 以堪久長? 一旦松柏被地, 墳壟刺天, 何時復能銜杯酒者乎? 忽忽若狂, 願足下自愛也。[151]

. . . Take good care of yourself, for the sake of the state and the people.

. . . 為國自重。為民自愛。[152]

. . . Take good care of yourself for the sake of the Way.

. . . 為道自愛。[153]

The last two examples demonstrate that the wish for the recipient's health was sometimes connected to a higher cause, such as the state, when writing to the politician Cao Cao, or the Way (*dao*), when writing to the Buddhist recluse Liu Qiu. There are also many letters that do not use formulaic wishes for the recipients' well-being but address them in a more individual way.

. . . I hope that you will receive treatment and that your strength may gradually be restored to good health.

[Sima] Pi deserves death punishment, once and again.

. . . 想得治力漸佳。丕死罪死罪。[154]

. . . Protect yourself well against wind and cold to make me feel comforted in my worry and longing for you. Let me stop here. I am impatiently awaiting your letter [*shu*] of response.

This is what a certain person writes to you.

. . . 善護風寒, 以慰懸想, 指復立此, 促遲還書。某疏。[155]

Requests for letters are an important part of the communicative agenda of the epilogue, since they assure the recipient of the continued interest of the writer in maintaining their relationship. They often conclude the epilogue, but their degree of formulaity is astonishingly low. Even if there are a good number of letters in which the writers are impatiently watching out for the messenger, "standing for a long time" (*zhu*), "on tiptoe" (*qi*) or "craning their necks" (*zhu wang*, *qi wang*, *he wang* 佇/企/鶴望), the wish for the continuation of correspondence is expressed in very different ways. Like the acknowledgment of letters in the proem, the request for letters in the epilogue sometimes provides information about early medieval modes of transmission, especially the dependence on carriers and the frequency of correspondence.

> . . . May you consider my humble words closely and quickly send me your answer.
>
> . . . 詳思愚言。速示還報也。[156]
>
> . . . No letter [*shu*] can express it all. Sir, do send me many letters [*gao*, notes] to comfort me!
>
> . . . 非書能悉。君數告以慰之耳。[157]
>
> . . . I am waiting to receive your virtuous letters [*yin*, messages].
>
> . . . 遲聞德音。[158]
>
> . . . I am waiting for the messenger to return with news [*zhi wen*].
>
> . . . 遲信還知問。[159]
>
> . . . Because I now seek advice in several matters, I long to perceive your fine teachings [*hui*, i.e., receive a letter from you] in order to dissolve my doubts.
>
> [Wang] Qia knocks his head on the ground and obeisantly salutes you.
>
> . . . 今故諮其數事。思聞嘉誨。以啟其疑。洽頓首和南。[160]
>
> . . . I only wish [*yuan*] that you may do your best to take care of yourself. I am waiting for the return of this messenger to learn more about what you are doing.
>
> . . . 惟願盡珍重理。遲此信反復知動靜。[161]
>
> . . . If there are messengers, then do not make your letters [*yin*, messages] as rare as jade.
>
> . . . 如有信唯不玉音。[162]
>
> . . . I am waiting for the messenger to arrive soon, that I may be comforted in my longing for you [lit., "my prolonged standing"].
>
> . . . 遲比來 (卸)〔郵〕。慰其延佇。[163]

. . . Having tethered my horse at the Jiang, I watch out on tiptoe for messengers, only waiting for a letter [*shu*] from you. This is all, I am not more comprehensive.
This is what a certain person named Xiao lets you know.

. . . 臨江總轡, 企望音郵, 唯遲來書, 此不多具。蕭某白。[164]

. . . Now I wait to receive a letter [*yin xi*, messages] from you. My head raised high, I watch out for a letter [*han*, brush] of reply that may comfort me in my longing for you [lit., "my stretched neck"].

. . . 今遣候承音息, 矯首還翰, 慰其引領。[165]

Xiao Gang's letter to Xiao Ziyun (487–549) contains an exceptionally elaborate request for letters that employs intra-epistolary allusions, specifically to letter writing in the late Han dynasty.

. . . 若使	. . . Assuming that
弘農書疏, 脫還鄴下	letters from Hongnong [i.e., Yang Xiu] returned to Ye and[166]
河南口占, 儻歸鄉里	dictations from Henan reached [Chen Zun's] hometown,[167]
必遲青泥之封	I am certainly waiting for a letter sealed with black clay
且覯朱明之詩	only to set eyes on a poem of "Red Brilliance."[168]

The last line is another reminder that correspondence was not only a means of exchanging personal information and affection but also an important medium for the distribution of literary and calligraphic works.

A number of writers conclude their letters with remarks about the *motivation of the letter.* Depending on the character of the particular letter, the reasons for writing range from the wish to update the correspondent about the latest family news, or lack thereof, to declarations of intent or admonitions.

. . . This is my opinion, which I wanted to explain to you. At the same time, this letter is meant to be a parting.
This is what Xi Kang lets you know.

. . . 其意如此既以解足下。幷以為別。嵇康白。[169]

. . . There is no time to lose! Make haste!

. . . 時不可失。足下速之。[170]

. . . May you make an effort.

> . . . 汝其勉之。[171]

> . . . I have sincerely written this letter to put forward my opinion.
> This is what Ying Qu lets you know.

> . . . 謹書起予。應璩白。[172]

> . . . Because your letter [*ming*, directive] was so detailed, I have briefly expressed my deep feelings.
> [Wu] Zhi deserves death punishment, once and again.

> . . . 以來命備悉。故略陳至情。質死罪死罪。[173]

> . . . I just offer these honest words. It would be fortunate if you could take them to heart.

> . . . 聊贈至言。幸能納之。[174]

> . . . Because it is difficult to adapt to cold and heat, you should take particular care of yourself. Be on your guard from morning to night and do not think of me. Because I was afraid you wanted to know about it, I have just written down what I saw. I wrote it on the way and in a hurry; neither the words nor the meaning are satisfactory.

> . . . 寒暑難適, 汝專自慎。夙夜戒護, 勿我為念。恐欲知之, 聊書所睹。臨塗草蹙, 辭意不周。[175]

> . . . I have just set this out because of my past affection for you. May you, sir, contemplate it.
> [Qiu] Chi knocks his head on the ground.

> . . . 聊布往懷。君其詳之。丘遲頓首。[176]

The motivation of the letter may take a special form of mentioning presents or enclosures, from literary and calligraphic works to flowers, fruits, and medicine.

> . . . It has been more than twenty years that I have not set my mind on literature. If one abandons it for too long, one's writing is left without rhyme or reason. But since I think that you certainly want a response to your poem, I accord with your wishes and send you one piece. It will just suffice to highlight the greater beauty of the poem you sent me.
> [Liu] Kun knocks his head on the ground, once and again.

> . . . 不復屬意于文。二十餘年矣。久廢則無次。想必欲其一反。故稱指送一篇。適足以彰來詩之益美耳。琨頓首頓首。[177]

. . . Qu Yuan was saddened by the gradual approach of old age and longed to feast on the blossoms that are shed by the chrysanthemums in autumn.[178] To benefit one's body and prolong one's years there is nothing more precious. I sincerely offer a bunch of chrysanthemums to support you in the arts of [the legendary methuselah] Pengzu.

. . . 故屈平悲冉冉之將老。思飡秋菊之 (樂)〔落〕英。輔體延年。莫斯之貴。謹奉一束。以助彭祖之術。[179]

. . . Your fine bestowal [of a jade ring] is excessively generous. How dare I not respectfully accept it? I sincerely offer you a rhapsody, in which I praise the the ring's intrinsic beauty.

This is what [Cao] Pi lets you know.

. . . 嘉貺益腆。敢不欽承。謹奉賦一篇以讚揚麗質。丕白。[180]

. . . Now the envoy is going to present you with a statue studded with pearls in many different colors, fifty bolts of brightly shining brocade, five ivory mats, and five gold ingots. I emphatically wish [*yuan*] that you may accept these presents.

. . . 今遣使者送五色珠像一軀。明光錦五十疋。象牙簟五領。金五枚。到願納受。[181]

Postscript

About a fifth of the letters from early medieval China that we have today were transmitted with a postscript. Since postscripts are thus found more often than prescripts, the postscript may have been more important, perhaps because the address on the envelope could substitute for the prescript. Generally speaking, postscripts read like prescripts without a date, although irregularities are not infrequent. Postscripts usually repeat the verb or verbs used in the prescript, sometimes with an additional expression of reverence, which seems appropriate in closing a letter, and they indicate the full name of the writer, that is, the family name (*xing*) plus given name.

On the twenty-fourth day of the twelfth month, [Wang] Xizhi reports: . . .

This is what Wang Xizhi reports.

十二月二十四日羲之報. . . 王羲之報。[182]

[Che] Yong lets you know: . . .

This is what Che Yong lets you know.

永白. . . 車永白。[183]

[Liu] Chao, deserving death punishment, lets you know: . . .
This is what [Liu Chao] sincerely lets you know.

超死罪白. . . 謹白。[184]

TERMS OF ADDRESS AND SELF-DESIGNATION

Because of the distinct dialogicity of letters, terms of address and self-designation are of particular importance to the genre.[185] Their choice is determined by the relationship between the correspondents in terms of social and familial hierarchy and distance as well as by the occasion of writing. Letter-writing manuals from the Tang dynasty onward usually provide elaborate lists of such terms along with instructions on how to use them,[186] but no systematic early medieval material of this type has been transmitted, so the letters themselves must suffice for drawing conclusions about contemporaneous conventions.[187] In doing this, we must be aware that terms of address and self-designation in letters, even if they are usually very good indications of the relationship between the correspondents, reflect not the actual hierarchical relationship and distance between them but rather the communicative intentions of letter writers who had a spectrum of rhetorical choices at their disposal. When Liu Xie in *The Literary Mind* praised Mi Heng for his ability to "achieve propriety" in his letters to addressees "close and distant," he certainly also referred to Mi Heng's command of the diverse terms of address and self-designation.[188]

In accordance with the general epistolary principle of securing the goodwill of the addressee, letter writers generally attempted to elevate their addressees by way of various rhetorical strategies, such as humbling themselves, focusing on the correspondents' concerns, or using honorifics when addressing them. Regarding terms of address and self-designation in letters, writers would use self-denigrating terms for themselves along with elevating terms for the addressees and their relatives. This was especially important and was even required in letters to superiors and in official communication, but letters written between equals or to inferiors also display similar strategies of politeness. Another way to denigrate oneself and elevate the addressee was to avoid terms of address and self-designation altogether. Grammatically, this is perfectly possible in Chinese, although it is often obliterated in translations into English, which requires a higher degree of referential explicitness.

Since focusing on oneself was regarded as diverging from the principle of self-denigration, writers often refrained from mentioning themselves. Accordingly, first-person pronouns appear only in letters written to equals or close addressees, most frequently *wu* 吾 (I, we), while *yu* 余 (I) is much rarer.[189] Writers also avoided their personal names as self-designations, although one's given name could be used in letters to equals or superiors. Another self-denigrating strategy was the use of *mou* 某 (a certain person) instead of one's name.[190] In polite and submissive letters, self-designations are usually pronominal substitutes derived from words that describe social or official positions, such as *pu* 僕 (your servant), *chen* 臣 (your vassal), and *xiaguan* 下官 (this lowly official).[191] All of these self-designations are rare in personal letters, as is *yu* 愚 (humble, lit., "stupid"). The same holds true for the condescending self-designations *zhen* 朕 (We), reserved for the emperor, and *gu* 孤 (I, the orphan), used by other sovereigns.[192]

Regarding terms of address, the most conspicuous phenomenon is again the scarcity of personal names and pronouns. Pronouns are used only in letters to inferiors, especially within a family, in which one addressed one's children or other members of the younger generation condescendingly by their given names and the pronouns *ru* 汝 or, very rarely, *er* 爾 (you). Even courtesy names (*zi*) are largely avoided, although they do occur in letters among equals. More common terms of address are either derived from kinship terms, ranks, and titles or are indirect forms of address. As for kinship terms, letter writers could use "elder brother" (*xiong* 兄) and "younger brother" (*di* 弟) to address their own brothers but more often used these terms as honorifics when addressing equals. Terms of address derived from ranks, such as the polite *jun* 君 (lord) and *zi* 子 (baron) among equals and *gong* 公 (duke) and *xiansheng* 先生 (master) when addressing superiors, are not as frequent in early medieval Chinese personal letters as terms derived from official titles, such as *qing* 卿 (minister)[193] among equals and the polite *lang* 郎 (gentleman-attendant) or *zhishi* 執事 (officer). The most common terms of address are indirect, usually referring to attendants of the addressee, who are supposed to stand "beneath the steps" (*bixia* 陛下, "Your Majesty"), a form of address reserved for the emperor; "below the hall" (*dianxia* 殿下, "Your Highness") in the case of other sovereigns; "below your knees" (*xixia* 膝下, "my father or mother"); or "left and right" (*zuoyou* 左右) when generally addressing superiors. The most common address among equals, "at your feet" (*zuxia* 足下), is also indirect.

The diversity of self-designations and terms of address, which by far exceeds the more general options just mentioned, is apparent in these excerpts from letters written by the Liang literatus and official Wang Yun, one of Wang Sengqian's grandsons:

> [Wang] Yun knocks his head on the ground, once and again:
>
> How is your health during the cool of high autumn? . . . Your servant's old ailment has worsened and turned into consumption. Lame and poverty-stricken, I cannot obtain leave from office, which makes me more and more resentful. I wish [*yuan*] respectfully to encourage you. I cannot write on.
>
> Wang Yun knocks his head on the ground, once and again.
>
> 筠頓首頓首。高秋淒爽。體中何如 . . . 僕夙疾增瘵。蹇廢蓬門。不獲執離。彌深傾懣。願敬勖。白書不次。王筠頓首頓首。[194]

> The disciple of the bodhisattva precepts Wang Yun, dharma-name Huiju, bows his head to the ground and obeisantly salutes you:
>
> I send my regards to dharma-teacher Sheng from Dongyang. Formerly, your disciple, on account of my good fortune, early on was granted an audience with you. Since then, years and months have passed by; it has been more than three decades. . . .
>
> Your disciple Wang [Yun] bows his head to the ground and obeisantly salutes you.
>
> 菩薩戒弟子王筠法名慧炬稽首和南。問訊東陽盛法師。弟子昔因多幸早蒙覲接。歲月推流踰三十載 . . . 弟子筠稽首和南。[195]

> Your disciple, the orphan [Wang] Yun, knocks his head on the ground, bows his head to the ground and obeisantly salutes you: . . .
>
> Leaning over the paper, I collapse sobbing.[196] The words I put forward are without rhyme or reason.
>
> Your disciple, the orphan Wang Yun, knocks his head on the ground, bows his head to the ground and obeisantly salutes you.
>
> 弟子孤子筠頓首稽首和南 . . . 臨紙崩衄。厝言無次。弟子孤子王筠頓首稽首和南。[197]

In these three letters, Wang Yun uses three different self-designations along with other adaptations of the frame. While the first example uses the standard form of a polite letter addressed to a superior (with *dunshou*, his given and family names, and *pu*), the second and third are addressed to a member of the Buddhist clergy. In the prescript of the second letter, Wang Yun uses a combination of two verbs (*qishou* and *henan*), refers to himself as "your disciple" (*dizi* 弟子), and, in addition to his given and family names, indicates his dharma-name (*faming* 法名). The self-designation "orphan" (*guzi* 孤子) as well as the overall tone of distress suggest that the third letter was written during mourning for Wang Yun's parents. This letter also provides examples of the practice of combining self-designations (*dizi* and *guzi*) as well as verbs in prescripts and postscripts (*dunshou*, *qishou*, and *henan*). Combining terms of address was also common, especially for official titles. However, since official titles are usually not mentioned in personal letters, prescripts such as the following indicate a piece of official or at least semiofficial communication:

> On the fourth day of the eleventh month Wang Xizhi from Langye, General of the Right and Administrator of Kuaiji, dares to address you, your lordship Xi from Gaoping, Minister of Works: . . .
>
> 十一月四日右將軍會稽內史瑯琊王羲之敢致書司空高平郗公足下。 . . .[198]
>
> Huan Qian, general of the Capital Army, secretarial court gentleman, and dynasty-founding marquis from Yiyang, and others are terrified and deserve death punishment: . . .
>
> 中軍將軍尚書令宜陽開國侯桓謙等惶恐死罪。 . . .[199]

The principle of self-denigration and elevation of the addressee was also applied to mutual acquaintances. Writers could choose from a variety of denigrating or elevating prefixes to communicate their rhetorical goals, such as *jia* 家 (house, family) for elder members of one's family (as in *jia xiong* 家兄) and *she* 舍 (guest house) for younger family members (as in *she di* 舍弟). Persons connected with the addressee could be prefixed by honorifics such as *ren* 仁 (benevolent, as in *ren xiong* 仁兄), *gui* 貴 (noble, as in *gui qie* 貴妾), *xian* 賢 (virtuous, as in *xian zi* 賢子), *zun* 尊 (venerable, as in *zun men* 尊門), and *ling* 令 (excellent, as in *ling di* 令弟).[200] *Xian* is often used to refer to a deceased person in the family of the addressee, for example, *xian di* 賢弟 (your virtuous [late] younger brother).

The letters that Cao Pi wrote to Wu Zhi and Zhong You (151–230) are telling with regard to the rhetorical choices writers had in referring to themselves and their addressees.[201] Although Cao Pi was not yet heir apparent or emperor of the Wei dynasty when he wrote these letters in 214/15, he was still the eldest son of Cao Cao, the most powerful man during the last decades of the Han dynasty. However, Cao

Pi's letters do not reveal this strong position of power but instead display deep respect for his addressees, who were not only much older—Wu Zhi by ten and Zhong You by thirty-six years—but also, at least in the case of Zhong You, of considerable eminence. Cao Pi's self-designations fall between neutral and submissive. He not only uses the personal pronouns *wu* and *yu* and his given name but also marks his ideas as "vulgar" (*bi zhi* 鄙旨), his reading as "deferential" (*qie jian* 竊見), and his presentation of a gift as "sincere" (*jin feng* 謹奉). Writing about Cao Zhi, he uses his younger brother's courtesy name but also the self-denigrating expression *shedi*. The terms of address used by Cao Pi are neutral or polite as well. He uses *zhishi* and *junhou* 君侯 (my lord) for Zhong You and, for Wu Zhi, his correspondent's courtesy name and *zuxia*. If Cao Pi's letters read like polite letters of friendship to equals that do not betray his superior position, the decidedly submissive responses of his addressees most certainly do, since they obviously could not choose to disregard the epistolary conventions that obliged them to properly recognize their addressee's exalted status.[202] Wu Zhi uses the self-designations *chen*, his given name, and various self-denigrating honorifics, such as "to have the honor" (as in *feng du* 奉讀), "deferential" (as in *qie chi zhi* 竊恥之), and "respectful" (as in *fu wei* 伏惟). Addressing Cao Pi, he once uses *zuoyou* but otherwise avoids all terms of address (just like Zhong You). Instead, he uses elevating honorifics throughout the text whenever he is referring to Cao Pi, for instance, calling his letter a "directive" (*ming* 命).

Cao Zhi's "Letter to Yang Xiu" illustrates a phenomenon found in many early medieval letters: the coexistence of different terms of address and self-designation. Referring to himself, the author uses three kinds of terms: his given name Zhi, *pu*, and the personal pronouns *wu* and *yu* as well as the archaic *wo* (in an allusion to early Chinese literature). Addressing Yang Xiu, he uses *zi* and *zuxia*.[203] The fact that different terms of address and self-designation are employed in the same letter could be an indication that early medieval personal letter writing was less strictly determined by conventions than official communication or even personal letter writing in later periods of Chinese history. However, speculations such as these remain unfounded due to the dearth of knowledge about the epistolary rules of early medieval China or even about how strictly they were expected to be obeyed.

Apart from choosing the appropriate words of address and self-designation, letter writers, in order to comply with the principle of

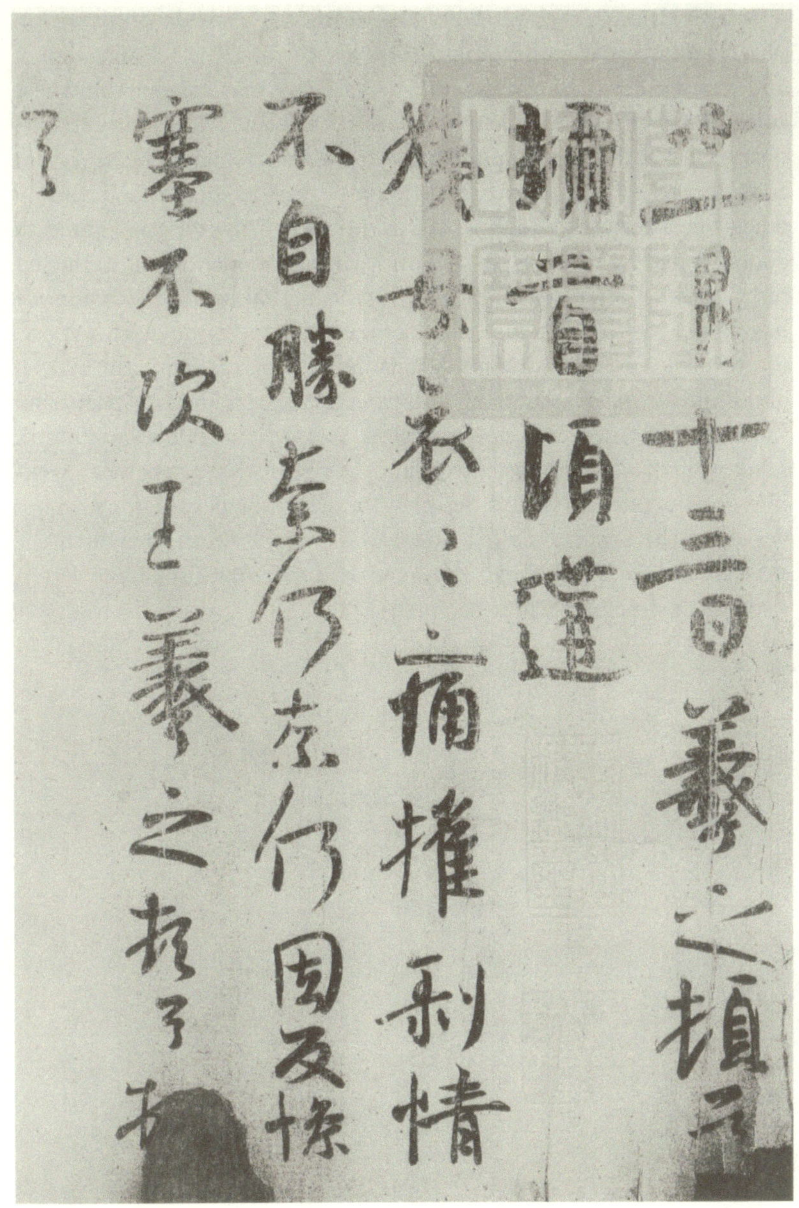

Figure 3.1. Wang Xizhi (303–361), "Yimu tie," Tang dynasty ink tracing copy on semitransparent beeswax paper, H 26.3 cm. Liaoning Provincial Museum, Shenyang

self-denigration and elevation of the addressee, were also expected to observe nonverbal, calligraphic rules concerning the relative size of and spacing between characters.[204] Again, we may assume that these rules about the textual arrangement of a letter were more strictly observed in official communication than in personal letters. A very conspicuous elevating feature of this kind was to start a new column whenever a term of address occurred or when the writer wanted to communicate veneration toward another person mentioned in the letter. Copies of letters by Wang Xizhi indicate that he may occasionally have observed this spacing rule (fig. 3.1).[205] Another device for showing respect for the addressee was to leave a blank space the size of about one or two characters in front of terms of address. Apart from these spacing rules, commonly referred to as *pingque* (level and omit), letter writers were supposed to adapt the size of characters when writing terms of address or self-designation. Early medieval letters do not yet show the practice called *taitou* (raising the head), in which the new column started above the general upper margin of the letter, making the line break more emphatic.[206]

CHAPTER FOUR

Topoi

It is long since I received a letter from you. You will allege, perhaps, you have nothing to write: but let me have the satisfaction at least of seeing it under your hand, or tell me merely in the good old style of exordium, "If you are well, I am so." I shall be contented even with that; as indeed that single circumstance from a friend includes every thing. You may possibly think I jest: but believe me I am extremely in earnest. Let me know how it is with you; for I cannot be ignorant of that, without the utmost anxiety. Farewell.

—PLINY, letter to Fabius Justus

Letters are distinguished not only by their particular materiality, structure, and phraseology but also by epistolary topoi, or "commonplaces."[1] Unlike epistolary phrases, these elements of a letter are characterized not so much by set expressions but rather by set ideas or sentiments. They may or may not be expressed in fixed phrases and usually concern the affirmation of the correspondents' relationship. Epistolary topoi commonly occur in the frame of a letter but frequently penetrate the main text as well, where they help to enhance a letter's epistolarity by emphasizing its dialogicity as well as the amalgamation of interpersonal concerns with other communicative intentions. The employment of certain commonplaces is vital for successful epistolary communication, especially in delicate situations such as condolences. Despite their overwhelming conventionality, epistolary topoi should thus not be dismissed as mere rhetorical clichés. Not only do some authors display astonishing variation and sophistication in wielding these topoi, but many of the topoi themselves articulate authentic human experiences that are at the heart of life and literature.

This chapter introduces three complex topoi that arise from the epistolary situation: the lament of separation, the perception of letters as substitutes for face-to-face conversation, and evocations of the insufficiency of one's letter along with that of language and writing in general. These topoi may all be interpreted as manifestations of the self-referentiality of a letter, for, as Roger Chartier so succinctly expressed it, "the real subject matter of letter-writing is the writing of the letters."[2] It will become evident that these topoi are commingled in many ways. One reason for their interrelatedness is that they are all expressions of close relationships, situated in the continuum of kinship and friendship relations.[3] Since only a small part of the transmitted letters are correspondences between family members and epistolary evidence for marital relations is almost nonexistent, much of the epistolary literature from early medieval China could be described as letters of friendship. This concept embraces very different aspects of human relationships: they are self-chosen (which may extend to family members), nonhierarchical (which does not exclude partners of different social standing), built on trust, based on the recognition of personality (or "understanding" the other),[4] enjoy a certain personal autonomy, and are dedicated to mutual support.

Many discussions of the notion of friendship, whether in the East or the West, focus on the last, utilitarian criterion and its implications for the character of a friendship, assuming that "pure" friendship is incompatible with the pursuit of personal or familial benefits. This seems to be an unproductive approach, because it confuses the establishment of an ideal with its realization in social practice. Although early Chinese literature created narratives of friendship unblemished by utilitarian purposes, a concept that remained powerful in later periods as well—as, not the least, early medieval letters prove—actual friendships were formed and tested in a sober reality, meaning, as Thomas Jansen put it, "in a society where political and social prominence was increasingly dependent on connections to the court or the participation in webs of patronage, the ability to form 'beneficial friendships' (*yiyou* 益友), to use Confucius' own words, [was] essential for every person hoping to achieve political influence."[5] However, this "setting in life" of every friendship does not mean that it is determined primarily by the pursuit of benefit, which is, after all, only one of its features.[6]

Letters from early medieval China do not meditate on friendship in an analytical or systematic way. There is no essay about friendship in letter form, but there are many amicable letters, each an instantiation of friendship. This quality is reflected not so much in the subject matter of these letters but rather in their interpersonal, dialogic nature and their choice of epistolary topoi. The fact that the lament of separation ranks first among these is certainly expressive of the importance attached to the continuation of personal relationships.

LAMENTING SEPARATION

Parted by death, we swallow remorse;
Apart in life we always suffer.
死別已吞聲，生別常惻惻。
—DU FU, "Dreaming of Li Bai" (Meng Li Bai er shou)[7]

The lament of separation, from lovers, siblings, or friends, has been one of the major topics of Chinese poetry since the *Book of Odes.* It has inspired poetic subgenres, such as the farewell poem, and a host of poetic motifs, such as the long and lonely night, the dusty mirror, and the letter that betrays a separation, to name but a few. The lament of the song "The Lesser Master of Fate" (Shao si ming), in the *Songs from Chu* (Chu ci), that "no sorrow is greater than the parting of the living,"[8] has since been repeated again and again, perhaps most famously by Du Fu.[9] Grief at parting and its complement, the anticipation of reunion, have always been "part of our social definition,"[10] or, as Wang Xizhi put it in one of his letters, "To meet and to part again is a constant in the texture of human life."[11]

It is not surprising that most personal letters from early medieval China in one way or another express the writer's affection and concern for the addressee by lamenting that they are apart. The prevalence of this topos in epistolary writing testifies to the self-referentiality of the letter, for to profess sorrow about a separation virtually spells out the raison d'être of the letter: the physical distance between the correspondents that places their bond in jeopardy and thus needs to be bridged by written communication.[12] There are but few epistolary subgenres, such as admonitions and recommendations, that do not require this physical distance. These types of letters may also be addressed to someone who is present, because the emphasis clearly is on the written nature of the communication, which is intended to be available for future rereading, reference, and documentation. However, the notion of separation does figure in these letters as well, because the hope for the durability of the written word virtually anticipates future separations, including death, the final parting.

If reasons for a separation are mentioned at all, the letters usually note the civil or military duties that required most scholar-officials to continually travel, often over considerable distances, either to new assignments or as part of their official responsibilities. But although most letters were written while the correspondents were apart, they only occasionally lament the spatial distance between author and addressee. The temporal dimension was felt more keenly, not the least because the passing of time during separation was closely associated with aging and death. Sometimes the time spans mentioned in the letters are breathtaking: Wang Yun laments that he has not met his correspondent for more than thirty years, Wang Xizhi cites twenty-six, and Ren Fang twenty-four.[13] To enhance the emotional impact of the lament of separation, allusions to the *Book of Odes* are common, since it provides a stock of highly iconic depictions of the grief of parting.

> To receive news that you are safe and sound, Wenxiu, was very good indeed [*shen shan shen shan*]. Can you imagine that we have been separated for more than thirty years already? And still there is no opportunity to see you! In the *Odes*, people compare a separation lasting for one day with years and months. How would they have coped if it had lasted dozens of years? After our separation, I have often felt as though I were drowning and rising to the surface again, or were broken apart and joined together again. As it is now, so it will continue to be in the future. . . .
>
> 文休足下。消息平安。甚善甚善。豈意脫別三十餘年。而無相見之緣乎。詩人比一日之別于歲月。豈況悠悠歷累紀之年者哉。自與子別若沒而復浮。若絕而復連者數矣。而今而後。 . . .[14]

Wang Lang alludes to the ode "Plucking Flax" (Cai ge), the first stanza of which famously declares that "a day without seeing you is like three months," only to amplify this declaration in subsequent stanzas by comparing a day to three autumns and finally to three years.[15] This ode is mentioned in other letters as well, many of which prove that separations did not need to be long to be lamented. Cao Zhi is aggrieved after only "a few days" of parting from Yang Xiu and writes him a long letter, although they will meet the next day.[16] For Wang Xizhi, "days turn into years waiting for a meeting with you,"[17] and Xie An's longing for Zhi Dun (ca. 313–366) not only "grows by the day," but for him, "a day amounts to a thousand years."[18] Aiming beyond the actual longing toward the fundamental transitoriness of life, the hyperbole of these comparisons emphasizes the connection of separation with aging and death.

Impressive examples of the lament of separation may also be found in letters written on the occasion of a parting, either before or immediately afterward, as in the following letter by Xiao Gang, written in late 531 upon Xiao Ziyun's impending departure from the capital to take up office as administrator of Linchuan (*Linchuan neishi*):

零雨送秋	A fine rain sees autumn off;[19]
輕寒迎節	a slight cold welcomes the next season.
江楓曉落	The maples along the Jiang are shedding their leaves at dawn;
林葉初黃	the woods have begun to turn yellow.
登舟已積	That you would board a ship has long been due,
殊足勞止	but it is more than enough to make me extremely weary with longing for you.[20]
解維金闕	Casting off the mooring lines that keep you in the capital,
定在何日 . . .	on what day is it fixed? . . . [21]

In this famous piece of parallel prose, Xiao Gang has found subtle ways to express the grief of parting. He explicitly mentions neither the separation nor the ode "Eastern Mountain" and the three years of separation it laments, as Cao Pi had done in "Further letter to Wu Zhi," no. 1, in 218. Instead, the separation appears mediated through images of the increasingly cold and stark autumn and through the "fine rain" (*ling yu*) that shapes each of the four stanzas of the ode "Eastern Mountain."

Many letter writers also mention bodily expressions, such as aches, tears, and sleepnessness, in order to convey their grief at parting, just as Wang Lang did, a practice that helps to inscribe their physical presence into their letters. The language they employ can be quite severe and may even resemble that of letters of condolence or mourning, which also frequently speak of pain, flowing tears, and failing voices.

> . . . My heart is injured; my tears flow. Discarding my brush, I stop writing.
>
> . . . 心傷淚灑。投筆無宣。[22]
>
> . . . "The length of the Jiang!"[23] Waking and sleeping, I am longing for you. Whenever I receive a letter from you, my aches subside and my diseases disappear. . . .
>
> . . . 江之遠矣, 寤寐相思。每得弟書輕痾 (遺)〔遣〕疾。 . . . [24]

The literary and rhetorical effect is strongest when the topos of the lament of separation is not only treated in the frame but pervades the whole text, as in a famous letter that Cao Pi wrote to his friend Wu Zhi around 215.

On the eighteenth day of the fifth month, [Cao] Pi lets you know:

May you, Jizhong, be unharmed. The roads that separate us may be short, but exercising office imposes restrictions on us. "The longing I want to speak about"[25] is hardly bearable. The district you are governing is awkwardly situated, so that letters [*shuwen*] are very scarce, which increases the weariness of longing for you.

I often think of our former travels in Nanpi; they are truly unforgettable. We deeply pondered the Six Canonical Books and roamed through the writings of the Hundred Philosophers. We set some time aside for pellet chess and finished our evenings with a game of six sticks.[26] Lofty talks delighted our hearts, and sorrowful zithers pleased our ears. We galloped through the fields to the north and feasted in the lodges to the south. We floated sweet melons in clear springs and sank red plums in cold water. When the white sun had set, we continued under the bright moon. Sitting in the same carriage or driving side by side, we rolled through the rear garden, the wheels slowly turning and none of the servants making a sound. When a fresh wind arose at night and sad flutes sounded faintly, joy made way for sorrow and we felt melancholy and sad. Turning to you, I said that this joy would hardly last, and you and your companions all agreed.

Now we are indeed separated; everyone is living somewhere else. Yuanyu [i.e., Ruan Yu] has gone forever and transformed into another being.[27] Whenever I think of all this, I wonder when we will be able to talk about it.

It is just midsummer, and southern winds are fanning the land. It is warm, and all the fruits grow in abundance. I often go for a ride to the north following the bends of the Yellow River. A servant blows a flute to clear the way, and the instructors ride in the rear carriage. The season is the same, but the times are different. Things have remained right, but people have not. "How can I describe the weariness of longing that I feel?"[28]

Since I am just about to dispatch a rider to Ye, I will have him detour by you. Go and take good care of yourself.

This is what [Cao] Pi lets you know.

五月十八日丕白。季重無恙。塗路雖局。官守有限。願言之懷。良不可任。足下所治僻左。書問致簡。益用增勞。每念昔日南皮之游。誠不可忘。既妙思六經。逍遙百氏。彈碁間設。終以六博。高談娛心。哀箏順耳。馳騖北場。旅食南館。浮甘瓜於清泉。沈朱李於寒水。白日既匿。繼以朗月。同乘并載。以游後園。輿輪徐動。參從無聲。清風夜起。悲笳微吟。樂往哀來。愴然傷懷。余顧而言。斯樂難常。足下之徒。咸以為然。今果分別。各在一方。元瑜長逝。化為異物。每一念至。何時可言。方今蕤賓紀時。景風扇物。天氣和暖。眾果具繁。時駕而游。北遵河曲。從者鳴笳以啟路。文學託乘於後車。節同時異。物是人非。我勞如何。今遣騎到鄴。故使枉道相過。行矣自愛。丕白。[29]

The letter is a gentle and very personal celebration of friendship, unencumbered by any ancillary communicative agenda such as a survey of the literary scene. The proem begins with Cao Pi's wish for good health and is immediately followed by the explicit lament of separation, which extends to the scarcity of correspondence. The focus on the personal relationship with the addressee is sustained in the body of the letter, during Cao Pi's nostalgic reflections, following the signal word *xi* (former), and during his musings about the present, marked by the signal word *jin* (now). Cao Pi resumes the lament of separation, now associated with the relentless passing of time and thus equated with the unavoidable separation by death.

Three years later, in "Further letter to Wu Zhi," no. 1, Cao Pi writes with increased urgency about these topics, now under the influence of the great epidemic of 217 that had cost many of his friends their lives. Again, he closely connects the sentiments of passing time and youth with the lament of separation.

> . . . Because I am already advanced in years, I am preoccupied by a myriad of things. Often there is something to consider that keeps me from sleeping for whole nights. When will my intentions and ideas ever be as they were in former days? I have already become an old man, only my hair has not turned white yet. Guangwu once said: "I am over thirty and spent ten years in the military, which has changed me in more than one way."[30] My virtue may not compare with his, but we are of the same age.
>
> Equipped with the substance of a dog or sheep, I wear the patterns of tigers and panthers.[31] Lacking the brightness of the stars, I borrow the light of the sun and the moon.[32] All my moves are watched and observed. When will this ever change? I am afraid I will never be able to go on travels as in the former days. We really must take advantage of our youth.[33] A year, once passed, can never be retrieved.[34] The ancients longed to wander all night long, a candle in hand—there is certainly something to be said for that.[35]
>
> How have you been amusing yourself recently? Surely there is something to tell. Are you writing? I am looking east, full of distress. I have written this letter [*shu*] to relieve my heart.[36]
>
> This is what [Cao] Pi lets you know.
>
> . . . 年行已長大。所懷萬端。時有所慮。至通夜不瞑。志意何時。復類昔日。已成老翁。但未白頭耳。光武言年三十餘。在兵中十歲。所更非一。吾德不及之。年與之齊矣。以犬羊之質。服虎豹之文。無眾星之明。假日月之光。動見瞻觀。何時易乎。恐永不復得為昔日遊也。少壯真當努力。年一過往。何可攀援。古人思炳燭夜遊。良有以也。頃何以自娛。頗復有所述。造不。東望於邑。裁書敘心。丕白。[37]

Although it is not exactly remarkable that the thirty-year-old Cao Pi has not yet turned white, his professions of feeling like an old man may sound exaggerated unless they are seen as part of an established literary practice that seems to have been accepted in China for long stretches of its literary history.[38] At the end of the epilogue, Cao Pi expresses the hope that writing a letter may help to "relieve my heart" and thus alleviate the grief of separation, a notion that is reminiscent of Liu Xie, who declared in *The Literary Mind* that letters are meant to "dispel pent-up emotions."[39]

The association of separation with aging and death is prevalent in other, less renowned letters as well. When Lu Yun in a letter to Yang Yanming ruminated on the passing of time and youth, he was probably not much older than Cao Pi when he wrote to Wu Zhi less than a century earlier.

> Lu Yun lets you know:
>
> Perusing the many sheets of paper of your letter [*shi*, instruction] has brought our past meetings to life again and increasingly made me sigh. How very fast the happy years go by!
>
> In former (*xi*) years, when we were still young, seeing a fifty-year-old man, we would feel that he was very far removed from us. These days we ourselves are slowly getting to this age already.[40] And if we have turned sixty,[41] we will sigh full of sorrow again. Branches coming into leaf are always delightful. But before we have become tired of enjoying the spring, autumn winds arrive to warn us, and we are already saddened by fallen leaves. Life is full of misadventures, while pleasures are always scarce. How long will we still travel this world?
>
> Although we have been separated for an eternity and every hope for a good meeting has come to nothing, I cannot forget my heartfelt longing for you, whom I dearly love, whether waking or sleeping. A letter [*shu*] cannot express all.
>
> 陸雲白。省示累紙。重存往會。益以增歎。年時可喜。何速之甚。昔年少時。見五十公。去此甚遠。今日冉冉。己近之 (己)〔已〕。耳順之年。行復為憂歎也。柯生而多悅。樂春未厭。秋風行戒。已悲落葉矣。人道多故。懽樂恆乏。敖遊此世。當復幾時。各爾永隔。良會每闕。懷想親愛。寤寐無忘。書無所悉。[42]

It is a sobering thought that Lu Yun, disturbed by the prospect of turning fifty or even sixty, would not live to either age but would die prematurely on the execution ground at just forty-one. Although his letter does not show the poetic density and force that characterize Cao Pi's letter to Wu Zhi, it is still moving in its immediacy and apparent artlessness, qualities that bring the letters of Wang Xizhi to mind. Just as in these, the lack of any particular message or communicative purpose highlights its affectionate nature. The "purposelessness" of many intimate personal letters may have been a reflection of the notion of "pure" friendship that had been an important ideal since early China, because it seems to be an attempt to create a sphere unblemished by the utilitarian purposes that necessarily dominated much of social life and relationships. Even if epistolary "purposelessness" may serve more substantial purposes, it still remains a reminder of the ideal of "pure" friendship.

In many letters, lamenting separation goes hand in hand with the celebration of reunion. Given the close association of separation with aging and death, reunions and being together almost appear as antidotes, especially in those letters that articulate the hope for a meeting with the addressee in an exalted tone. However, the spectrum of expressions is broad, ranging from the terse and restrained to the flowery and effusive.

> . . . We have been separated for long. What day can you come here?
>
> . . . 隔久。何日能來。[43]
>
> I have not seen you for a stretch of time, and it has been very long. I am waiting to meet you. Tomorrow when I go out to attend a meeting, I hope to get the chance to see you.
>
> 此段不見足下。乃甚久。遲面。明行集。冀得見卿。[44]
>
> . . . I only hope that you can return soon. Holding my brush, I am feeling sad.
>
> . . . 想不久可得還耳。執筆惻慼。[45]
>
> . . . We are going to see each other soon, so I do not write more. Take good care of yourselves, now, during the summer.
> This is what [Ying] Qu lets you know.
>
> . . . 相見在近。故不復為書。慎夏自愛。璩白。[46]
>
> . . . We won't be sitting knee to knee anytime soon. I am looking east with deep emotion. I only hope that the days and months will pass easily and that the time of your return may not be far away. . . .
>
> . . . 促膝未近。東望慨然。所冀日月易得。還期非遠耳。 . . .[47]
>
> . . . But Mounts Heng and Wu are extremely high and the Han River is so long. When will we be able grasp our sleeves again and open our hearts to each other?[48]
>
> . . . 但衡巫峻極。漢水悠長。何時把袂。共披心腹。[49]

Especially when letter writers express their longing for their addressees' physical presence, separation becomes quite tangible: holding hands (*di zhang*, *xie shou*, *zhi shou*), grasping the other's sleeve (*ba mei*), and sitting knee to knee (*cu xi*)—an especially appealing idea if we keep in mind that in early medieval China people sat not on chairs but on mats or low, rather large beds or couches, legs bent or tucked under the body.[50] These images evoke the immediacy and intimacy of a meeting between friends and are thus very suitable to conveying appreciation of the other beyond the current epistolary exchange.

While the quoted letters express the writers' hopes to see the addressees in the near future, many more writers just lament that there is no reunion within sight. Among the different ways of expressing this sentiment is a formulaic phrase consisting of or starting with *wu yin* 無因, *wu yuan* 無緣, or *wu you* 無由, literally, "there is no reason/opportunity" to meet you.

> . . . There is no opportunity to set eyes on each other. Although words do not fully capture the mind, I hope you may frequently grant me a letter [*hui*, teaching] to comfort me in my longing for you in the far distance.
>
> [Lu] Yun bows repeatedly.

. . . 無因覩對。言不盡心。屢垂誨。以慰遠思。雲再拜。[51]

> . . . That there is no opportunity to get together makes me sigh. I am waiting for messages [*zhi wen*] from you.

> . . . 無緣同為歎。遲知問。[52]

> . . . I am longing for a meeting with you. That there is no opportunity to meet you is lamentable, lamentable.

> . . . 思卿一面。無緣可歎可歎。[53]

> On the sixteenth day of the third month, [Lu] Yun lets you know:
>
> It is spring, but I am not well. Having received your letter [*shi*, instruction], I know that you are safe and sound. I long to meet you but do not know of an opportunity yet. . . .

> 三月十六日雲白。春節餘不適。得示。知足下平安。為思面。未知何由。 . . .[54]

> . . . There is no opportunity to talk to you in person. Holding my brush, I am filled with eternal longing for you.
>
> Xie Lingyun obeisantly salutes you.

> . . . 無由言對。執筆長懷。謝靈運和南。[55]

As in the last example, the core of the phrase may, like an abbreviation, stand alone, omitting the semantically decisive "meeting" or a similar complement.[56]

In these letters, the lament of separation emerges as a powerful epistolary topos. One reason for this efficacy is rhetorical in nature: lamenting separation draws attention to the letter itself and thus reinforces its epistolarity. Lamenting separation is also the perfect expression of friendship or another close relationship: separation amounts to waiting, to aging, and to getting closer to death, the ultimate separation, while being together signifies the release into immediacy that promises to alleviate the fears associated with parting.

LETTERS AS SUBSTITUTES FOR FACE-TO-FACE CONVERSATION

You'll get my Letter by
The Seventeenth; Reply
Or better, be with me—
Your's, Fly.
—EMILY DICKINSON, "Bee! I'm expecting you!"[57]

When there is no opportunity to get together, letters are perceived as substitutes for the presence of the other. Weighing a letter against a meeting, correspondence against conversation, is a common epistolary topos in early medieval Chinese letter writing. While *The Literary Mind* expresses this idea explicitly when Liu Xie praises letters in which "the words resemble those spoken face-to-face,"[58] Yan Zhitui's *Family Instructions* cites a "dictum from the south that says 'letters carry their writers' faces across a thousand miles.'"[59] These two approaches cover both the textual and the material aspects of letter writing: Liu Xie was concerned with literary composition; Yan Zhitui quoted the saying from the south in the context of calligraphy and was thus talking primarily about the handwriting of a letter. The general assumption was that letters are most effective if they manage to turn the writer into a speaker or reading into a face-to-face conversation. We have already seen that many epistolary phrases suggest the bodily presence of the correspondents and that it is very common indeed to write about "speaking" or "hearing" in a letter. In Western epistolary thought, the power of a letter to simulate the presence of its writer in the mind of the reader (*parousia*) has been a prominent topos since antiquity as well.[60]

In extant Chinese letter writing, the first author who articulated the idea of the letter as a substitute for face-to-face conversation appears to have been Cai Yong, who declared that "without hope of seeing each other, we have only the traces of the brush substituting for meeting face-to-face."[61] Although Cai was referring to both his own and his addressee's letters, many writers who later employed the topos differentiated between the two, because they present rhetorically very different situations: while talking about oneself and thus also one's own skills at letter writing required humility, the literary productions of the addressee, including their letters, needed to be praised. Expressing confidence about the communicative powers of one's own letter, as in the following examples, was therefore rather uncommon.

> . . . There is no opportunity to see you, sir. Therefore I have expressed all I have in mind, hoping that my letter may substitute for a meeting.
>
> . . . 無緣見君。故悉心而言。以當一面。[62]
>
> . . . There is no opportunity to talk to you in person. May this chit-chat substitute for a meeting.
>
> This is what He Chengtian lets you know.
>
> . . . 未緣言對。聊以代面。何承天白。[63]
>
> . . . I am gone, Scholar He![64] Tall trees are richly fragrant. I have written this letter [*shu*] to substitute for a meeting. Brush and tears fall down together.
>
> . . . 去矣何生。高樹芳烈。裁書代面。筆淚俱下。[65]

Much more often, letter writers emphasize their own epistolary inadequacy. (This well-developed topos is explored in the next section.)

Explicit references to letters as substitutes for face-to-face conversation most often occur as reflections on the act of reading a letter, when writers express admiration for the letter they have received from the addressee.

> . . . The ways across heaven are lofty and far away. For very long there has been no opportunity to meet you. My fond feelings for you make me toss and turn. What can I do? What can I do? I have received the letter [*xun*, message] you sent me. The beauty of your literary style is intricate: luminous as spring blossoms, clear as the fresh wind. Straightening out the paper and chanting again and again, I felt lighthearted as if we had met again. . . .
>
> . . . 天路高邈。良久無緣。懷戀反側。如何如何。得所來訊。文采委曲。曄若春榮。瀏若清風。申詠反覆。曠若復面。 . . .[66]
>
> . . . To straighten out and peruse your letter [*shu*] is almost as good as talking to you face-to-face.

> . . . 申省次若言面。[67]
>
> . . . When the monk Huiming arrived, I received your letter [*shu*] of the twelfth month of last year and your good wishes. Having opened your letter and scrutinized it again and again, I was filled with joy as if I had momentarily come face-to-face with you. . . .
>
> . . . 慧明道人至。得去年十二月疏并問。披尋返覆。欣若暫對。 . . . [68]

Since letters, after all, can only simulate a meeting, they not only fail to bridge a separation but even call attention to its persistence. In a paradoxical way, praise for someone's letter could therefore be coupled with pretended censure and thus express an even higher degree of appreciation of its writer. This would happen when the addressee's letters were perceived and described as insufficient substitutes for a meeting. The following letter by Wang Xizhi, written to his friend Zhou Fu in Yizhou, demonstrates this emotional and rhetorical conundrum:

> I reckon twenty-six years have passed since I said good-bye to you. Although we frequently exchange letters [*shuwen*], they cannot dispel the longing for you that I have harbored for so long. Perusing your last two letters [*shu*] has only increased my sadness. Lately, it has been snowing heavily, and it is colder than it has ever been in fifty years. I hope everything is going well for you these days. I only hope to receive further news [*wen*] from you in the next summer or autumn. Of late, I have been missing you more than I can say. I have been taking cold-food powder for a long time, but I am still weak.[69] However, on the whole and considering my age, I am fairly well.[70] Do take the greatest care of yourself! Leaning over my letter, I feel nothing but disappointment and frustration.
>
> 計與足下別。卄六年於今。雖時書問。不解闊懷。省足下先後二書。但增歎慨。頃積雪凝寒。五十年中所無。想頃如常。冀來夏秋閒。或復得足下問耳。比者悠悠。如何可言。吾服食久。猶為劣劣。大都比之年時。為復可耳。足下保愛為上。臨書但有惆悵。[71]

Letters can offer only something that resembles a meeting, so the desire for the presence of the addressee ultimately remains unsatisfied, as Wang Xizhi makes clear by his statement "Perusing your last two letters has only increased my sadness." Although he hopes for his friend's letters, he also finds fault with them: unable to relieve his longing, they even arouse it. This contradictory attitude toward the other's letters—constantly and urgently requested but also regularly and principally found inadequate—is a variation on the theme "there is no opportunity to meet you" and thus closely related to the lament of separation. The stance was also employed by Cao Pi in a letter to Wu Zhi ("although we exchange letters, they do not suffice to relieve the weariness of longing"[72]) and in a letter by Suo Jing (239–303).

> On the twenty-sixth day of the seventh month, [Suo] Jing writes to let you know:
>
> Although I frequently hear from you, this cannot dispel the weariness of longing for you. . . .
>
> 七月二十六日具書靖白。雖數相聞。不解勞倦。 . . .[73]

The fact that letters have strengths and are not simply deficient compared to conversation was rarely expressed in letters themselves, which mostly strive to win the goodwill of the addressee and hence generally profess to prefer a meeting over a letter. A writer who expressed the opposite idea was Wang Wei (415–453), who wrote in a letter to his cousin that "even a meeting could not surpass reading this letter."[74]

Rhetorically successful as this approach may be, it does not do justice to the potential of epistolary communication. The benefits of letter writing result mainly from writing itself, which allows as well as demands greater attention to the wording of a message,[75] has a more binding nature, permits the convenient timing of a dispatch, and so forth.[76] Another advantage arises from the indirectness of epistolary communication, because it may embolden writers if they do not have to face their addressees—a feature that has been famously characterized by Cicero who, in 55 BCE, in a letter to Lucius Lucceius, justified a somewhat reckless request with the words "a letter does not blush" (*epistula enim non erubescit*).[77] The recipients could also profit from epistolary communication in various ways. At first sight, the most appealing of these is the possibility of completely ignoring a letter, illustrated by the anecdote about the late Han official Du An, who prudently left letters unopened because he feared they might politically compromise him. The unopened letters later helped him prove his innocence.[78] However, the opposite was probably more relevant: the ability to freely reread and ponder a message, which was, incidentally, also one of the strategies for compensating for the frequently invoked insufficiency of letters.[79]

Generally, these strategies aim at intensifying the "epistolary experience," which could be achieved by the temporal extension of the act of reading and by deriving benefit from the nonverbal dimensions of a letter. While the temporal extension of reading may serve as compensation for a letter's inevitable brevity, sensual reading—such as enjoying the touch or even scent of a letter—may complement the extremely reduced form of communion that a written text provided. Descriptions of reading the addressee's letters, usually placed in the proem, are frequent in epistolary writing since Han times.[80] Authors mention multiple readings and reading aloud, at times even to others, along with references to actually "handling" a letter.[81]

> [Yang] Xiu deserves death punishment, once and again:
> It has been only a few days [since we parted], but it feels like a whole year to me. Isn't it because the abundance of your love and consideration have deepened my feelings of admiration and reverence? You have condescended to send me a fine letter [*ming*, directive]. What a splendid piece of literature! I recited it again and again. . . .
>
> 修死罪死罪。不侍數日。若彌年載。豈由愛顧之隆。使係仰之情深邪。損辱嘉命。蔚矣其文。誦讀反覆。 . . .[82]
>
> . . . I have received your letter [*shu*] of the twelfth day of the ninth month. Reading it, I smiled happily. I grasped and cherished it without getting tired of it. . . .
>
> . . . 得九月二十日書。讀之喜笑。把玩無厭。 . . .[83]
>
> . . . Your letter [*hui*, teaching] is full of affection and serious devotion that become ever more abundant. Reciting and cherishing it a thousand times over was like meeting you. . . .
>
> . . . 來誨綢繆。篤眷彌隆。誦翫千周。以當侍會。 . . .[84]
>
> [Liu] Kun knocks his head on the ground:
> You have condescended to send me a letter [*shu*] and a poem. Using bitter words of misery, you unfold lasting and far-reaching ideas. Again and again I held your writings to cherish them; I would not let them out of my hands. I sighed with sadness and was filled with joy. . . .
>
> 琨頓首。損書及詩。備辛酸之苦言。暢經通之遠旨。執玩反覆。不能釋手。慨然以悲。歡然以喜。 . . .[85]
>
> . . . Having perused your letter [*gao*, note], one may well say that it is full of the highest devotion and consideration. I scrutinized and cherished it three or four times over but still sighed with sadness. . . .
>
> . . . 省告。可謂眷顧之至。尋翫三四。但有悲慨。 . . .[86]
>
> Shi Daogao lets you know:
> I had the honor to receive another profound letter [*hui*, teaching] from you. Its meaning is magnificent, and its ideas are far-reaching.

> Only after I had read it three times over and pondered it nine times over could I unlock its depths. . . .
>
> 釋道高白。重奉深誨。義華旨遠。三讀九思。方服淵致。 . . . [87]
>
> I received your letter [*shu* 疏] of the twenty-eighth of the fifth month and the enclosed poem. Perusing them over and over again, I felt comforted as if I had sat knee to knee with you. You have always been a natural genius and have complemented this with your fondness for literature and your awareness of your abilities. You are getting better every day. The opening and closing [of the letter?] are clean-cut; it can be regarded as a fine piece of writing. I chanted and cherished it again and again. I could not bring myself to stop, even if I had wanted to. . . .
>
> 得五月二十八日疏幷詩一首。省覽周環。慰同促膝。汝本有天才。加以愛好。無忘所能。日見其善。首尾裁淨。可為佳作。吟玩反覆。欲罷不能。 . . . [88]

Most of these examples mention both compensatory strategies at the same time: reading more than once and actually holding a letter in one's hands. Guglielmo Cavallo and Roger Chartier have pointed out that "readers are never faced with an abstract, ideal text detached from everything material: they manipulate objects" whose properties guide the reading process and influence the understanding of a text.[89] While this observation certainly applies to every type of reading,[90] letters are distinguished because they are not only complex material objects providing a text but also objects that carry diverse physical traces of their writers and may therefore represent them more fully than a disembodied text could.[91] The material features of a letter—from its handwriting to the texture of the paper and its smell—thus appear as filling the inevitable gap between a letter and an actual meeting with all its physical components. This becomes very obvious when the tactile aspects of reading are spelled out: the letter is held (*zhi*, *ba*), just like the hand of the other that one does not want to let go of. The sensual delight of holding a letter is effectively accentuated by the word *wan* (to play, amuse oneself).[92] Its English translation as "to cherish" is slightly unsatisfactory, because it does not emphasize the tactile aspects of the word strongly enough. *Wan* suggests the playful handling of an object in a broad range of meanings, from fondling a haptically pleasing object, to carelessly or teasingly toying with something, to the joyful contemplation of a literary or philosophical text. Although the latter semantic facet already occurs in the "Commentary on the Appended Words,"[93] the tactile dimension of *wan* played a decidedly stronger role, especially in early and medieval Chinese, when *wan* referred to a piece of writing, be it a letter or another literary text. When Liu Kun, for example, uses *wan* in his letter, the tactile dimension is quite clear: "The pearl that could illuminate the night—why should only the hand of the marquis of Sui cherish it?"[94]

If letters are in this way perceived as material objects, they appear similar to gifts that are also handed from one person to another and often represent the givers as well as the bond between givers and recipients. In early China, words were often praised as the most valuable kind of present, surpassing carriages or other treasures such as gold and jade.[95] While this long tradition refers to content only, the admonishing or otherwise enlightening qualities of a text, in Han times the focus shifted to include a regard for the written word's materiality, especially the calligraphic value of writings. This meant that in China the materiality of letters was even more relevant than in other cultures, which also contain the idea of the letter as a present for the addressee although handwriting did not enjoy the particular Chinese appreciation apart from being a tangible representation of the writer.[96] However, Chinese letter writers also expressed delight about someone's handwriting as such, irrespective of its calligraphic qualities, as in this letter from Lu Jing to his brother:

> It has been roughly three years since I have joined the army. It is certainly because of your sincere amity that I have survived this time. I treasure and collect your letters [*shu*]; they already fill a basket. When I do not get a new letter [*ming*, directive], I have nothing to comfort myself. Then I often warm over an old one to quench my longing for you. Because the messenger is here, I forget so many words [that I wanted to write]. Whenever I see your handwriting, I feel as if I had temporarily met you again.
>
> 自尋外役。出入三年。緣兄之篤睦。必時存之。寶錄兄書。積之盈笥。不得新命。無以自慰。時輒溫故。以釋其思。有信忘數字。每見手跡。如復暫會。[97]

Lu Jing does not even mention the content of his brother's letters but describes the pleasure he takes in his handwriting, similar to Xu Ling's letter quoted in chapter 1. Unlike Xu Ling, however, who praises the calligraphic qualities of his relative's hand, Lu Jing enjoyed his brother's handwriting not on account of of aesthetic criteria but because it represented its writer. This appreciation, together with the treasuring and collecting he mentions, is a perfect example for the illocutionary force of letters that is independent of any propositional content.[98] For Lu Jing and many other correspondents, the primary value of letters was as a manifestation of the writer's affection for the addressee that reaffirmed the bond between them, or, as Peter Gay describes it, "a letter was a token, *the* token, of true affection, proof that the other was ready to set aside valuable time to visualizing, and addressing, the loved one."[99]

THE LIMITS OF WRITING AND LANGUAGE

While reflections on the act of reading a letter are closely connected to the idea of the letter as a substitute for a meeting and are often enough optimistic as to the letter's ability to provide this impression, reflections on writing usually take a darker view, focusing on the limits of letter writing, which extends to the limits of language and writing in general. The invocation of the insufficiency of letters was a major topos in early medieval letter writing, as many of the examples quoted so far prove, and it continued to be popular in later centuries as well.[100] The locus classicus of the topos is the dictum "writing does not fully capture words, words do not fully capture meaning," which the "Commentary on the Appended Words" ascribes to Confucius.[101] In his own interpretation of these words, Confucius declares that the gap between language and meaning is filled by the *Book of Changes* itself, whose hexagrams and explanations are capable of counteracting the fundamental inadequacy of words and writing. The idea was a prominent subject of philosophical and literary disputes in early medieval China, especially in third- and fourth-century "mysterious learning" (*xuanxue*).[102] Although it has been elaborated on or alluded to in many genres, not the least poetry, it fits the rhetorical requirements of epistolary writing particularly well. It not only fulfills the imperative of showing humility about everything related to oneself, including the ability to write, but, as a reflection on the act of writing, is also an effective way of enhancing a letter's self-referentiality and thus rhetorical success. Evoking the limits of language and writing moreover hints at the dimension of the unwritten or even inexpressible behind one's own paltry lines and thus provides a most welcome excuse for any writer.

A famous letter by Lu Chen to Liu Kun explicitly mentions the locus classicus of the dictum by quoting the *Book of Changes* verbatim.

... The *Book of Changes* says: "Writing does not fully capture words, words do not fully capture meaning." Writing is thus no tool with which to fully capture words; words are no device with which to fully capture meaning. If even words fail to fully capture meaning, how could writing fully capture words? Overcome by [my feelings of] frustration and resentment, I nevertheless sincerely present you with a poem. . . .

...易曰。書不盡言。言不盡意。然則書非盡言之器。言非盡意之具矣。況言有不得至于盡意。書有不得至于盡言邪。不勝猥懣。謹貢詩一篇。 ...[103]

Epistolary references to the idea of the general imperfection of spoken and written language abound, many of them modifying the phrasing of the *Book of Changes*. They are usually placed toward the end of the epilogue, where they resemble a declaration of defeat. The ambiguity of the word *shu*, which can refer to writing in general but also to letters and specifically one's own letter, was certainly regarded as an additional boon for the employment of this topos.

... We will meet tomorrow morning. Writing does not fully capture the heart.

This is what [Cao] Zhi lets you know.

...明早相迎。書不盡懷。植白。[104]

... Writing expresses the mind. But of the myriad things accumulated in the mind, not even one can be told.

[Lu] Yun bows repeatedly.

...書以言心。心之所積萬不敘一。雲再拜。[105]

... That there is no opportunity to talk face-to-face makes me sigh. How could a letter [*shu*] express it all?

...無緣言面為歎。書何能悉。[106]

... No letter [*shu*] can express it all. When I see you, we will talk in detail.

...非書所悉。見卿一一。[107]

... Holding my brush, I am disappointed and frustrated. It is impossible to fully express oneself.

...執筆惆悵。不能自盡。[108]

... Take good care of yourself. Writing does not fully capture words.

...心乎愛矣。書不盡言。[109]

> . . . This poor monk's words are shallow, and his diction is clumsy. Language cannot express the mind. I hope on the day when I have the honor to see you, I will be able to express myself in debate.
> This is what [Shi Daogao] sincerely lets you know.

> . . . 貧道言淺辭拙。語不宣心。冀奉見之日。當申之於論難耳。謹白。[110]

Another conventional way to invoke the insufficiency of a letter was to lament its incompleteness and general deficiency, implicitly casting blame on both language and writing as well as on one's own authorial inadequacy. However, brevity as such was of no particular concern in Chinese letter writing, unlike in the West, where it was valued highly since antiquity.[111] Conventional phrases referring to the deficiencies of one's letter, usually placed toward the end of the epilogue, are *bu ci*, *bu ju*, *bu xi*, *bu bei*, and *bu yiyi*. They are used either on their own or with various additions, as these examples demonstrate:

> . . . Choked by cruel grief, I cannot write on [*bu ci*].
> Wang Xizhi knocks his head on the ground, once and again.

> . . . 因反慘塞不次。王羲之頓首頓首。[112]

> . . . Despite all my efforts, I cannot write on [*bu ci*].
> Wang Shao bows repeatedly.

> . . . 力及不次。王劭再拜。[113]

> . . . I cannot be more comprehensive [*bu fu ju*].
> This is what [Zhong] You lets you know.

> . . . 不復具。繇白。[114]

> . . . My letter is not comprehensive [*bu ju*].
> Your disciple Mao Xi obeisantly salutes you.

> . . . 白書不具。弟子毛喜和南。[115]

> . . . I am just entertaining honored guests, so my dictation cannot express all [*bu xi*]. May I henceforth often hear from you.
> This is what Cao Zhi lets you know.

> . . . 適對嘉賓。口授不悉。往來數相聞。曹植白。[116]

> . . . My sincere words are sparse and not complete [*bu bei*].
> This is what [Wang] Xianzhi says.

> . . . 謹言疏不備。獻之言。[117]

. . . I am in fairly good health again. I cannot go into more detail [*bu yiyi*].
This is what Wang Xizhi lets you know.

. . . 復平平。不一一。王羲之白。[118]

As some of these letters demonstrate, reflections on the act of writing occasionally couple expressions of longing for the addressee with despair about the inadequacy of the letter one is writing. This sentiment is usually expressed with the help of a phrase that consists of two words referring to the materiality of writing, such as "leaning over my letter" (*lin shu*) or "holding my brush" (*zhi bi*), followed by another two words that indicate discontent with one's letter or an emotional state that makes it impossible to continue writing, in some cases even to continue speaking. These phrases appear either addressed to superiors or accompanying a more serious tone, often, but not exclusively, in the context of mourning and condolence. Accordingly, they occur along with other formal features, such as verbs other than *bai* in prescripts or postscripts.

. . . Leaning over my letter, I feel wretched and depressed.
[Xie] An knocks his head on the ground, once and again.

. . . 臨書淒悶。安頓首頓首。[119]

. . . Why is my longing for you so deep? Leaning over my letter, my mind feels obstructed.

. . . 何其相思之深。臨書意塞。[120]

. . . Leaning over the paper, I collapse wailing. I will not go on writing.
Xiao Yuanming knocks his head on the ground, once and again.

. . . 臨紙崩號。不復多及。蕭淵明頓首頓首。[121]

. . . Leaning over the paper, I feel frustrated. I do not know what else to say.
Sincerely put forward.

. . . 臨紙罔罔。不知復所言。謹啟。[122]

. . . Holding my brush, I choke with sobs. I do not know what to say.
This is what [Wang] Qia says, knocking his head on the ground.

. . . 執筆哽涕。不知所言。洽頓首言。[123]

. . . Holding my brush increases my longing for you. It truly cannot be expressed in words.
This is what [Wang] Hong respectfully says.

. . . 執筆增懷。真不可言。王弘敬謂。[124]

. . . Leaning over my letter, I choke with sobs. Discarding my brush, I am mortified.

. . . 臨書鯁塞。投筆傷情。[125]

. . . There is nothing I can do but discard my brush. What else could I say?

. . . 投筆而已。夫復何言。[126]

. . . Writing does not fully capture meaning. There is nothing I can do but abandon my brush.

. . . 書不盡意。絕筆而已。[127]

An interesting feature of these phrases is that they invoke the insufficiency of letter writing by declaring surrender to language, often expressed as choking, and revert to physical manifestations of emotional states, such as sighing, sobbing, crying, or breaking down. This is not only another expression of the underlying philosophical problem that "writing does not fully capture words, words do not fully capture meaning"; it seems to go one step further, implying that nonlinguistic, physical expressions of one's mind are more authentic. The classical reference here would be the *Zhuangzi*'s wheelwright Bian, who valued that which lies beyond language much more highly than everything that can be expressed by words.[128] The conventional invocation of the limits of letter writing thus appears as a perfect example of a complex epistolary topos: not only does it fit pragmatic requirements of the genre, such as communicating humility and enhancing the self-referentiality of a letter; it also has distinct philosophical connotations that may lend depth to a letter.

CHAPTER FIVE

Normativity and Authenticity

I had (and have all my life) observed that conventional phrases are a sort of fireworks, easily let off, and liable to take a great variety of shapes and colours not at all suggested by their original form.

—CHARLES DICKENS, *David Copperfield*

The easily recognizable homogeneity of personal letters written in a certain culture and during a certain period suggests that letter writing has been a highly regulated form of communication since the earliest periods of its history. In Western literature, this assumption is supported by early model letters and letter-writing guides that, in the case of ancient Egypt, appear as early as 1800 BCE.[1] Since these types of normative texts that set out the rules of epistolary communication are highly revealing about other forms of social intercourse and etiquette, they have been the objects of comprehensive investigation in the West, especially concerning the Middle Ages.[2]

LETTER-WRITING GUIDES

Thanks to the bibliographic catalogs in Chinese dynastic histories, we know that in China, epistolary guides (*shuyi*, lit., "writing etiquette") date back to at least early medieval times and existed in considerable variety.[3] Some of them targeted a general audience or writers of different social standing and thus communicative needs, such as Tang Jin's (6th century) *Letter-Writing Etiquette for Women* (Furen shuyi) and Shi Tanyuan's *Letter-Writing Etiquette for the Sangha* (Sengjia shuyi). Others focused on specific occasions, as the two, probably complementary guides *Letter-Writing Etiquette for Inauspicious Occasions* (Diaoda shuyi), for deaths, and *Letter-Writing Etiquette for Auspicious Occasions* (Ji shuyi), for all other life-cycle events, by Wang Jian (452–489). None of these early manuals has been transmitted, probably because their communicative advice was prone to become obsolete whenever social or literary conventions changed significantly. The loss of these texts is regrettable indeed. Tang Jin's *Letter-Writing Etiquette for Women*, in particular, highlights a blank spot on the map of our knowledge of early medieval epistolary culture.

More than one hundred letter-writing guides, many of them fragmentary, from the Tang and the Five Dynasties periods (908–60) were found among the Dunhuang manuscripts and have in recent years been studied extensively.[4] The first letter-writing manuals that were transmitted in their entirety come from the Song dynasty (960–1279).[5] Late imperial China then saw the publication of an increasing number of epistolary guides and model-letter collections.[6] Although some of these books are designed as purely epistolary guides, most manuals of this kind place the rules of letter writing within the framework of other social practices and conventions, an approach that is common in the West as well.[7] Epistolary guides were thus typically not only used in the composition of appropriate letters but also consulted as encyclopedias of social life, or, as Roger Chartier put it, "through a process of readings that were often not followed by any attempt at writing, they nourished a social knowhow and a social imaginary."[8]

The only extant epistolary guide from early medieval China, Suo Jing's (239–303) *Monthly Etiquette* (Yueyi), is a model-letter collection that was transmitted for its calligraphic value (fig. 5.1).[9] Although the letters of the fourth to sixth months are missing, the guide probably originally consisted of one letter and its reply per month and may thus have been inspired by the early Chinese "monthly commands" (*yueling*), which seek to harmonize human behavior with changing seasonal conditions throughout the year.[10] That the letters in *Monthly Etiquette* are not actual letters but rather models or templates, and thus a normative type of text, is indicated by their structural uniformity, peculiar noncommittal blandness, and lack of concrete information. Model-letter collections of this monthly type seem to have been common in medieval China.[11] While the transmitted calligraphy of *Monthly Etiquette* is usually regarded as dating from the Tang dynasty, most scholars today do not share Yao Nai's doubts about the Jin dynasty origin of the text itself.[12]

The following translation of two model-letter pairs demonstrates the character of *Monthly Etiquette*. The letters lack an invented letter

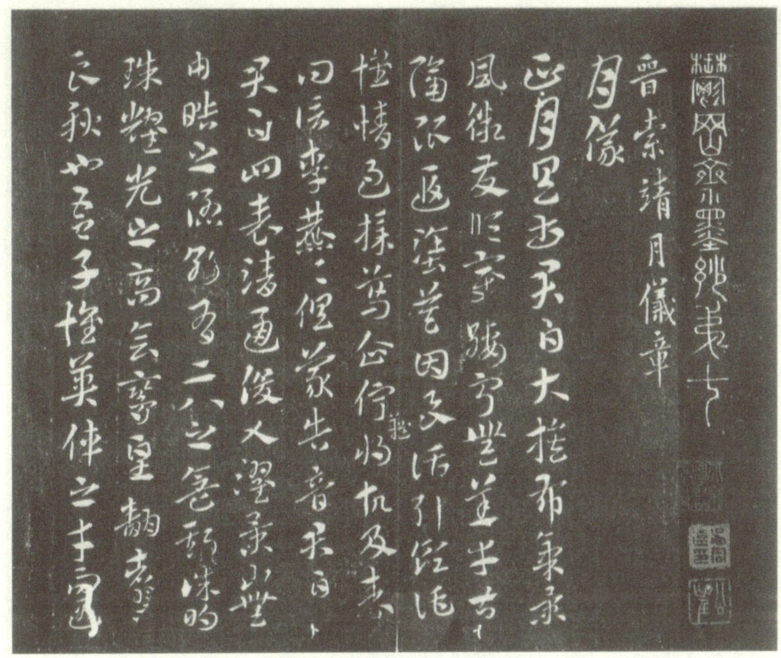

Figure 5.1. Suo Jing (239–303), *Monthly Etiquette* (Yueyi), ink imprint of A's letter of the first month (detail). National Library of China, Beijing.

body and consist only of frames—prescript, proem, epilogue, and postscript—that are rich in familiar topoi and allusions. In order to avoid confusion, the term "lord, sir" (*jun*) that appears in the prescript and postscript of each letter as a placeholder for the names of the two supposed writers is rendered as A and B.[13]

正月具書	"Letter written in the first month"
君白	A lets you know:
大蔟布氣	In the first month of spring, the *yang* energies are spreading.[14]
景風微發	Gentle winds are subtly rising;
順變綏寍	following the changes, there will be peacefulness.
無恙幸甚	May you be unharmed; this would be very fortunate.
隔限遐塗	We are separated and constrained by the long road between us;
莫因良話	there is no opportunity to have a good talk.
引領託懷	Stretching my neck looking out for you, I am filled with longing.

情過採葛	My feelings surpass those described in the ode "Plucking Flax";
企佇難將	I have long been standing on tiptoe and can hardly go on;
故及表問	therefore I would like to express my regards.
信李麃麃	May messengers be aplenty,[15]
俱蒙告音	so that I may receive letters [*gao yin*, messages] from you.
君白	This is what A lets you know.

The model letter is followed by a model reply.

君白	B lets you know:
四表清通	The whole realm is peaceful throughout;
俊乂濯景	outstandingly talented men are bathed in the sun light of imperial grace.
山無由皓之隱	In the mountains, there are no recluses such as Xu You and the four hoaries;[16]
朝有二八之盛	at court prevails the lunar abundance of the sixteenth day.[17]
斯誠	This is truly
明珠燿光之高會	a lofty meeting in the dazzling luster of the "bright pearl,"[18]
鸞皇翻翥之良秋也	a good season under a soaring pair of phoenixes.[19]
吾子懷英偉之才	You possess a flourishing and imposing talent
而遇清升之祚	and have encountered the blessing of a clear rise.
想已天飛	I hope that you, who have already flown into the sky
奮翼紫闥	and are spreading your wings at the purple palace doors,
使親者有通賴也	will allow those close to you to rely on you fully.
君白	This is what B lets you know.[20]

The second pair of letters demonstrates the repetitive structure and recurring topoi among the letters of *Monthly Etiquette*.

十月具書	"Letter written in the tenth month"
君白	A lets you know:
應鍾導運	The first month of winter is moving along.[21]
嚴霜稍隆	Severe frosts have slightly increased;
時變物移	all beings transform with the seasonal changes.
感候增懷	Feeling the season, my longing for you increases;
馳心繫想	my galloping heart is bound to thoughts of you.
言存所親	Words uphold our close relationship,
山川路限	although mountains and rivers obstruct the ways between us.
不能翻飛	Unable to flutter and fly,
登彼崇丘	I climbed that high mountain;

逍遙長望	free and unfettered, I watched out for you constantly.
延佇莫及	I stood there for a long time, but nobody came,
思積情疲	so that my longing for you grew and my feelings became exhausted.
不勝鬱陶	I am overwhelmed by melancholy
眷然之感	and feelings of affection.
裁復白書不悉	Even if I continued writing, my letter [*shu*] cannot express all.
君白	This is what A lets you know.

The reply to this model letter reads like this:

君白	B lets you know:
往春執手	Last spring when we held hands,
刻會來秋	we promised each other to meet again next autumn.
迎期待面	Looking forward to the time and waiting for a meeting,
慊然遲想	I was resentful when my hopes were deceived.
正以逸驥之跡	Just like the traces of a thoroughbred horse,
騁于雲漢之路	you are galloping along the roads of the Milky Way.
龍驤天府	A dragon raising its head at the heavenly court,
忘此友信	you may have forgotten this agreement between friends.
飛沈壹殊	Once the rising and the sinking each go their separate ways,
何緣言 (嬿)〔燕〕	what opportunity will we have to talk and feast?
厚為時節	Wishing you may take care of yourself in the season,
寶愛光儀	I treasure your radiant appearance.[22]
君白	This is what B lets you know.[23]

The overall tenor of these letters as well as details such as the reciprocal terms of address suggest that the letters in Suo Jing's *Monthly Etiquette* were meant to be models for a correspondence between friends of equal rank. Their separation appears to be due to the move of one writer, A, to the capital, while his friend, B, stayed behind. A's letters invariably start with a reference to the season, usually the corresponding notes of the chromatic scale and the weather, in some cases complemented by other information, for instance, a reference to an annual festival, such as the Mid-autumn Festival (Zhongqiu) in the letter of the eighth month. While only two letters continue with a health wish, every single letter features the lament of separation, often in colorful terms and taking up most of the space. All of the facets of the topos of the lament of separation are covered in these letters: expressing grief and misery, lamenting the length of separation—often supported by allusions to the *Book of Odes*, the *Analects*, or other ancient texts—mourning the passing of time, expressing hope for letters and a meeting with the addressee, reveling in the other's letter while also lamenting the limitations of letter writing. The overall effect of this high concentration of conventional topoi is one of verbosity and vapidity at the same time.

B's messages are different in nature, mostly because they are devised as replies, although there are no specific references to A's letters or formal repercussions, similar to Wu Zhi's mirroring of Cao Pi's letter.[24] B does not start his letters by mentioning the seasons but employs other elements of the conventional proem, such as references to A's letters and, of course, the lament of separation. Regarding the receipt of letters, B's letter of the eleventh month offers an interesting example of thinking in terms of stimulus and response (*ganying*), although wishful thinking is a term that comes to mind as well.

望塗延思	Watching the roads, I am filled by a protracted longing for you.
精誠所感	If our feelings are perfectly true,
無物不應	there will be no being that does not respond.
果□來況	And indeed [I received?] a letter [*kuang*, bestowal] from you.[25]

There is also a definite difference in authorial voice that seems to be due to the different positions of A and B. While A's letters are devoted exclusively to personal matters and the maintenance of the friendship between the correspondents and do not pursue any other communicative aims, B's letters are partly concerned with non-personal subjects, such as the political situation or A's superior talents, his position in the capital, and his influence at court. This difference in emphasis reflects A's relative independence as well as B's lesser social standing and his attempts to maintain a relationship that is not only personally important for him but also potentially useful for his social position and advancement. B's accolades may strike modern readers as overly submissive, even ingratiating, and consequently counterproductive, but in the eyes of a contemporary reader, they were probably no more overblown than A's excessive professions of longing. Actual friendships did not exist in a societal vacuum, nor do they today, but, as characterized by Thomas Jansen, "were inextricably intertwined with the political fabric of the state in early medieval China."[26]

Regrettably, the intended uses for the letters in *Monthly Etiquette* are unknown. Were they primarily calligraphy models, or was the emphasis on content? And how normative were they? Was a writer expected to slavishly follow these templates or rather to be loosely inspired by them? It is most likely that this depended first of all on the writer's degree of literacy. A fully competent writer would hardly have to rely on a letter-writing guide but would be able to easily emulate and even transcend the advice given in such a text, which, after all, not only attempted to shape but also represented contemporary letter writing. This also means that the resemblance of an actual letter to a template in a letter-writing manual is not necessarily the result of copying.

The degree of adherence to letter-writing etiquette further depended on the occasion for letter writing. While casual letters between friends may have enjoyed a certain freedom from etiquette, there were situations, such as condolences, that demanded a more rigid adherence to epistolary conventions, irrespective of the writer's literary proficiency. Referring to the Tang dynasty, Patricia Ebrey remarks that "condolence letters were gestures, like bows, intended not so much to be read as to be recognized,"[27] an observation that can doubtlessly be extended beyond the Tang dynasty or even China. Another intriguing question would be whether the model letters in *Monthly Etiquette* were supposed to be complete letters or to provide merely an epistolary frame that needed to be filled in with a main body. While any main body would probably temper the frame's overblown tone by diluting its highly concentrated topicality, the particular intention of a main body—continuing in a predominantly amicable vein or incorporating a clear-cut communicative purpose, for instance, a request relating to A's connections at court—could give the final letter a very different character.

EXPRESSING INDIVIDUALITY WITHIN THE BOUNDS OF CONVENTION

As demonstrated by many of the examples quoted throughout this book, there are quite a few letters from early medieval China, especially the casual, informal kind aiming at the maintenance of a relationship for its own sake, that consist of little but epistolary phrases and topoi and may at first sight appear to be taken straight out of a letter-writing manual. This raises the question of if and how letters that are bound by conventions can still be voices and images of the mind—a notion originally expressed by Yang Xiong and later highlighted by Liu Xie in his *The Literary Mind.*[28] In other words, how is it possible to abide by the normative rules of letter writing and still create an authentic, perhaps even original expression of one's mind? A letter by Yang Xin, another well-known calligrapher, who lived about a century after Suo Jing, provides a starting point for this inquiry. It is neither a letter of condolence nor does it expressly mention death, but its characteristics indicate that it was either written during mourning or addresses someone who was in mourning.[29]

> On the sixth day of the third month, [Yang] Xin knocks his head on the ground:
>
> At the end of spring, I feel a cutting grief that I can hardly endure. What shall I do? What can I do? Having received your letter [*gao*, note] of the sixth, I feel deeply comforted. How are you now? Are your feet getting better every day? I am worse every day and find it difficult to recover. This makes me regard myself with sorrowful sighs, a mood that has become quite persistent. Holding my brush increases my chagrin. Take good care of yourself! What can a letter [*shu*] hope to say!
>
> Yang Xin knocks his head on the ground.

> 三月六日欣頓首。暮春感摧切割。不能自勝。當奈何奈何。得去六日告深慰。足下復何如。腳中日勝也。吾日弊難復。令自顧憂歎。情想轉積。執筆增惋。足下保愛。書欲何言。羊欣頓首。[30]

This short and unassuming letter does not boast much of a main body and clearly resembles the models in *Monthly Etiquette*, yet it manages to move us in all its directness and simplicity, something that certainly cannot be said of the bland letters in *Monthly Etiquette.* If we try to identify why Yang Xin's letter does not come across as a piece of mechanical imitation of epistolary conventions but as an authentic, believable message, an image of the mind, three features emerge: dialogicity, self-referentiality, and personalized epistolary language.

The most conspicuous feature is the pronounced dialogicity of this letter. After the conventional reference to the season that situates the letter in time, Yang Xin immediately turns to his correspondent, expressing gratitude for the other's letter and inquiring after his health. Moreover, he does so in quite specific terms, mentioning the addressee's feet, which makes his concern and affection very convincing. The following brief health report may also be read as a manifestation of the close relationship between writer and addressee. Yang not only entrusts the other with information about his deteriorating health but also unreservedly reveals the psychological repercussions of his illness. All this is expressed in a straightforward, unadorned fashion. The set phrase *naihe* 奈何 (what to do?), which is used mostly in condolences or during mourning, also enhances the letter's dialogicity. Expressing absolute helplessness in the face of death or another blow of fate, the writer accepts the inevitability and magnitude of this event and thus creates a shared situation for himself and the addressee.

The second feature that sets Yang Xin's letter apart is its marked self-referentiality. This is accomplished mainly through epistolary topoi and phrases that allude to the act of letter writing, especially its limitations, and thus draw the reader's attention to the letter itself. Yang Xin is successful in this task because he manages to personalize the formulaic epistolary language, which is the third feature that distinguishes this letter. Unlike *naihe*, which is a set phrase that, apart from reduplication, is hardly ever modified, the phrases and topoi in the epilogue of Yang's letter are less fixed in character and allow for individual modification and thus personalization, a potential that the writer fully exploited. While early medieval letter writers used many different phrases starting with "holding my brush" in order to express disappointment about the deficiency of their own letters or, more generally, their communicative abilities, Yang's "holding my brush increases my chagrin" may well have been a unique coinage, at least as far as is known from the corpus of transmitted literature. The same could be true for Yang Xin's particular variant of the statement "writing does not fully capture words, words do not fully capture meaning" from the *Book of Changes*. The phrase he chose, "What can a letter hope to say?" (an alternative translation would be "What can writing hope to say?"), is unique in transmitted literature, despite the ubiquity of the topos and the utter conventionality of this reference to the "Commentary on the Appended Words."

Although epistolary conventions are indispensable for successful letter writing, they easily produce a dulling effect that may undermine a letter's authenticity, let alone any aspirations to literary creativity. The subtle modification or situational tweaking of set phrases and topoi that leaves their basic communicative functions intact is not only an effective means of personalizing a letter and achieving emotional authenticity; it may even produce true originality. Even an inconspicuous modification of sequence may add to this effect. Yang

Xin's interruption of the conventional order of two topoi through the insertion of a valediction ("Take good care of yourself!") may appear as a lack of literary refinement, but the seemingly clumsy disruption of the customary rhythm produces an impression of spontaneity and thus enhances the individuality of the statement and the authenticity of the message.[31]

Yang Xin's letter, in its own modest way, exemplifies the fusion of normativity and convention, on the one hand, and authenticity and individuality, on the other. It also proves the fundamental possibility of this fusion in letters whose literary character is more pronounced, which is an important concern for many kinds of transmitted literature, not only that of China. Klaus Thraede remarked that in Greek and Roman antiquity the "cultivated letter of friendship, neither 'purely' literary form nor 'purely' bubbling spontaneity, but individually tinted convention and socially conventionalized individuality," was considered the epitome of epistolary writing.[32] Giles Constable made similar observations about medieval Europe, where letters were "designed to be correct and elegant rather than original and spontaneous, and they often followed the form and content of model letters in formularies."[33] In letters transmitted from early medieval China, the same phenomena may be observed and need to be taken seriously in order to do justice to a letter-writing culture that is as far removed as possible from our modern communicative sensibilities and practices. Moreover, carrying the awareness of this ambiguity over into our practice of reading and interpreting letters even today will certainly afford us deeper insights into our own communicative culture as well.

Epistolary authenticity is a complex and elusive issue, not the least because of the apparently artless and unaffected attitude of many letters. However, as Lu Xun famously remarked, the writer of a letter does not enter the stage stark naked, but "in fact he is still wearing a flesh-colored, tight-fitting dress and even a brassiere, something he normally should never put on."[34] With the costume that pretends nudity while presenting its wearer as he or she wants to be seen, Lu Xun has created a powerful counterimage to the naive identification of the actual, living writer of a letter and the first-person narrator emerging in an epistolary text. The idea of the nakedness of the letter writer has long been popular in the West, where it became popular in the wording of Samuel Johnson (1709–1784) and has since been repeated many times. Although Johnson's famous quote, "in a

Man's Letters you know, Madam, his soul lies naked, his letters are only the mirrour of his breast, whatever passes within him is shown undisguised in its natural process,"[35] is actually offered in a context of teasing mockery in a letter that clearly betrays that its writer was very well aware of epistolary role-play, Johnson's words are mostly cited without disclosing this decisive circumstance. Such are the dangers of irony.

Lu Xun's image of the artist wearing a dress that simulates nudity fits the complexity of epistolary writing very well: in producing images of their minds, letter writers are expected to take not only existing conventions into account but also their intended readers, which is an essential requirement arising from the dialogicity of letters, as suggested by Liu Xie in *The Literary Mind*.[36] Going one step further, Lu Xun highlights the conscious self-fashioning of the letter writer and the resulting plurality of self-images, which complicate the notion of authenticity and of the "image of the mind" well beyond simple mirroring. This approach makes it quite clear how important it is to take the fundamentally literary character of letters into account.

Conclusion

It is an enlightening experience to read letters from early medieval China at a time when the modes of personal communication are going through changes whose magnitude and ramifications are not yet foreseeable. Paper and ink are largely abandoned, as is the rest of the material culture of letter writing, to be replaced by the completely different material culture that enables digital communication; the time lag between writing, reading, and responding to a written message has shrunk from months, weeks, or days to seconds; epistolary conventions have all but dissolved and are in the process of transforming into new languages of correspondence. As these changes and their consequences for individuals, small networks, and society as a whole are passionately debated in the public sphere, one keeps encountering important topics explored in this book in unexpected contexts and on surprising occasions. Although the majority of current discussions of media change lack any historical perspective extending beyond the past century, the problems that are discussed nowadays are astonishingly similar to those faced in early medieval letters. Even if the counterpart of face-to-face communication is no longer seen in letter writing but appears in various types of computer mediated communication, which involves all sorts of new questions, basic problems of written communication have unmistakably remained the same: the effective engagement of an absent addressee (who can no longer be sure that he or she alone is addressed);[1] the convincing presentation of oneself (which involves coping with unprecedented freedom in the choice of a persona);[2] the tension between face-to-face and digital modes of communication (accompanied by anxieties about the fragmentation of society, since the former seems to be losing ground);[3] and the possibilities and limitations of the medium itself (which allows new distortions of the underlying communicative framework). While the mode of exchange does make a difference, core parameters of written communication remain intact even in e-mails and text messages.

This essential awareness of basic questions of correspondence that we all share, along with basic epistolary skills, also affects the study of ancient Chinese letters. Reading them, we immediately recognize them for what they are and grasp their potential, but we are also easily disconcerted by unfamiliar conventions that make it difficult to unlock the wealth of information they hold. Modern readers may find themselves excluded from personal letters, especially if they are hundreds of years removed from the cultural, familial, and individual worlds that once occasioned these written exchanges. Some of the obstacles to fully comprehending and appreciating early medieval epistolary texts were created by the letter writers themselves, either inadvertently, because the particular directedness of a letter tends to exclude non-intended readers from fully understanding a message in all its implications, or deliberately, because the authors wanted to shield their messages from unauthorized eyes. These obstacles to sharing the correspondents' "universe of discourse," to use Qian Zhongshu's words again, may forever withstand our efforts. But with some persistence, obstacles caused by a lack of familiarity with epistolary culture and conventions of the time can be overcome. They are at the center of this book, which seeks to make Chinese epistolary culture fully visible in its potential and Chinese letters more accessible for future research and appreciation.

The amount of material witnesses left behind from more than two millennia of Chinese written communication is enormous. Personal letters alone represent an impressively voluminous and multifaceted source that remains to be explored. It promises not only participation in past personal exchanges from a wide variety of relationships but also, since letters are unlimited in their subject matter, a wealth of information about all kinds of subjects: language, history, philosophy, religion, everyday life, psychology, medicine, trade, law, and so forth. What is most important, however, is to keep the connection between these two aspects in mind: the personal exchange and the factual information it contains.

The potential of letters as important complementary sources in so many fields of inquiry could only be hinted at in this book, which is, after all, focused on the literary workings of epistolarity, especially its rhetorical potential and its ability to inscribe not only the writer but also the addressee in a text and therefore to be a unique reflection of personal relationships. That many letters came down to us in the more or less "de-epistolarized" form their editors gave them does not detract from their source value. Many of the most famous early medieval letters resemble essays and are usually appreciated as non-epistolary texts, but this needlessly reductive treatment fails to take the original genre character of the texts into account and can lead only to a limited understanding. In order to fully realize the potential of letters, we need to take a different interpretative approach and acknowledge that these texts were once part of a correspondence, that they, on account of an authorial decision, were written as letters (whether actual or fictitious) and meant to be read as such. Restoring their proper genre affiliation and incorporating it into our interpretations may occasionally entail a certain element of conjecture, but bearing this condition in mind, the interpretative gain is considerable. An example of such an amalgamation of the two aspects—the personal exchange and the factual information it contains—is the analysis of letters of literary thought in chapters 2 and 3, which, in the case of Cao Pi, includes comparison with an equivalent non-epistolary text. Viewing the factual information of letters as being embedded in a personal exchange, the analysis demonstrates that it is indeed consequential whether a text was composed as a letter or not.

However rewarding personal letters may be as sources of information, they are not mere mines and reservoirs of knowledge but invaluable in themselves—as rare testimonies of unique lives and experiences, as works of calligraphic art, or as literary masterpieces. Liu Xie's emphasis on aesthetic criteria had already made a convincing case for this early on. Letters certainly deserve to be appreciated as literature, and their study will thus add an important new facet to our picture of Chinese literary history, particularly our understanding of the development of prose styles. This is true not only of the exemplary letters transmitted in *Selections of Refined Literature* but also of many humble, everyday letters that lack or fail any literay ambitions but may still provide glimpses into past lives that are unavailable elsewhere.

Ultimately, the study of letters, as that of any other kind of literature or art, may help us to fathom what it means to be human.

Among the handful of details that differentiate us from "vegetables or birds"—such as language, self-determination, lying, and the awareness of time and death—W. H. Auden also registered that we "count some days and long for certain letters."[4] This longing to connect with those from whom we are separated is close to human nature, indeed. It can be easily observed in these times of ever-present text messaging, which has turned the reception and composition of written communications into a public event (again). Watching how anxiously messages are expected and how facial expressions and body postures change through the joy of connecting recalls Kafka's "passion for letters," this seemingly obsolete form of written communication, his confession that he "doesn't want to stop drinking." The unquenchable thirst for the continuation of human relationships with those who are not present informs much of the epistolary literature left from early medieval China.

NOTES

EPIGRAPH

Kafka, *Letters to Milena*, 18. In German, the passage reads: "Was meinen Sie? kann ich noch bis Sonntag einen Brief bekommen? Möglich wäre es schon. Aber es ist unsinnig, diese Lust an Briefen. Genügt nicht ein einziger, genügt nicht ein Wissen? Gewiß genügt es, aber trotzdem lehnt man sich weit zurück und trinkt die Briefe und weiß nichts als daß man nicht aufhören will zu trinken." Kafka, *Briefe an Milena*, 23.

INTRODUCTION

Epigraph: *Wenxin diaolong zhu* 25.460.

1. Notable studies include Eriksen, *Tyranny of the Moment*, and Baron, *Always On*.

2. A prominent voice among those who emphasize the positive creative potential of the new media is the linguist David Crystal, whose publications on the subject include *Txtng: The Gr8 Db8*.

3. Arthur Conan Doyle's (1859–1930) story "A Case of Identity" (1891) is an early example of the literary use of typewriting in letters. It not only serves to conceal the identity of a writer, but this writer himself expressly asks his lover for handwritten letters, because "when they were typewritten he always felt that the machine had come between" them. See also one of Franz Kafka's letters to Felice Bauer, written on December 29, 1913, in which he insists that she reply in her own hand, since "to be convinced, and understand it properly, I want to see your writing." Kafka, *Letters to Felice*, 333. See also Kafka, *Briefe an Felice*, 482.

4. Steinhausen, *Geschichte des deutschen Briefes*, 410, and Benjamin, *Deutsche Menschen*, 128. For a discussion of the end of letter writing, see also Nickisch, *Brief*, 59–70.

5. Brown, "Whatever Happened to Mme de Sévigné?" 215–20.

6. Mittleman, "The Twentieth-Century English Letter," 223.

7. An outstanding example is Martha Hanna's *Your Death Would Be Mine: Paul and Marie Pireaud in the Great War.*

8. Exemplary works regarding the cultures mentioned above include Oppenheim, *Letters from Mesopotamia;* Koskenniemi, *Studien*; Malherbe,

Ancient Epistolary Theorists; Schnider and Stenger, *Studien*; and Constable, *Letters and Letter Collections.* Recent anthologies of translations include Trapp, *Greek and Latin Letters*, and Rosenmeyer, *Ancient Greek Literary Letters.*

9. The following studies may give an idea of the breadth of research: Chapa, *Letters of Condolence in Greek Papyri*; Poster and Mitchell, *Letter-Writing Manuals*; Grünbart, *Formen der Anrede im byzantinischen Brief*; Bagnall and Cribiore, *Women's Letters from Ancient Egypt*; Goitein, *Letters of Medieval Jewish Traders*; White, *Cicero in Letters*; and Beebee, *Epistolary Fiction in Europe.*

10. Among the most influential works regarding the theoretical approach to letters are Jacques Derrida's *The Post-Card: From Sokrates to Freud and Beyond* and Janet Gurkin Altman's *Epistolarity.* To gain a glimpse of the quantity and diversity of secondary literature in Western scholarship, see Institut für Textkritik, BRIEFkasten, a bibliography of personal letter writing in Germany from 1750 to 2000, which lists approximately 450 titles.

11. Eva Chung's "Study of the 'Shu'" is a groundbreaking survey of Han dynasty personal letter writing. David Pattinson's dissertation "The *Chidu* in Late Ming and Early Qing China" is dedicated to an individual letter collection, Zhou Lianggong's (1612–1672) anthology *Chidu xinchao* (1662); Suzanne Wright's "Visual Communication and Social Identity in Woodblock-Printed Letter Papers of the Late Ming Dynasty" studies printed stationery. Additionally, there are one monograph and one unpublished dissertation dedicated to official communication during the Han dynasty: Metelmann, "Schriftverkehr," and Giele, *Imperial Decision-Making.* There are also dissertations that include sections about letters, such as Wu Sujane's "Clarity, Brevity, and Naturalness: Lu Yun and His Works" and Ditter's "Genre and the Transformation of Writing in Tang Dynasty China."

12. Kádár, *Historical Chinese Letter Writing.* See also Kádár's *Model Letters in Late Imperial China.*

13. This number includes studies that deal with letters but do not raise or pay only marginal attention to genre-specific questions. For example, Cimeddorji in his monograph *Die Briefe des K'ang-Hsi-Kaisers* follows a purely historical approach that neglects literary or genre features of the texts he explores. Modern and contemporary letters have hardly received more attention than their premodern predecessors. Studies include McDougall, *Love-Letters*; Findeisen, "From Literature to Love"; Goodman, "'Words of Blood and Tears'"; and Zeng, "The Past Revisited."

14. See also von Zach's articles "Auszüge aus einem chinesischen Briefsteller" and "Ein Briefwechsel in Versen."

15. See Schnider and Stenger, *Studien*, as well as Klauck's *Ancient Letters*, in particular the bibliography on pp. xix–xxviii.

16. Brook, "Communications and Commerce," 579–707.

17. An example of the latter approach is Janet Theiss's forthcoming book, tentatively titled *The Perils of Intimacy: Family Scandal and Family Fortune in Qing China*, which draws on personal letters incorporated into court files of a divorce case. See also Theiss, "Love in a Confucian Climate."

18. This trend is attested to by a number of commercial websites and nonacademic books on the collection and appreciation of letters, not just calligraphy in general, such as Gu, *Ming Qing chidu*; Cheng and Fang, *Zizi zhenzang*; and Cui, *Chidu baifa*. See also the list of prices that letters achieved at auctions, quoted in Hu Chuanhai, *Chidu shi jiang*, 83–84, and Cheng and Fang, *Zizi zhenzang*, 30–47. See a recent report about the sale of a Tang dynasty copy of one of Wang Xizhi's (303–361) letters, "Hand Scroll Copy of Ancient Chinese Calligrapher Sold for 308 Mln Yuan."

19. See Zhao Shugong's historical survey *Zhongguo chidu wenxue shi*.

20. One of the few comprehensive approaches that even considers Western research on letter writing is Zou Zhenhuan's "Qingdai shuzha wenxian." For a thorough study of Wang Xizhi's letters, see Qi, *Mai shi zhi feng*, 97–252.

21. This also applies to the only chapter on letters in a general literary history that is known to me, Zhang Mengxin's *Zhongguo sanwen fazhan shi*, 198–226.

22. Scholars working on letters from different historical periods have mentioned this issue. See Ebrey, "T'ang Guides," and Campbell, "The Epistolary World of a Reluctant 17th Century Magistrate." There are also indications that pieces of official communication were edited before they were incorporated into other literary texts. See *Lunheng jiaoshi* 84.1182 and, for an example from early medieval China, Tian, *Beacon Fire*, 183–85. On the lack of the epistolary frame in letters by Pliny (61/62–ca. 113), see Thraede, *Grundzüge*, 77. On the same phenomenon in European medieval letters, see Constable, *Letters and Letter Collections*, 18.

23. For example, Bao Zhao's (d. 466) "Letter to his younger sister Bao Linghui about ascending the bank of Great Thunder Lake" (Deng Dalei an yu mei shu) (439), famous as one of the earliest pieces of travel literature in China, was transmitted with only traces of the frame (see the translation of the epilogue in chapter 3). However, in the anthology *Classical Chinese Literature* by John Minford and Joseph S. M. Lau, even these meager markers of the text's epistolarity were omitted from the translation that thus forgoes the chance to clearly characterize the text as a letter. See Minford and Lau, *Classical Chinese Literature*, 607–8, and, for another example, 614–15.

24. Issues of calligraphic transmission have been extensively studied for the letters ascribed to Wang Xizhi. Studies include Ledderose, *Mi Fu*, 7–44, and two articles by Robert Harrist, "Copies, All the Way Down" and "Replication and Deception."

25. See Metelmann, "Schriftverkehr," and Li and Liu, *Jiandu wenshu*, esp. 268–71.

26. On the huge archaeological finds of third-century personal and administrative letters in Zoumalou, Hunan, see Tsien, *Written on Bamboo and Silk*, 112.

27. Yan Kejun's (1762–1843) collection of ancient and early medieval prose writings *Quan shanggu Sandai Qin Han Sanguo Liuchao wen* is an important tool for accessing epistolary literature of the period, although one

needs to be aware that it does not cover all transmitted texts. The Daoist tradition, for example, is largely ignored.

28. On this problem, see Violi, "Letters," 157–59.

29. Luo, "Jiandu yiwen kaoshi," 215.

30. 家庭瑣事, 戚友碎語, 隨手信筆, 約略潦草, 而受者了然, Qian Zhongshu, *Guanzhui bian* 1109, trans. in Egan, *Limited Views*, 236–38.

31. See the two transcriptions in Liu Zhengcheng's *Zhongguo shufa quanji 20*, 20, 328. One of them is part of Qi Gong's article discussing the letter in this volume. It does not offer a translation.

32. So far, about 150 of approximately 2,100 early medieval letters have been translated, including very short partial translations. See Richter, "Table of Non-Official Letters from Early Medieval China," which tries to keep track of scholarship and translations of individual letters.

CHAPTER 1. MATERIALITY AND TERMINOLOGY

Epigraph: act 3, scene 2, lines 264–67.

1. On bamboo, wood, and silk as writing supports, see Tsien, *Written on Bamboo and Silk*, 96–144.

2. For more detailed information about these long-established Chinese writing implements, see Tsien, *Written on Bamboo and Silk*, 175–93. See also Nishibayashi and Chen, *Xin Zhongguo chutu shuji*, 67, 85, 93, 96.

3. Tsien, *Written on Bamboo and Silk*, 194–98.

4. Bamboo also offered the possibility of writing on both sides of a slip, but this was apparently not as common as in the case of wood. Usually there are only titles or corrections on the verso of bamboo manuscripts.

5. These letters were discovered in 1975–76 in tomb no. 4 of Shuihudi, Hubei. See transcriptions and reproductions in Yunmeng Shuihudi Qin mu bianxiezu, *Yunmeng Shuihudi Qin mu*, 25–26, figs. 167–68. For a translation of one of the letters, see Shaughnessy, "Military Histories of Early China," 181.

6. See an oft-quoted letter by Cui Yuan (2nd century) in which he mentions that he cannot afford to write on silk, "Letter to Ge Gong" (Yu Ge Yuanfu shu), *Quan Hou Han wen* 45.1a.

7. For a reproduction and an annotated transcription of this letter, see "Yuan's letter to Zifang" (Yuan zhi Zifang shu), in Hu and Zhang, *Dunhuang Xuanquan Han jian*, 187–91.

8. On the early history of paper, see Tsien, *Written on Bamboo and Silk*, 145–69.

9. Tsien, "Zhi de qiyuan xinzheng," 6.

10. *Hou Han shu* 78.2513.

11. On the superior qualities of paper, see also Fu Xian's (239–294) "Rhapsody on Paper" (Zhi fu). *Quan Jin wen* 51.5a; *Yiwen leiju* 58.1053.

12. Nishibayashi and Chen, *Xin Zhongguo*, 141.

13. See Tsien, *Paper and Printing*, 76–79, 85–96; Harrist and Fong, *The Embodied Image*, 206–7. "Five-colored" (*wu se*) stationery is mentioned

several times, e.g., in Xu Ling's (507–583) preface to his anthology *New Songs from a Jade Terrace* (Yutai xinyong), 13, or in one of Yang Xi's (330–386?) letters in the collection *Declarations of the Perfected* (Zhengao) edited by Tao Hongjing (452–536) (Yoshikawa and Mugitani, *Zhengao jiaozhu*, 535). On five-colored paper used for official communication, see *Record of All Within Ye* (Ye zhong ji), 1.

14. Wu Zhi (177–230), "Letter in reply to Cao Zhi" (Da Dong'a wang shu), *Wen xuan* 42.1908–12; *Quan Sanguo wen* 30.9b–10.b. The word "affection" (*choumou*) alludes to *Mao shi* 118.

15. Xiao Tong, "Letter in reply to Xiao Yi 蕭繹 requesting his *Collected Writings* and *Illustrious Blossoms in the Garden of Poetry*" (Da Xiangdong wang qiu *Wenji* ji *Shiyuan yinghua shu*), *Quan Liang wen* 20.2a–b (發函伸紙, 閱覽無輟); Xu Mian (466–535), "Letter in reply to Fu Ting" (Bao Fu Ting shu), *Quan Liang wen* 50.5b–6a (發函伸紙, 倍增憤歎); Wang Sengru (465–522), "Letter in reply to Jiang Yan" (Da Jiang Yan shu), *Quan Liang wen* 51.6a–b (發函伸紙, 朗若披雲). Variations of this phrase use different words for "envelope"; see the anonymous "Further letter on behalf of Wang Sengbian in reply to Xiao Yuanming" (You wei Wang taiwei da Zhenyang hou shu), *Quan Liang wen* 69.3b (披函伸紙), and Xu Ling's "Further letter on behalf of Xiao Yuanming to Pei Zhiheng" (Wei Liang Zhenyang hou chong yu Pei Zhiheng shu), *Quan Chen wen* 9.2b. (披封伸紙).

16. 臨紙累歎, Xie Lingyun (385–433), "Letter in reply to Fan Tai" (Da Fan guanglu shu), *Quan Song wen* 32.4a. On other phrases of this type, see the "Limits of Writing and Language" section of chapter 4.

17. Liu Heng, *Lidai chidu shufa*, 3; Liu and Zhao, *Zhongguo gudai youyi shi*, 177–78.

18. See Eastern Han letters written on wood in both running cursive and draft cursive in Liu and Wang, *Changsha Dongpailou*, 17–36.

19. 性善書, 與人尺牘, 主皆藏去以為榮, *Han shu* 92.3711.

20. 及寢病, 帝驛馬令作草書尺牘十首, *Hou Han shu* 14.557. For the anecdotes about Chen Zun (d. ca. 24) and Liu Mu, see Ledderose, *Mi Fu*, 30, and Bai, "Chinese Letters," 381.

21. Ledderose, *Mi Fu*, 7–44.

22. Harrist, "A Letter from Wang Hsi-chih."

23. Harrist, "Reading Chinese Calligraphy," 5. On letters as calligraphic models in late medieval China, see McNair, "The Engraved Model-Letters Compendia" and "Engraved Calligraphy in China."

24. Bai, "Chinese Letters," 385. See also Richter, "Beyond Calligraphy."

25. Translations of official titles throughout this book follow Hucker's *Dictionary of Official Titles*.

26. Xu Ling, "Letter in reply to Xu Changru" (Da zuren Liang Donghai taishou Changru shu), *Quan Chen wen* 10.1a–b.

27. *Ti*, here translated as "layout," refers to a whole that is composed of a number of components in a certain arrangement. When *ti* is used in reference to calligraphy, as in this letter, it denotes the particular structuring of a calligraphy as a whole as well as that of individual characters.

28. Xiao Ziliang (460–494), "Letter in reply to Wang Sengqian" (Da Wang Sengqian shu), *Quan Qi wen* 7.8b–9a. The last sentence quotes Liu Kun's "Letter in reply to Lu Chen" (Da Lu Chen shu), *Wen xuan* 25.1169.

29. See Sivin, *Traditional Medicine*, 52, 147–67, and Catherine Despeux's entry in Pregadio, *Encyclopedia of Taoism*, 562–65.

30. See Hay, "Human Body as a Microcosmic Source," 74–102; Nylan, "Calligraphy, the Sacred Text," 16–77.

31. Hay, "Human Body as a Microcosmic Source," 88.

32. See, in particular, chapters 4 and 5 of this book.

33. See Branner and Feng, *Writing and Literacy in Early China*. Studies on literacy in late imperial China include Rawski, *Education and Popular Literacy*, and Yu Li, "A History of Reading." For a short description of the range of scribal roles in Western antiquity, see Klauck, *Ancient Letters*, 59–60.

34. Emperor Wu of the Han dynasty (r. 141–87 BCE) famously employed a poet-scribe, Sima Xiangru (179–117 BCE), for one of his letters to Liu An (179–122 BCE). *Han shu* 44.2145.

35. To cite only two examples, Sun Chu's (d. 293) "Letter on behalf of Shi Bao to Sun Hao [Emperor Mo of the Wu dynasty (r. 264–80)]" (Wei Shi Zhongrong yu Sun Hao shu) (see the "Letter Body" section of chapter 3) and He Xun's 何遜 (d. ca. 518) "Letter on behalf of Xiao Gong to his wife" (Wei Hengshan hou yu fu shu), *Quan Liang wen* 59: 11a.

36. We may safely assume that this profession existed during early medieval China, as it did in later times in Chinese history. See McDougall, *Love-Letters*, 90 and 246 n. 9. One of the earliest literary proofs of the existence of scribes is an anecdote in *Hanfeizi*, which describes a nighttime dictation (of a letter?) during which the instruction "Raise the light!" (舉燭) inadvertently became part of the text. *Hanfeizi* 32.37: 801.

37. Shen Qingzhi's "Letter to Liu Yixuan" (Yu Nanjun wang Yixuan shu) is preserved in *Quan Song wen* 41.4b. Regarding his illiteracy, see *Song shu* 77.2003 and Mather, *The Poet Shen Yüeh*, 9.

38. 遠近書疏莫不手答, *Jin shu* 66.1774.

39. 口授不悉, Cao Zhi, "Letter to Wu Zhi" (Yu Wu Jizhong shu), *Wen xuan* 42.1905–7; *Quan Sanguo wen* 16.6b–7b; trans. in Cutter, "Cao Zhi's Symposium Poems," 5–6. On the dictation of letters in the Middle Ages, see Constable, *Letters and Letter Collections*, 42–44.

40. Hu and Zhang, *Dunhuang Xuanquan Han jian*, 187. See also Trevor Evans's study of subscripts "Orality, Greek Literacy."

41. A small number of transmitted letters from early medieval China are specified as "secret" (*mi*), but I have not found letters that emphasize privacy or secrecy, e.g., by asking the addressee not to show the letter to anyone else or to destroy it. Ronald Egan points out similar requests in his article "Su Shih's 'Notes'," 570. The earliest evidence for the importance of secrecy in military communication seems to be the chapter "Secret Documents" (Yin shu) in the military text *Six Secret Teachings* (Liu tao).

42. See, e.g., Jan Vermeer's (1632–1675) *The Love Letter* in the Rijksmuseum in Amsterdam. In early twentieth-century Chinese pictorial depictions of scenes involving the reception of letters, a similarly conspicuous

element, though different in function, is the red address band running across the envelope.

43. Apart from documents and letters, the archaeological site in Xuanquan near Dunhuang, Gansu, also yielded writing and sealing materials. See the excavation report and illustrations in Gansu sheng wenwu kaogu yanjiusuo, "Gansu Dunhuang Handai Xuanquan zhi yizhi fajue jianbao," 4–20, as well as Hu and Zhang, *Dunhuang Xuanquan Han jian*. See also Liu and Wang, *Changsha Dongpailou*, nos. 6, 15–16; Li and Liu, *Jiandu wenshu*, 429–37; Liu Heng, *Lidai chidu shufa*, 8. Xiao Gang (503–551), Emperor Jianwen of the Liang dynasty (r. 549–51), in his "Letter to Xiao Ziyun" (Yu Xiao Linchuan shu), *Quan Liang wen* 11.2a, uses the poetic phrase "seals of black clay" (*qing ni zhi feng*) to designate letters. See the translation of this letter in the "Epilogue" section of chapter 3.

44. For two silk letters in envelopes from Dunhuang, dated 15–56, see Tsien, *Written on Bamboo and Silk*, 131–32, and Chung, "Study of the 'Shu'," 206–7.

45. Tsien, *Written on Bamboo and Silk*, 57–61, 122–25; Tsien, *Paper and Printing*, 137; Chung, "Study of the 'Shu'," 220–25.

46. Huan Wen (312–373), one of the most the influential figures at the Eastern Jin court.

47. 後溫將以浩為尚書令, 遺書告之。浩欣然許焉。將答書, 慮有謬誤, 開閉者數十, 竟達空函。大忤溫意, 由是遂絕。永和十二年卒, *Jin shu* 77.2047.

48. Qian Nanxiu, *Spirit and Self*, 3–5, 47–52.

49. Chen Pan (*Han Jin yijian*, 23–24) argues that this semantic change happened during the Han dynasty.

50. A particular kind of network in early medieval China is under scrutiny in Liu Yuejin's paper "Monks of the Six Dynasties: Special Envoys of Cultural Exchange" (Liuchao senglü: Wenhua jiaoliu de teshu shizhe), presented at the workshop "Pratiques culturelles et vie sociale sous les Six Dynasties" in Paris in 2004.

51. For a number of examples, see Harrist, "Replication and Deception," 44. In He Jianjun's 1995 movie *The Postman* (Youchai), the title character obsessively reads other people's letters, which becomes a powerful metaphor for other interpersonal transgressions, among them incest.

52. 殷洪喬作豫章郡。臨去, 都下人因附百許函書。既至石頭, 悉擲水中, 因祝曰。沈者自沈, 浮者自浮, 殷洪喬不能作致書郵, *Shishuo xinyu jiaojian* 23.31.400. In citing Mather's translation (*Shih-shuo Hsin-yü*, 411), I have converted spellings for proper names to pinyin and used Hucker's translation of the title *taishou* (*Dictionary*, no. 6221). Mather notes emendations in his translation that are based on the commentary by Xu Zhen'e and on two versions of the story collected in *Taiping yulan* and *Beitang shuchao*. The anecdote is found also in *Jin shu* 77.2043 and *Yiwen leiju* 58.1041.

53. 儒者學; 學, 儒矣。傳先師之業, 習口說以教, 無胸中之造, 思定然否之論。郵人之過書, 門者之傳教也, 封完書不遺, 教審令不 (遺) 誤者, 則為善矣。(傳)〔儒〕者傳學, 不妄一言, 先師古語, 到今具存, 雖帶徒百人以上, 位博士、文學, 郵人、門者之類也, *Lunheng jiaoshi* 80.1114–15.

54. 述而不作, 信而好古, *Lunyu* 7.1.

55. *Shishuo xinyu jiaojian* 25.23.428, trans. in Mather, *Shih-shuo Hsin-yü*, 443.

56. 久無家問, 笑語犬曰。我家絕無書信, 汝能齎書取消息不。犬搖尾作聲。機乃為書以竹筩盛之而繫其頸。犬尋路南走。遂至其家, 得報還洛。其後因以為常, *Jin shu* 54.1473. Another version of the story is collected in *Yiwen leiju* 94.1639.

57. In the German poet Jean Paul's (1763–1825) novel *Hesperus oder 45 Hundposttage: Eine Lebensbeschreibung* (1795), the canine messenger is carrying not a bamboo cane but a calabash at his neck, dispatching the raw material for a serial novel.

58. On the Chinese postal relay system through the ages, see Liu and Zhao, *Zhongguo gudai youyi shi.* There is no Western equivalent to this study, as, e.g., Adam Silverstein has presented with his *Postal Systems in the Pre-modern Islamic World.* Joseph Needham dedicated a few pages to the post station system; see his *Science and Civilisation in China, Vol. 4*, 34–38. Other Western studies are focused on late imperial China, such as Brook's "Communications and Commerce" and Cheng Ying-wan's *Postal Communication.* Aspects of the transmission of letters in the ancient Western world are introduced in Klauck, *Ancient Letters*, 60–65.

59. We have no concrete data about the distances between the various types of postal stations in ancient China (*you*, *ting*, *zhi*, etc.). Joseph Needham's conclusions (*Science and Civilisation in China, Vol. 4*, 35) seem unrealistic, since he assumed that, in the second through thirteenth centuries, on important roads the distance between *you* stations was five *li* 里 (about 1,500 meters), ten *li* between *ting* stations, and thirty *li* between *zhi* stations. Modern Chinese studies interpret *li* not as a measure of length but as referring to a settlement. See Liu and Zhao, *Zhongguo gudai youyi shi*, 130–37. For Ming dynasty China, Timothy Brook ("Communications and Commerce," 582) assumes that the distances between postal stations amounted to roughly a day's journey, i.e., 35–40 kilometers.

60. 德之流行速於置郵而傳命, *Mengzi* 2A1.14. See the analysis of this dictum from the perspective of postal history in Liu and Zhao, *Zhongguo gudai youyi shi*, 91–96.

61. See the definition in Liu and Zhao, *Zhongguo gudai youyi shi*, 5.

62. The archaeological finds of the last decades promise new insights into Chinese postal legislation and procedures. To mention only two important finds, tomb no. 11 in Shuihudi, Hubei, yielded the oldest evidence of courier legislation so far, a Qin dynasty document titled *Laws Concerning the Transportation of Documents* (Xing shu lü). See the reproductions of the bamboo slips and the transcriptions in Shuihudi Qin mu zhujian zhengli xiaozu, *Shuihudi Qin mu zhujian*, 30, 61, as well as Liu and Zhao, *Zhongguo gudai youyi shi*, 97–119. Another discovery of great relevance for the culture of letter writing and postal history was made in Xuanquan near Dunhuang, Gansu, where the written remains of a Han dynasty postal station yielded both letters and postal documents. See Hu and Zhang, *Dunhuang Xuanquan Han jian*, and Zhang Defang, "Xuanquan Han jian zhong de 'Zhuanxin jian' kaoshi."

63. Dien, "The Stirrup," 33–56.

64. Liu and Zhao, *Zhongguo gudai youyi shi*, 208.

65. As stated for the Jin dynasty (1115–1234) by Herbert Franke, in Franke and Twitchett, *The Cambridge History of China, Vol. 6*, 297–98.

66. See Sun Zhiping, "Yi you chuan qing," 610–22. Timothy Brook in his *Confusions of Pleasure* (185–90) gives a vivid account of the difficulties of correspondence in Ming China.

67. 足下所治僻左, 書間致簡, Cao Pi, "Letter to Wu Zhi" (Yu Wu Zhi shu), *Wen xuan* 42.1895. See translations of parts of this letter in chapter 4.

68. 冀因行李數有承問, Liu Chengzhi (aka Liu Yimin), "Letter to Shi Sengzhao requesting an explanation of his 'Disquisition on the Not-knowing of Knowledge [*prajñā*]'" (Zhi shu Shi Sengzhao qing wei 'Banruo wuzhi lun' shi), *Quan Jin wen* 142.5b–7a, trans. in Liebenthal, *Book of Chao*, 86–95.

69. 儻值行李輒復承問, Xie Lingyun, "Letter in reply to Fan Tai," *Quan Song wen* 32.4b.

70. 信南返不悉, Shi Sengzhao, "Letter in reply to Liu Chengzhi" (Da Liu Yimin shu), *Quan Jin wen* 164.1a–4b, trans. in Liebenthal, *Book of Chao*, 96.

71. 有信忘數字, Lu Jing (ca. 250–ca. 280), "Letter to his elder brother Lu Yan" (Yu xiong shu), no. 2, *Quan Sanguo wen* 70.1b.

72. Wang Xizhi, "Qiuyue tie" (aka "Qiyue tie"), *Quan Jin wen* 25.9b. Emendations to the *Quan Jin wen* edition of Wang Xizhi's letters based on Morino and Satō, *Ō Gishi zen shokan*, are not identified individually.

73. See the Jin dynasty example quoted in Chung, "Study of the 'Shu'," 213–15.

74. This anecdote about Wang Xianzhi and Xie An is quoted from Sun Qianli's (ca. 648–687/702) *Manual of Calligraphy* (Shupu), as translated in Chang and Frankel, *Two Chinese Treatises on Calligraphy*, 2, 82. See also Bai Qianshen's translation ("Chinese Letters," 382) of the anecdote as found in Yu He's (fl. ca. 470) "Memorial Discussing Calligraphy" (Lunshu biao). Two other anecdotes in this memorial mention Wang Xianzhi's high opinion of his own artistic achievements: one tells of Wang Xianzhi at the end of a letter expressly asking its recipient, the emperor, to keep it; the other describes how Wang Xianzhi once went to see his young nephew Yang Xin (370–442) and, finding him asleep, left a few lines of his handwriting on the boy's new silk dress, obviously not doubting that this addition would enhance the garment. *Quan Song wen* 55.4b, 5a.

75. Wang Xizhi, "De dan shu zhi jia tie," *Quan Jin wen* 23.2a–b. Apart from "this morning," other interpretations of *dan* are possible as well; it could refer to the first day of the month or to the name of an unidentified person. Morino and Satō, *Ō Gishi zen shokan* no. 313.

76. Wang Xizhi, "Qiuri ganhuai shen tie," *Quan Jin wen* 24.2a.

77. Wang Xun 王珣 (349–400), "Letter" (Shu), *Quan Jin wen* 20.1b. Phrases that mention that the writer "knows of" or "learned about" (*zhi* 知) the addressee's affection, consideration, etc., imply an expression of gratitude that I have made explicit in my translations.

78. Lists of terms are provided in many publications. Two examples that include annotations are Chung, "Study of the 'Shu'," 253–60, and Liu Heng, *Lidai chidu*, 5–7.

79. Compounds that show this kind of ambiguity include *shuji* 書記 (which, in addition to "writing" and "letter," may also denote a "scribe") and *shuhan* 書翰 (writing, letter, to write).

80. See Nickisch, *Brief*, 22, and Meisner, *Archivalienkunde*, 29.

81. For example, in "I have again received a letter [*jian*] from you" (重獲來簡) in Liu Shanming's (432–480) "Further letter in reply to Shi Sengyou" (Zai da Shi Sengyan shu), *Quan Qi wen* 18.9b–10a. Certain compounds containing *jian* (such as *jiandu* 簡牘) could also refer to both letters and other writings.

82. Liu Jun, "Further letter in reply to Liu Zhao" (Chong da Liu Moling Zhao shu), *Wen xuan* 43.1950–51; *Quan Liang wen* 57.1b; trans. in Zach, *Die chinesische Anthologie*, 800–801.

83. Yan Shigu (581–645), in his commentary on Ban Gu's (32–92) *History of the [Western] Han Dynasty*, remarks that *zha* are smaller and thinner than *du* (*Han shu* 57A.2533).

84. In modern Chinese, literary letters are usually called *chidu* or *shudu* 書牘, while the more comprehensive term *shuxin* 書信 includes all kinds of nonelectronic written communication. There have been various attempts to determine these words terminologically. Zhou Zuoren (1885–1967) in the "Prefatory letter" (Xu xin) to his 1933 letter collection defines *shu* as literary letters, e.g., those that are included in an author's collected works, and regards *xin* or *chidu* as private letters that had not been intended for publication. Zhou Zuoren, *Zhou Zuoren shuxin*, 1–2. See also Findeisen, "From Literature to Love," 85, and McDougall, *Love-Letters*, 92–93. Zhu Guangqian in his 1948 essay "Reading Letters" (Du shudu) takes a similar approach as Zhou Zuoren, regarding *shu* as formal, scholarly, or serious and *du* as private and informal. Zhu, "Du shu du," 162.

85. See Tsien, *Written on Bamboo and Silk*, 116–17, and, in more detail, Li and Liu, *Jiandu wenshu*, 89–96.

86. For *chishu*, see the ballad "The Orphan" (Gu'er xing), *Yuefu shiji* 38.567. The locus classicus of *chisu* is the famous "Song about Watering the Horses in a Cave at the Great Wall" (Yin ma Changcheng ku xing), *Wen xuan* 27.1277–8; trans. in Zach, *Die chinesische Anthologie*, 476–77. Another compound denoting letters in early medieval China is *chizhi* 尺紙 (a foot of paper).

87. See Ying Qu's (190–252) poem "One Among a Hundred" (Bai yi) (*Wen xuan* 21.1016) and Lu Ji's "Rhapsody on Literature" (Wen fu) (*Wen xuan* 17.761–82).

88. On the carp and geese metaphors, see the "Epilogue" section of chapter 3.

89. For example, *sushu* (silk letter) in Fu Zhidao's "Letter on behalf of Wang Kuan to his wife Yi Anzhu [?]" (Wei Wang Kuan yu fu Yi Anzhu shu) (*Quan Chen wen* 16.8b). I am not sure if the interpretation of 義安主 as the personal name of Wang Kuan's wife is correct.

90. Ledderose, *Mi Fu*, 10.

91. He Xun 何遜 in his "Letter on behalf of Xiao Gong to his wife" (*Quan Liang wen* 59: 11a) uses *han* as a letter designation. Compounds include the just mentioned *chihan* as well as *shuhan* 書翰. See *Yanshi jiaxun jijie* 7.133.

92. For example, both Cao Pi's "Letter to Wu Zhi" (*Wen xuan* 42.1895), which complains about the rarity of *shuwen* (書問致簡), and Wang Xizhi's "Ji xue ning han tie" (*Quan Jin wen* 22.6b–7a), which laments "although we frequently exchange *shuwen*, they cannot dispel my longing for you" (雖時書問不解闊懷), could as well refer to letters alone or to letters and orally transmitted messages. These letters are translated in chapter 4.

93. Wang Cuo (late 6th century), "Always Thinking of You" (Chang xiang si), *Yuefu shiji* 69.993.

94. Liu Xiaowei (ca. 496–549), "Resentment" (Yuan shi), *Yuefu shiji* 41.612–13.

95. Mendelson, *Auden*, 132–33.

96. Similar definitions may be found in Western epistolary research. See, e.g. Müller, "Der Brief," 67, or Trapp, *Greek and Latin Letters*, 1.

97. As E. M. Forster (1879–1970) put this so succinctly, "Letters have to pass two tests before they can be classed as good: they must express the personality both of the writer and of the recipient" (*Goldsworthy Lowes Dickinson*, 204).

98. Violi, "Letters," 160.

99. Guillén, "Notes," 80.

100. Zott, "Die unzeitgemäßen Hundsposttage," 44.

101. MacLean, "Re-siting the Subject," 177.

102. Speaking of "host genres, those forms one of whose roles is to provide a hospitable environment for the other form or forms that are regularly incorporated within them," Heather Dubrow (*Genre*, 116) points out the potential of letters to "mitigate both the harshness of formal verse satire and the imperiousness often associated with its speaker by suggesting his close relationship with the recipient, putative or actual, of the letter."

103. Referring to the Middle Ages, Giles Constable (*Letters and Letter Collections*, 12) remarked that "almost any material could be caste [*sic*] in the form of a letter if the writer chose to do so."

104. Patricia Rosenmeyer in her *Ancient Epistolary Fictions* traces epistolary fiction back to early Greek literature.

105. See, e.g., Beebee, *Epistolary Fiction in Europe*; Day, *Told in Letters*; Kauffman, *Special Delivery*.

106. See Yip, "The Reception of *Werther*," and Ng, "Li Ang's Experiments."

107. Guillén, "Notes," 86.

108. See the discussion of Qiu Chi's "Letter to Chen Bozhi" (Yu Chen Bozhi shu) in chapter 3 .

109. *Quan Hou Han wen* 66.3a and 96.8b–9b, trans. in Chung, "Study of the 'Shu'," 646–51, and Malmqvist, "Letters Between Qin Jian and His Wife Xu Shu." See also Chung, "Study of the 'Shu'," 657–63, for a positive judgment on the authenticity of these letters.

110. *Yiwen leiju* 23.418; *Quan Han wen* 25.12a; Zhang Pu, *Han Wei Liuchao baisan mingjia ji* 1.37a–b.

111. These labels, as well as the titles in which they occur, were never part of a letter but are later editorial additions. While they are often based on the wording that introduced a letter in a historical source, such as the biography of a letter writer in a standard history or an encyclopedia, they generally reflect the interpretation of a text by the editor of an anthology. See Metelmann, "Schriftverkehr," 98–102, 270.

112. See a letter written by Chen Lin (d. 217), "Memorandum in reply to Cao Zhi" (Da Dong'a wang jian), *Wen xuan* 40.1823–24; *Quan Hou Han wen* 92.4a; trans. in Zach, *Die chinesische Anthologie*, 756–57. On these inconsistencies, see also Hightower, "The *Wen Hsüan* and Genre Theory," 525 n. 65.

113. Sima Yu (321–72), Emperor Jianwen of the Jin dynasty (r. 371–72), "Memorandum in reply to Yin Hao" (Da Yin Hao jian), *Quan Jin wen* 11.5a.

114. Xie Wan (320–361), "Letter to Lang and his other sons" (Yu zi Lang deng shu), *Quan Jin wen* 83.4a. On *ji* 記 and *shu* 疏 as synonyms for *shu* 書, see Chen Pan, *Han Jin yijian*, 25–26, and Chen Lanlan, "Handai jiandu," 61.

115. *Wen xuan* 37.1671–75; trans. in Zach, *Die chinesische Anthologie*, 665–67. See also Robert Joe Cutter's exploration of Cao Zhi's memorials in "Personal Crisis and Communication."

116. *Wen xuan* 37.1693–96; *Quan Jin wen* 70.10a–11a; trans. in Zach, *Die chinesische Anthologie*, 679–81; and David Knechtges, "Memorial Expressing My Feelings," in Minford and Lau, *Classical Chinese Literature*, 597–99.

117. *Quan Song wen* 47.2a.

118. Steinhausen, *Geschichte des deutschen Briefes*, vii–viii.

119. The impossibility of clearly differentiating between official and personal communication has been noted by scholars in China and the West alike. Liu Heng (*Lidai chidu shufa*, 6) observed that it is often very difficult to differentiate between official and private communication, because letters "frequently possess qualities of both." Western voices are numerous, including Meisner, *Archivalienkunde*, 76, and Zott, "Die unzeitgemäßen Hundsposttage," 49–50. Peter Bürgel appositely called the letter a "tragelaph" (a hybrid animal in Greek mythology) in his *Literarische Kleinprosa*, 179.

120. *Quan Liang wen* 45.6a–9a. See Schmidt-Glintzer, *Das "Hung-ming chi,"* 120, and Jansen, *Höfische Öffentlichkeit*, 215–18, 252–53.

121. Takakusu and Watanabe, *Taishō*, 1856. See Zürcher, *Buddhist Conquest*, 226–30, and Wagner, "The Original Structure," 28–48.

122. Referring to the Song dynasty (960–1279), Stephen Owen (*Anthology*, 597) described letters and other forms of written communication as "means by which those outside the discussion-making inner circle of government could comment on and participate in the formulation of public policy."

123. Reinhard Nickisch (*Brief*, 19–21) spoke of the "'improper' utilization ['*uneigentliche' Verwendung*] of letters," which is given if the pragmatic text type letter is employed in the service of nonpragmatic or literary

intentions or if a letter, contrary to the archetypal epistolary situation, is addressed to a limited or unlimited public audience.

124. Genette, *Paratexts*, 371.

125. See also Belke, *Literarische Gebrauchsformen*, 144.

126. The biblical scholar Adolf Deissmann established the epistle/letter distinction in the 1920s. For a concise review of his ideas and later critics, see Rosenmeyer, *Ancient Epistolary Fictions*, 5–10.

CHAPTER 2. LETTERS AND LITERARY THOUGHT

Epigraph: *Lu Xun quanji* 6: 409.

1. Nickisch, "Der Brief und andere Textsorten," 358.

2. Chen Wuyun, *Shuxin daquan*, 11–12. On speculations about a Shang or even Xia dynasty origin of the courier system, see Liu and Zhao, *Zhongguo gudai youyi shi*, 36.

3. *Zuo zhuan* "*Xiang*" 24.280. See also Chung, "Study of the 'Shu'," 56–60, and a list of *Zuo zhuan* letters in Schaberg, *A Patterned Past*, 137 n. 13.

4. Sima Qian, "Letter in reply to Ren An" (Bao Ren Shaoqing shu), *Wen xuan* 41.1854–69; *Quan Han wen* 26.5a–9a. The letter was frequently translated and discussed; see Fuehrer, "The Court Scribe's *Eikon Psyches*," 175 n. 29, and Knechtges, "Key Words," 75 n. 1. See also Stephen Durrant's study "Self as the Intersection of Traditions."

5. Bauer, *Das Antlitz Chinas*, 83.

6. Ma Yuan, "Letter admonishing his nephews Yan and Dun" (Jie xiong zi Yan Dun shu), *Quan Hou Han wen* 17.9a–b, trans. in Frankel, "Ma Yuan." See also Chung, "Study of the 'Shu'," 148–49, and Richter, "Between Testament and Letter."

7. Kong Rong, "Letter criticizing Cao Cao's declaration and implementation of a wine prohibition" (Nan Cao gong biao zhi jin jiu shu), *Quan Hou Han wen* 83.8b–9a, trans. in Chung, "Study of the 'Shu'," 496–98.

8. Ruan Yu, "Letter written on behalf of Cao Cao to Sun Quan [182–252, Emperor Da of the Wu dynasty (r. 229–52)]" (Wei Cao gong zuo shu yi Sun Quan), *Wen xuan* 42.1887–94; *Quan Hou Han wen* 93.2a–4a; trans. in Zach, *Die chinesische Anthologie*, 773–78.

9. Studies of literary thought in this period include Holzman, "Confucius," and Owen, *Readings*, 19–56.

10. 文學的自覺時代, Lu Xun, "The Style and the Literature of the Wei and Jin Periods and Their Connection to Drugs and Wine" (Wei Jin fengdu ji wenzhang yu yao ji jiu zhi guanxi), in *Lu Xun quanji* 3: 491.

11. Holzman, "Literary Criticism," 114.

12. *Wen xuan* 52.2270–73; trans. in Owen, *Readings*, 57–72. Apart from the works listed in Owen's bibliography (p. 640), see Hughes, *The Art of Letters*, 231–48; Holzman, "Literary Criticism," 128–31; Wong, *Early Chinese Literary Criticism*, 19–25.

13. 文人相輕自古而然 . . . 不自見之患, *Wen xuan* 52.2270.

14. *Wen xuan* 52.2271.

15. See Plato's (427–347 BCE) *Republic* (Bloom, *"The Republic" of Plato*, 70–75) and Aristotle's (384/383–322/321 BCE) *Poetics* (Aristotle, *On Poetics*, 253–54; and Halliwell, *Aristotle's "Poetics,"* 92–96). Johann Wolfgang Goethe's characterization of epic, poetry, and drama in his *Noten und Abhandlungen zu besserem Verständnis des West-östlichen Divans* (1816–18) resembles Cao Pi's in succinctness, because he uses only two words to describe each genre. Trunz and Schrimpf, *Goethes Werke*, 2: 187–88.

16. Belke, *Literarische Gebrauchsformen*, 7–11.

17. Cai Yong's (132–192) *Independent Decisions* (Duduan) provides the first classification of official communication. Cai differentiates writings addressed to the emperor (such as *zou* [presentation], *yi* [appeal], *zhang* [petition], and *biao* [memorial]) from writings that the emperor addressed to officials and other subjects (such as *zhishu* [decision], *zhaoshu* [edict], *ceshu* [diploma], and *jieshu* [admonition]). Giele, *Imperial Decision-Making*, 96–297.

18. On Han dynasty precursors who described disquisitions as structured, see Wang and Yang, *Wei Jin Nanbeichao wenxue*, 40–41.

19. On the Greek demand for clarity, see Koskenniemi, *Studien*, 27–28. Horst Belke (*Literarische Gebrauchsformen*, 147) speaks of the proximity of essays and letters on account of the "subjective, casually improvising, dialogic form of the letter." Wolfgang Müller ("Der Brief als Spiegel der Seele," 138) points out similarities between Michel de Montaigne's (1533–1592) *Essais* and personal letters of the sixteenth to eighteenth centuries, especially because they shared a "radical self-expression and disclosure of their innermost feelings," based on a "plain and unaffected style."

20. See Pollard, "*Ch'i* in Chinese Literary Theory," and Cutter, "To the Manner Born?"

21. *Wen xuan* 52.2271.

22. Translations include Fang, "Rhymeprose on Literature"; Wong, *Early Chinese Literary Criticism*, 39–60; Owen, *Readings*, 73–181; Knechtges, *Wen Xuan*, 3: 211–31.

23. 奏平徹以閒雅, *Wen xuan* 17.766.

24. Coincidentally, Lu Ji's oeuvre of transmitted letters is relatively large. It includes his correspondence with his brother Lu Yun (262–303), which comprises forty-four short letters that are, unfortunately, only partly comprehensible today. See Fu, "'Wen gui qingsheng'"; Satō, *Riku Un kenkyū*; Yu Shiling, "Lu Yun 'Yu xiong Pingyuan shu'."

25. *Wen xuan* 17.765.

26. Stephen Owen (*Readings*, 119–20) eliminates the reading "letter" explicitly.

27. See, e.g., Ye Youming, *Lidai shuxin xuan*, 5; Cheng and Fang, *Zizi zhenzang*, 1; Zou, "Qingdai shuzha wenxian," 183.

28. 尺素書, *Wen xuan* 27.1278; trans. in Zach, *Die chinesische Anthologie*, 477.

29. Complete translations into English include Shih, *The Literary Mind*; Wong, *The Book of Literary Design*; Yang and Zhou, *Wenxin Diaolong*. For translations of selected chapters, see Wong, *Early Chinese Literary*

Criticism, 115–36, and Owen, *Readings*, 183–298. On the preface of *The Literary Mind*, see also Richter, "Empty Dreams and Other Omissions."

30. 各照隅隙, 鮮觀衢路 . . . 亦幾乎備矣, *Wenxin diaolong zhu* 50.726–27.

31. James Hightower's 1965 article "Some Characteristics of Parallel Prose" is still the best introduction to this style of writing, elements of which are common in literary Chinese well beyond the Six Dynasties, when it was at its height.

32. While chapters 6–25 are commonly regarded as representing the typological part, some scholars have included all five or selected chapters of the first part, most often chapter 5 detailing the elegy (*sao*). However, since Liu Xie explicitly described chapters 1–5 as dealing with the "pivot of literature" (文之樞紐, *Wenxin diaolong zhu* 50.727), I hesitate to include any of them in the typological part.

33. The theoretical frame of *The Literary Mind* (chapters 1–5 and 26–50) is much more renowned than the massive typological block it encloses. Although references to the genre chapters are a normative part of any study of a specific genre in Chinese literature, Liu's expositions on genres are frequently berated for their shortcomings and usually excluded from comprehensive reflections on the book. The ratio found in Zhang Shaokang's comprehensive *Wenxin diaolong yanjiu shi*, in which only five out of six hundred pages (465–70) are dedicated to genre, is fairly representative of this situation.

34. Liu Xie introduces *yun* as the contemporary prevalent distinctive feature (今之常言, 有文有筆, 以為無韻者筆也, 有韻者文也, *Wenxin diaolong zhu* 44.655). However, not only is his understanding of *yun* controversial (actual rhyming or other prosodic features, possibly tonality); Liu Xie also appears to question a formalistic approach to this question in chapter 44 and in *The Literary Mind* in general, without offering an alternative criterion of differentiation. A further complication arises because *wen bi* also occurs as a compound referring to "writings" as a whole. An oft-quoted phrase in Liu Xie's preface, for example, could also be read as a metonymical reference to the various kinds of literary writing (若乃論文敘筆, *Wenxin diaolong zhu* 50.727).

35. See Pauline Yu, "Formal Distinctions," and *Guanzhui bian* 1420–21, trans. in Egan, *Limited Views*, 248–50.

36. The passage appears as a quote from the now lost treatise "Forms of Refined Literature and Utilitarian Texts" (Wen bi shi), which is probably of early Tang provenance. See Miyasaka, *Kōbō Daishi Kūkai zenshū*, 716, and Pauline Yu, "Formal Distinctions," 35–36.

37. To give a few examples, Liu Shipei regarded chapters 6–15 as *wen* and chapters 16–25 as *bi* (*Zhongguo zhonggu wenxue*, 110); Fan Wenlan took chapters 5–13 for *wen* and chapters 16–25 for *bi*, assuming two chapters of mixed character in between (*Wenxin diaolong zhu* 4–5); Donald Holzman, drawing the line between chapters 13 and 14, regards chapters 5–13 as *wen* and chapters 14–25 as *bi* ("Liu Hsieh," 139).

38. While the other chapters of the *wen* section cover one or two genres each, very seldom mentioning a few subgenres as well, the "Za wen" chapter (*Wenxin diaolong zhu* 14.254–70) collects nineteen genres, of which three

are described in detail, while the rest are merely listed. The three genres described in detail are *duiwen* (response to questions), *qi* (seven), and *lianzhu* (linked pearls), while the following sixteen genres are only enumerated: *dian* (statute), *gao* (instruction), *shi* (speech), *wen* (inquiry from the throne), *lan* (survey), *lüe* (summary), *pian* (chapter), *zhang* (paragraph), *qu* (song), *zao* (song on given themes), *nong* (ditty), *yin* (prelude), *yin* (sad chant), *feng* (expostulatory poem), *yao* (ballad), and *yong* (topical poem).

39. In chapter 12, the epitaph (*bei*) is accordingly defined as a subgenre of the inscription (夫碑實銘器, *Wenxin diaolong zhu* 12.214).

40. Guillén, "Notes," 80. See "The Genre of Personal Letters" in chapter 1.

41. 敷奏以言, 明試以功, 故堯咨四岳, 舜命八元, 固辭再讓之請, 俞往欽哉之授, 並陳辭帝庭, 匪假書翰。. . .至太甲既立, 伊尹書誡, 思庸歸亳, 又作書以讚。文翰獻替, 事斯見矣, *Wenxin diaolong zhu* 22.406. According to traditional historiography, Yao ruled at the end of the third millennium BCE. *Shi ji* 1.31–35.

42. 昔唐虞之臣, 敷奏以言, *Wenxin diaolong zhu* 23.421.

43. 不專緩頰, 亦在刀筆, *Wenxin diaolong zhu* 18.329.

44. See also Liu Xie's definition of the brush as the servant of the spoken word in *Wenxin diaolong zhu* 44.655 (予以為發口為言, 屬筆曰翰 . . . 筆為言使).

45. The influential Qing scholar Yao Nai (1732–1815), famous for disparaging Six Dynasties literature, did not concur with Liu Xie's distinction between the written and the oral as far as letters are concerned. In his *Classified Collection of Ancient Literature* (Guwenci leizuan) (1779), Yao Nai not only combines letters (*shu*) and persuasions (*shui*) to form one of thirteen categories but also declares, in his preface, that "whether the officials of the various states in the Chunqiu period made their announcements when meeting face-to-face or whether they wrote each other letters, the meaning was the same." 春秋之世, 列國士大夫或面相告語, 或為書相遺, 其義一也, *Guwenci leizuan*, 3. See also Edwards, "A Classified Guide," and Kern, "'Persuasion' or 'Treatise'?".

46. In a corpus of pre-Tang literature in the database of Academia Sinica in Taipei, I found about 110 occurrences of *shu ji* as a compound, more than three-quarters of them referring to various kinds of "written records," including "books," and even "literature." This usage goes back to Han times; see *Shi ji* 123.3162 (晝革旁行以為書記) or *Liji* 12.52.79 (十年, 出就外傅, 居宿於外, 學書記). A considerable number of these occurrences denote "written records" as the field of responsibility of an official, which probably gave rise to the meaning "scribe"; see *Sanguo zhi* 21.600 (建安中都護曹洪欲使掌書記).

47. We also see this use in biographical sketches, e.g., in standard histories, when somebody's literary writings are listed, as in *Hou Han shu* 79B.2583 (所著賦、碑、誄、書記、連珠、九憤, 凡十餘篇).

48. Among the genre chapters, there are three types of titles: verb noun phrases, such as "Ming shi" (Elucidating lyric poetry); nominal coordinations that designate two genres, such as "Ming zhen" (Inscriptions and admonitions);

and subordinated phrases that designate one or more genres, such as "Zhu zi" (The masters) or "Za wen" (Miscellaneous kinds of refined literature).

49. In *The Literary Mind*, the term *ji* does not occur as an independent genre term, and the same holds true for *Selections of Refined Literature* and the above-mentioned list of genres transmitted in the *Disquisitions from the Secret Repository of the Literary Mirror.*

50. All in all, there are six occurrences; see *Wenxin diaolong zhu* 23.423, 25.456, 25.457.

51. Most scholars understand the chapter title as a coordination, such as "letters" and "records" (Knechtges, *Wen Xuan*, 1: 23; Chung, "Study of the 'Shu'," 25); "notes and letters" (Wong, *The Book of Literary Design*, 95); or "epistolary writing and miscellaneous records" (Yang and Zhou, *Wenxin diaolong zhu*, 351).

52. Behr, "Language Change in Premodern China," 16–17.

53. McDougall, *Love-Letters*, 84, follows Shih, *The Literary Mind*, 279, in reading the title as "letter records," "epistolary writing."

54. Richter, "Notions of Epistolarity," 143–44.

55. 若乃論文敘筆, 則 (囿)〔品〕別區分, 原始以表 (末)〔時〕, 釋名以章義, 選文以定篇, 敷理以舉統, 上篇以上, 綱領明矣, *Wenxin diaolong zhu* 50.727.

56. In the following, chapter 25 of *The Literary Mind* is given according to Fan Wenlan's edition of the text (*Wenxin diaolong zhu* 50.455–91). Line numbers are added for pragmatic reasons.

57. *Shangshu* 5.7.

58. In an alternative reading of lines 4–7, both occurrences of *shu* are interpreted as a title and thus understood as specifically referring to the *Book of Documents.*

59. *Fayan* 5.12.

60. *Zhou yi* 43.51–52.

61. 書實記言, *Wenxin diaolong zhu* 3.21.

62. 書契斷決以象夬, *Wenxin diaolong zhu* 2.16.

63. 上古結繩而治, 後世聖人易之以書契, 百官以治, 萬民以察, 蓋取諸夬, *Zhou yi* 65.88. See also *Han shu* 30.1720–21 and *Shuowen jiezi* 50a.753–54.

64. 符檄書移, 則楷式於明斷, *Wenxin diaolong zhu* 30.530.

65. 詔策章奏, 則書發其源, *Wenxin diaolong zhu* 3.22.

66. 詔命策檄, 生於書者也 . . . 書奏箴銘, 生於春秋者也, *Yanshi jiaxun jijie* 9.221. See also Dien, "A Sixth Century Father's Advice," 67–82.

67. *Zhou yi* 65.80.

68. This topos will be introduced in detail in the "Limits of Writing and Language" section of chapter 4.

69. Visual criteria for the choice of characters are discussed in chapter 39 of *Wenxin diaolong zhu*. See, e.g., *Wenxin diaolong zhu* 39.624 (心既託聲於言, 言亦寄形於字, 諷誦則績在宮商, 臨文則能歸字形矣).

70. Harrist, "Reading Chinese Calligraphy," 4.

71. Klauck, *Ancient Letters*, 186.

72. See Koskenniemi, *Studien*, 40; Thraede, *Grundzüge*, 17–24; Müller, "Spiegel der Seele."

73. Plato's *Phaedrus* 60 famously proves the awareness of the precarious autonomy of a written text in ancient Greece. See Cavallo and Chartier, *A History of Reading*, 5–6.

74. Differing interpretations of *ce* ("inscribed bamboo tablet," i.e., "written document," vs. "whip") in *Zuo zhuan* are introduced in the commentary in *Wenxin diaolong zhu* 50.462.

75. All four letters are mentioned in *Zuo zhuan*: Wen 13.2.143, Wen 17.4.151, Cheng 7.5.199, Xiang 24.2.280.

76. *Liji* 4.46.27.

77. Klauck, *Ancient Letters*, 185. The quote appears in *On Style*, attributed to Demetrius. See the introduction of the topos of the letter as a substitute for face-to-face conversation in chapter 4.

78. This letter by Dongfang Shuo—probably addressed to Gongsun Hong (200–121 BCE)—has not been transmitted. See the commentary in *Wenxin diaolong zhu* 25.468.

79. Yang Yun (d. 56 BCE), "Letter in reply to Sun Huizong" (Bao Sun Huizong shu), *Wen xuan* 41.1869–1873; trans. in Birch, *Anthology*, 159–62.

80. On the correspondence between Liu Xin (d. 23) and Yang Xiong, see Knechtges, "The Liu Hsin / Yang Hsiung Correspondence," 309–25.

81. *Wen xuan* 17.768; trans. in Knechtges, *Wen Xuan*, 1: 223.

82. Official letters by Cui Yuan are collected in *Quan Hou Han wen* 45.1a–2a.

83. This characterization of Ruan Yu's letters, mentioned again in chapter 45 (元瑜展其翩翩之樂, *Wenxin diaolong zhu* 45.673), harks back to Cao Pi's famous "Further letter to Wu Zhi," no. 1, introduced in detail in this chapter as well as chapters 3 and 4.

84. On Cao Pi's esteem for Kong Rong's works, see *Hou Han shu* 70.2279. *Ban jian* (lit., "half a bamboo slip") stands as a hyperbole for the tiniest fragments of his texts, emphasizing how highly they were valued.

85. Ying Qu is represented with the largest number of letters in *Selections of Refined Literature* (*Wen xuan* 42.1912–22). See also Lin, "Rediscovering Ying Qu."

86. Two of Xi Kang's letters are dedicated to severing a relationship, the long and famous "Letter to Shan Tao, severing their relationship" (Yu Shan Juyuan juejiao shu) (*Wen xuan* 43.1923–31 and *Quan Sanguo wen* 47.6a–8a), and the short, less well-known "Letter to Lü Sun, severing their relationship" (Yu Lü Changti juejiao shu) (*Quan Sanguo wen* 47.8a–b). On these two letters, including translations, as well as the older tradition of severing relationships, see Jansen, "The Art of Severing Relationships."

87. Liu Xie probably refers to Zhao Zhi's (ca. 247–283) "Yu Xi Maoqi shu" (Letter to Xi Fan), *Wen xuan* 43.1940–43; *Quan Jin wen* 67.3b–4b; trans. in Zach, *Die chinesische Anthologie*, 794–97.

88. Liu Xie alludes to Chen Zun's ability to dictate letters to ten scribes simultaneously, even with addressees requiring different kinds of etiquette (書數百封親疏各有意, *Han shu* 92.3711). Chen Zun's letters have not been transmitted.

89. The letters of Mi Heng, a contemporary of Cao Cao's, are largely lost. See *Hou Han shu* 80B.2652 and the commentary in *Wenxin diaolong zhu* 25.477.

90. Klauck, *Ancient Letters*, 186, quoting from *On Style*, attributed to Demetrius.

91. See commentaries on *Liji* 9 in *Shisanjing zhushu*, 9.76b and 76c. In *The Literary Mind*, *yutao* also describes a state between joy and sadness. See *Wenxin diaolong zhu* 46.693.

92. 諸子之徒, 心非鬱陶, *Wenxin diaolong zhu* 31.538.

93. *Wenxin diaolong zhu* 25.457.

94. The dictum (*yan*) is classified among the "written records" because it refers to literary quotations from transmitted literature; see the explanation in *Wenxin diaolong zhu* 25.460.

95. *Lüshi chunqiu* 20.8.138; *Huainanzi* 12.111.

96. On Xiao Tong and his *Selections of Refined Literature*, see Knechtges, *Wen Xuan*, 1: 1–70.

97. 深愛接之, *Liang shu* 50.710.

98. Richard Mather, in his foreword to Knechtges, *Wen Xuan*, 1: ix.

99. 文選序, *Wen xuan* 1–3, trans. in Hightower, "The *Wen Hsüan* and Genre Theory," 518–30; Knechtges, *Wen Xuan*, 1: 72–91; Wong, *Early Chinese Literary Criticism*, 149–63.

100. Of the thirty-eight genres that are mentioned in the preface, eleven are not represented in the anthology, and of the thirty-seven genres that are represented in *Selections of Refined Literature*, ten are not mentioned in the preface. Scholars have tried to account for these discrepancies, mainly by pointing out the requirements of parallel style in the preface. Hightower, "The *Wen Hsüan* and Genre Theory," 524 n. 57, 530–33.

101. Knechtges, *Wen Xuan*, 1: 21.

102. See Wu Na, "*Wenzhang bianti* xushuo," 41; Hightower, "The *Wen Hsüan* and Genre Theory," 531–33; Chung, "Study of the 'Shu'," 5.

103. One is an open letter or circular by Liu Xin addressed to his subordinates, the scholars (*boshi*) of the Taichang academy (Yishu rang Taichang boshi), *Wen xuan* 43.1952–56; trans. in Zach, *Die chinesische Anthologie*, 801–5; Chung, "Study of the 'Shu'," 482–95, see also 287–300. The other one is Kong Zhigui's (447–501) address to the natural forces of North Mountain (Beishan yiwen), *Wen xuan* 43.1957–61; trans. in Zach, *Die chinesische Anthologie*, 805–08; Birch, *Anthology*, 169–73; Hightower, "Parallel Prose," 108–39. Knechtges (*Wen Xuan*, 1: 44) assumes that these two communications could be the remnants of a now lost dispatch (*yi*) category in *Selections of Refined Literature*.

104. These are the five memorandums by Yang Xiu (175–219), Chen Lin, Wu Zhi, and Po Qin (d. 218) and possibly a sixth by Xie Tiao (464–499). The memorandums by Ruan Ji (210–263) and Ren Fang (459–507) seem to be pieces of official communication. Outside of *Selections of Refined Literature*, a similar mix of personally and officially motivated letters is labeled "memorandums."

105. It should be mentioned that one of these letters, Liu Jun's "Further letter in reply to Liu Zhao," was addressed to an already deceased person. *Wen xuan* 43.1950–51.

106. Lu Chen (284–350), "Presented to Liu Kun along with a letter" (Zeng Liu Kun bing shu), *Wen xuan* 25.1177; trans. in Zach, *Die chinesische Anthologie*, 418–19; *Quan Jin wen* 34.12a–b (here titled "Letter to Liu Kun, Minister of Works" [Yu sikong Liu Kun shu]) and Liu Kun (271–318), "Letter in reply to Lu Chen," *Wen xuan* 25.1168–74; *Quan Jin wen* 108.10a–b; trans. in Zach, *Die chinesische Anthologie*, 412–13. David Knechtges's "Liu Kun, Lu Chen" contains annotated translations of both letters.

107. 略其蕪穢, *Wen xuan* 2.

108. Toynbee, *Dantis Alagherii epistolae*, 160–211, and McClatchy, *The Whole Difference*, 69–79.

109. Ancient Greek examples, such as Philostratus of Lemnos (b. ca. 190) and Gregory of Nazianzus (ca. 329–390), are quoted in Koskenniemi, *Studien*, 20.

110. Famous early medieval Chinese letters on literary thought include Cao Pi "Letter to Wang Lang" (Yu Wang Lang shu) (*Quan Sanguo wen* 7.7a; trans. in Holzman, "Literary Criticism," 122); Cao Zhi, "Letter to Yang Xiu" (Yu Yang Dezu shu) (see chapter 3), along with Yang Xiu's reply "Memorandum in reply to Cao Zhi" (Da Linzi hou jian) (*Wen xuan* 40.1818–20; *Quan Hou Han wen* 51.10b–11b; trans. in Zach, *Die chinesische Anthologie*, 752–54; Holzman, "Literary Criticism," 120–21); Lu Yun, "Letters to his elder brother Lu Ji" (Yu xiong Pingyuan shu) (*Quan Jin wen* 102.1–10b; see Wu Sujane, "Clarity, Brevity, and Naturalness," 208–38); Lu Jue (472–499), "Letter to Shen Yue" (Yu Shen Yue shu) (*Quan Qi wen* 24.6b–7b; trans. in Mather, *The Poet Shen Yüeh*, 46–50); Xiao Tong, "Letter in reply to Xiao Gang" (Da Jin'an wang shu) (*Quan Liang wen* 20.1b–2a; trans. in Wang Ping, *The Age of Courtly Writing*, 100–102); Xiao Gang, "Letter to Xiao Yi 蕭繹" (Yu Xiangdong wang shu) (*Quan Liang wen* 11.3a–4a; trans. in Marney, *Liang Chien-wen Ti*, 137–47).

111. "Jian'an qi zi," i.e., Xu Gan (170–217), Ying Yang (d. 217), Chen Lin, Liu Zhen, Ruan Yu, Wang Can (177–217), and Kong Rong, who alone is not mentioned in this letter. For the dating of the letter, see the commentary in *Selections of Refined Literature*, *Wen xuan* 42.1896.

112. *Laozi* 19A.6.

113. An allusion to the recluse Xu You, who withdrew to Mount Ji after the legendary ruler Yao had offered him the throne (*Shi ji* 61.2121).

114. *Lunyu* 6.18 describes the gentleman (*junzi*) as having achieved a balance between *wen* (education) and *zhi* (natural substance).

115. This phrase was famously used by Sima Qian. *Shi ji* 130.3319.

116. *Lunyu* 5.22.

117. The interpretation of *zhu shu* as not just "to write a book" but as "to write a great book," i.e., a grand philosophical treatise in the tradition of early Chinese masters literature (*zi shu*), is inspired by ideas about this genre expressed in articles by Tian Xiaofei ("The Twilight of the Masters") and Michael Puett ("The Temptations of Sagehood").

118. *Chu ci* 4.6.16 (孤子吟而抆淚兮).

119. Cao Pi, "Further letter to Wu Zhi" (You yu Wu Zhi shu), no. 1. *Wen xuan* 42.1896–99; *Quan Sanguo wen* 7.5b–6b; trans. in Zach, *Die*

chinesische Anthologie, 780–82; Holzman, “Literary Criticism,” 123–25; Watson, “Cao Pi: Two Letters to Wu Zhi.”

120. See Liu Shao’s (ca. 186–245) *Treatise about Personality* (Renwu zhi), which was intended as a tool for the appointment of officials. The classification of literary talents reached a culmination in Zhong Rong’s (d. 518) *Gradings of Poets* (Shipin).

121. Examples include Lu Jue’s poem “Presented in Reply to his brother-in-law Gu Xi” (Fengda neixiong Xishu) (*Wen xuan* 26.1215) and Yu Xin’s (513–581) epitaph for Yuwen Guang (?–570), which praises the letters of the deceased as full of verve (Gu Zhou dajiangjun Zhao Gong muzhiming) (翩翩書記, *Quan Hou Zhou wen* 17.7b).

122. *Mao shi* 162, 171 (翩翩者鵻).

123. *Shi ji* 76.2376 (平原君, 翩翩濁世之佳公子也).

124. 太祖嘗使瑀作書與韓遂, 時太祖適近出, 瑀隨從, 因於馬上具草, 書成呈之。太祖擥筆欲有所定, 而竟不能增損, from Yu Huan’s *Dianlüe* (ca. 270) as quoted by Pei Songzhi (372–451) in his commentary on *Sanguo zhi* (21.601 n. 2); trans. in Holzman, *Poetry and Politics*, 3.

125. Nickisch, “Der Brief und andere Textsorten,” 358.

126. See also Guillén, “Notes,” 85.

127. Two other letters from this context are transmitted: Wang Rong’s 王融 (467–493) “Letter on behalf of Xiao Ziliang to the recluse Liu Qiu” (Wei Jingling wang yi yinshi Liu Qiu shu) (*Quan Qi wen* 12.9b–10b) and Ren Fang’s “Letter on behalf of Yu Gaozhi to the recluse Liu Qiu” (Wei Yu Gaozhi yu Liu jushi Qiu shu) (*Quan Liang wen* 43.9b–10a). See also Jansen, *Höfische Öffentlichkeit*, 77–79.

128. Xiao Ziliang, “Letter to Liu Yin” (Yu Nanjun taishou Liu Jingrui shu), *Quan Qi wen* 7.11a–b.

129. Although the date of neither Xiao Ziliang’s letter nor Liu Xie’s *The Literary Mind* is certain, it is probable that the letter was written earlier, perhaps around 490.

130. See his biography in *Liang shu* 33.469–74.

131. This line quotes Cao Zhi’s “Letter to Yang Xiu” (*Quan Sanguo wen* 16.5b).

132. See the stories of Laozi’s journey west as told in *Zhuangzi* 27.80 (老聃西遊於秦 . . .) and of the recluse Liang Hong’s (1st century) wanderings in his biography in *Hou Han shu* 83.2766 (因東出關, 過京師 . . .). The whole passage about Laozi’s and Liang Hong’s feelings of sadness at parting is moreover an allusion to the introduction to Zhao Zhi’s “Letter to Xi Fan” (昔李叟入秦, 及關而歎, 梁生適越, 登岳長謠), *Wen xuan* 43.1940.

133. This phrase seems to combine allusions to *Mao shi* 70 (雉離于羅) and Cao Zhi’s short “Rhapsody on a Parrot” (Yingwu fu) (*Quan Sanguo wen* 14.4a–b, 遇旅人之嚴網).

134. These phrases recall Sima Qian’s “Letter in reply to Ren An,” in which he says that “a scholar, if a prison was drawn on the ground, will not enter this form, nor will he, if a piece of wood was carved to look like a warden, address it in discussion” (故士有畫地為牢勢不入, 削木為吏議不對).

Wen xuan 41.1860–61; *Quan Han wen* 26.7b; trans. in Owen, *Anthology*, 140.

135. *Zhou yi* 29.36.

136. Both appear in *Kongcongzi* 4.2.48, weeping profusely at a parting (文節流涕交頤).

137. This line continues the allusion to *Kongcongzi* (子高徒抗手而已、分背就路).

138. Autumn is implied here through its traditional correlation with metal. For an introduction to correlative thinking based on *yin* and *yang* and the five phases (*wu xing*), see A. C. Graham's *Yin-Yang and the Nature of Correlative Thinking.* Until about the fourth century BCE, *yin* and *yang* mainly designated concrete entities: *yin* the shady northern slope of a hill or the sunlit southern bank of a river and *yang* the sunlit southern slope of a hill or the shady northern bank of a river. Toward the end of the Warring States period, *yin* and *yang* became key philosophical concepts designating the two poles or phases of a process.

139. An allusion to *Mao shi* 62, in which *shou ji* (headache) appears as a symptom of separation from a loved one (願言思伯, 甘心首疾).

140. The same praise for a letter is used in Wang Lang's "Letter to Xu Jing" (Yu Xu Wenxiu shu), no. 1. *Quan Sanguo wen* 22.10b–11b.

141. Wang Sengru, "Letter to He Jiong" (Yu He Jiong shu) (*Quan Liang wen* 51.4a–6a). See also *Guanzhui bian* 1435–38; trans. in Egan, *Limited Views*, 412–17.

142. Yang Yun's "Letter in reply to Sun Huizong" (*Wen xuan* 41.1869–1873) and Ren Fang's "Letter to Shen Yue" (Yu Shen Yue shu) (*Quan Liang wen* 43.9a).

143. I found only eleven occurrences of *shen shan shen shan* in pre-Tang literature, six of which came from letters.

CHAPTER 3. STRUCTURES AND PHRASES

Epigraph: Le Faye, *Jane Austen's Letters*, 121.

1. See Trapp, *Greek and Latin Letters*, 34–38; Klauck, *Ancient Letters*, 17–25 (on the New Testament); Constable, *Letters and Letter Collections*, 16–20 (on the Middle Ages).

2. For two concise descriptions, which employ slightly divergent terminologies, see Camargo, *Ars dictaminis*, 22–23, and Klauck, *Ancient Letters*, 17–42.

3. See, e.g., Dietz, *Die buddhistische Briefliteratur Indiens*.

4. Xiao Tong in his "Letter in reply to Xiao Gang" (*Quan Liang wen* 20.1b) (see the translation in chapter 4) remarks on Xiao Gang's "clean-cut opening and closing" (首尾裁淨), but it is more likely that these words refer to the poem Xiao Gang had sent him than to his letter.

5. In modern Chinese, different sets of terms are employed for the three main parts of a letter, such as *shangkuan* 上款 for the opening, *zhengwen* 正文 for the main text, and *xiakuan* 下款 for the closing (Zhao Shugong, *Zhongguo chidu wenxue shi*, 638) or, alternatively, *qishou* 起首 for the opening,

zhengwen for the main text, and *jiewei* 結尾 for the closing (Hu Chuanhai, *Chidu shi jiang*, 25–36). Qi Xiaochun (*Mai shi zhi feng*, 149) uses Hu Chuanhai's terms as well but further subdivides the opening into *riqi* 日期 (date), *shuming* 署名 (writer's name), and *kaitouyu* 開頭語 (opening words) and the closing into *jieshuyu* 結束語 (closing words) and *luokuan* 落款 (inscription). Chu Hui-liang, in her analysis of Song dynasty letters "Songdai ceye zhong de chidu shufa," differentiates nine parts: *juli* 具禮 (salutation), *chengwei* 稱謂 (appellation), *ticheng* 題稱 (expression of respect), *qianjie* 前介 (introduction), *benshi* 本事 (main text), *zhusong* 祝頌 (expressing good wishes), *jieshu* 結束 (closing), *riqi* (date), and *shuya* 署押 (signature). See also Cao Xianghong's analysis of pragmatic aspects of modern Chinese letter writing, *A Sociolinguistic Study of Addressing, Openings and Closings in Contemporary Personal Letters.*

6. Cao Pi, "Further letter to Wu Zhi," no. 1, *Wen xuan* 42.1896.

7. Wang Xizhi, "Da han tie," *Quan Jin wen* 23.12a.

8. Wu Zhi, "Memorandum in reply to Cao Pi" (Da Wei taizi jian), *Wen xuan* 40.1825–27; *Quan Sanguo wen* 30.8a–b; trans. in Zach, *Die chinesische Anthologie*, 757–58.

9. Sima Rui (276–322), Emperor Yuan of the Jin dynasty (r. 317–322), "Letter" (Shu), *Quan Jin wen* 8.12a.

10. Liu Zhilin (477–548), "Letter of condolence on the occasion of the demise of the Buddhist chief and metropolitan dharma-teacher" (Diao sengzheng jing fashi wang shu), *Quan Liang wen* 56.2b–3a. I could not identify the addressee of this letter. The salutation *henan*, used in letters to members of the Buddhist clergy or lay Buddhists, is a rendering of the Sanskrit term *vandanam* (prostration, bow, to worship). See Pulleyblank, *Lexicon*, 123, 221, and Zürcher, *Buddhist Conquest*, 408 n. 83.

11. On dating conventions in official communication based on archaeological finds, see Li and Liu, *Jiandu wenshu*, 144–48.

12. Cao Pi, "Letter on the ninth to Zhong You" (Jiu ri yu Zhong You shu), *Quan Sanguo wen* 7.3b–4a; trans. in Davis, "The Double Ninth Festival," 46.

13. Wang Xizhi, "Yueban nian zuxia tie," *Quan Jin wen* 25.8a.

14. Interpretations of *zaibai* differ. While Eva Chung translates "to bow repeatedly" ("Study of the 'Shu'," 155), Enno Giele translates "[bowed and] transmitted salutations," interpreting the phrase as a "mediated, transmitted salutation," i.e., a salutation that is first performed toward a representative, who then repeats it toward the addressee (*Imperial Decision-Making*, 89).

15. On these phrases, see Chung, "Study of the 'Shu'," 154–57; Giele, *Imperial Decision-Making*, 87–94.

16. See also Giele, *Imperial Decision-Making*, 136–37.

17. Tao Qian (365–427?), "Letter to Yan and his other sons" (Yu zi Yan deng shu), *Quan Jin wen* 111.7b–8a, trans. in Hightower, "Tao Qian."

18. Xie Wan, "Letter to Lang and his other sons," *Quan Jin wen* 83.4a.

19. Wang Xizhi, "Gao Li shi biao tie," *Quan Jin wen* 24.5a.

20. Rollins, *Letters of John Keats*, 1: 324.

21. Koskenniemi, *Studien*, 110–11.

22. Guillén, "Notes," 98.

23. Wang Xizhi, "Huran gai nian tie," no. 2, *Quan Jin wen* 24.10a.

24. Wang Yun (481–549), "Letter to the *vinaya*-master Shi Tanyuan" (Yu Yuan lüshi shu), *Quan Liang wen* 65.4a–b. Since the winter solstice, as the height of the *yin* forces, was an occasion to pay respects to family elders, the mourning (*aimu*) that Wang Yun expressed in this letter could refer to his deceased parents.

25. The phrase *yong guan san jun* 勇冠三軍 quotes Li Ling's (d. 74 BCE) "Further letter in reply to Su Wu [d. 60 BCE]" (Chong bao Su Wu shu), *Wen xuan* 41.1851; *Quan Han wen* 28.6b; trans. in Chung, "Study of the 'Shu'," 529–47.

26. The line alludes to the phrase *cai wei shi ying* 才為世英 in Su Wu's "Letter in reply to Li Ling" (Bao Li Ling shu), *Quan Han wen* 28.3a; trans. in Chung, "Study of the 'Shu'," 523–28. In the commentary in *Selections of Refined Literature*, the phrase in question appears as *cai wei shi sheng* 才為世生 (*Wen xuan* 25.1169, 43.1943).

27. Qiu Chi, "Letter to Chen Bozhi," *Wen xuan* 43.1943–49; *Quan Liang wen* 56.6b–7b; trans. in Zach, *Die chinesische Anthologie*, 797–800.

28. The correspondence is commonly regarded as an early medieval fabrication. See Whitaker, "Some Notes," and Chung, "Study of the 'Shu'," 316–65.

29. An allusion to the famous conversation about the joy of the fishes between the philosophers Zhuangzi and Huizi (ca. 4th century BCE) above the river Hao. *Zhuangzi* 17.47.

30. Xiao Gang, "Letter in reply to Xiao Yi 蕭繹" (Da Xiangdong wang shu), no. 2, *Quan Liang wen* 11.4b–5b; trans. in Marney, *Liang Chien-wen Ti*, 122–23. Marney erroneously dates this letter to 523. See also Wu Guangxing, *Xiao Gang Xiao Yi*, 168–70. On the term "mahāsattva" (*dashi*, lit., "great being"), here probably used as a synonym for "bodhisattva," see Soothill and Hodous, *A Dictionary of Chinese Buddhist Terms*, 87.

31. The image of the soaring eagle alludes to *Mao shi* 236 (時維鷹揚).

32. Cao Zhi, "Letter to Yang Xiu," *Quan Sanguo wen* 16.5b–6b; *Wen xuan* 42.1901–05; trans. in Holzman, "Literary Criticism," 116–19; Wong, *Early Chinese Literary Criticism*, 27–37; Richard M. W. Ho, "Cao Zhi."

33. 恃惠子之知我也, Cao Zhi, "Letter to Yang Xiu," *Quan Sanguo wen* 16.6b.

34. 恃鮑子之知我, *Wen xuan* 42.1904. See also *Shi ji* 70.2132 (生我者父母, 知我者鮑子也). "The one who understands me" (*zhi wo zhe*) also alludes to the *Book of Odes*, especially *Mao shi* 65.

35. The friendship between Zhuangzi and Huizi emerges throughout *Zhuangzi* but is a topic in *Zhuangzi* 24.69–70.

36. 竊備矇瞍誦詠而已, Yang Xiu, "Memorandum in reply to Cao Zhi," *Wen xuan* 40.20.

37. See the translation of this letter's epilogue in the "Limits of Writing and Language" section of chapter 4.

38. Müller, "Der Brief," 79–80.

39. *Mao shi* 156 (自我不見於今三年). It is intriguing to speculate whether this allusion could have been inspired by Ruan Yu's "Letter written on behalf of Cao Cao to Sun Quan" (*Wen xuan* 42.1887), which was written about seven years earlier and may have circulated within the Cao family.

40. Yang Yun in his famous "Letter in reply to Sun Huizong" has "with ears hot from wine, we looked up at the sky, goblets in our hands, singing" (酒後耳熱仰天撫缶而呼嗚嗚), *Wen xuan* 41.1871.

41. Cao Pi, "Further letter to Wu Zhi," no. 1, *Wen xuan* 42.1896–97.

42. This sentiment alludes in its first part to Qu Yuan's (ca. 340–ca. 278) "Encountering Sorrow" (Lisao) (老冉冉其將至兮, 恐脩名之不立朝) (*Chu ci* 1.1.20) and in its second part to *Lunyu* 17.1 (日月逝矣歲不我與).

43. Wu Zhi, "Memorandum in reply to Cao Pi," *Wen xuan* 40.1825.

44. Wang Xizhi, "Duo ri bu zhi wen tie" 多日不知問帖, *Quan Jin wen* 25.10b.

45. George Washington (1732–1799), in an oft-quoted letter of November 28, 1796, to his grandson George Washington Parke Custis, admonished him, declaring that "to acknowledge the receipt of letters is always proper, to remove doubts of their miscarriage."

46. Koskenniemi (*Studien*, 77) remarked on a similar phenomenon in ancient Greek letters.

47. Che Yong, "Letter in reply to Lu Yun" (Da Lu Shilong shu), *Quan Jin wen* 109.4a.

48. Lu Yun, "Letter in reply to Che Yong" (Da Che Mao'an shu), *Quan Jin wen* 103.5a–6a.

49. Wang Tian (4th century), "Letter" (Shu), *Quan Jin wen* 19.8a.

50. Wang Xizhi, "Chu yue tie" (aka "Xizhi lei shu tie"), *Quan Jin wen* 23.12b.

51. Cao Pi, "Letter in reply to Po Qin" (Da Po Qin shu), *Quan Sanguo wen* 7.3a–b.

52. Xu Ling, "Further letter on behalf of Xiao Yuanming to Pei Zhiheng," *Quan Chen wen* 9.2a–b.

53. Shi Huiyuan, "Letter in reply to Dai Kui" (Da Dai chushi shu), *Quan Jin wen* 161.1b. The phrase *bie shi*, translated here as "parting letter," could also refer to "another letter." For an analysis of compounds consisting of *bie* and a word denoting a letter, see Chen Jing "'Biezhi' kaoshi."

54. Fan Hongzhi (4th–5th century), "Letter to Wang Xun" (Yu Wang Xun shu), *Quan Jin wen* 125: 11b–12a. The letter to Yin Zhongkan (d. 399) was not transmitted.

55. Behr and Führer, "Einführende Notizen," 13–33.

56. Wang Dao (276–339), "Further letter to He Xun 賀循, in which he inquires after the emperor's announcement at the ancestral temple after ascending the throne" (You yu He Xun shu wen ji wei gao miao), no. 2, *Quan Jin wen* 19.5b.

57. Wang Xizhi, "Huran xiazhong tie" (aka "Xie Renzu tie"), *Quan Jin wen* 25.2b, 3b. Apart from his aptitude for calligraphy, not much is known about Yu Anji. See Cao and Cao, *Wang Xizhi shiqi tie*, 85. Xie An's elder

brother Xie Yi (d. 358) was the father-in-law of Wang Xizhi's second son Ningzhi (d. 399).

58. Che Yong, "Letter to Lu Yun" (Yu Lu Shilong shu), *Quan Jin wen* 109.3b–4a.

59. Wang Xizhi, "Zisong tie" 子嵩帖, *Quan Jin wen* 25.7b. I could not identify the son of Yu Ai (262–311).

60. Wang Xizhi, "Huran gai nian tie," no. 1, *Quan Jin wen* 23.10a.

61. Sima Daozi (364–403), "Letter to someone" (Yu ren shu), *Quan Jin wen* 17.7b–8a.

62. An allusion to *Mao shi* 204 (六月徂暑).

63. Wang Xizhi, "Chushu tie," *Quan Jin wen* 25.4b.

64. Wang Xun 王循, "Letter" (Shu), *Quan Jin wen* 143.9b.

65. Sima Rui, "Letter," *Quan Jin wen* 8.12a. Mid-autumn Festival (Zhongqiu) on the fifteenth day of the eighth month is an important occasion for getting together with family and friends.

66. The reference to the ninth month (when, lit., "[winter] clothes are distributed") alludes to *Mao shi* 154 (九月授衣).

67. Wang Ningzhi, "Letter" (Shu), *Quan Jin wen* 27.1b.

68. Du Yu (222–284), "Letter" (Shu), no. 1, *Quan Jin wen* 42.10a.

69. Wang Xizhi, "Da han tie," *Quan Jin wen* 23.12a. Great Cold, one of the twenty-four climatic periods (*jieqi*) of the solar year, starts on January 21 or 22 according to the Gregorian calendar.

70. On the *formula valetudinis* in ancient Greek and Roman letter writing, see Koskenniemi, *Studien*, 130–39.

71. See Richter and Chace, "Writing about Maladies and Moods" (unpublished manuscript).

72. John Muir (*Life and Letters*, 3) observed a similar phenomenon in Greek letter writing.

73. Wang Sui (fl. ca. 300), "Letter" (Shu), *Quan Jin wen* 21.12a.

74. Wang Xizhi, "Zuxia chai bu tie," *Quan Jin wen* 23.1a.

75. Wang Yi (276–322), "Letter" (Shu), no. 2, *Quan Jin wen* 20.11b.

76. Xi Yin (313–384), "Letter" (Tie), *Quan Jin wen* 109.12a.

77. Wang Xizhi, "Qishi tie," *Quan Jin wen* 25.11a–b.

78. Wang Xizhi, "Bu shen zunti tie," *Quan Jin wen* 23.6a.

79. Wang Xianzhi, "Letter" (Tie), *Quan Jin wen* 27.10a–b.

80. Mao Xi (516–587), "Further letter" (You shu), no. 2, *Quan Chen wen* 15.5b–6a.

81. Shi Sengzhao, "Letter in reply to Liu Chengzhi," *Quan Jin wen* 164.1a, trans. in Liebenthal, *Book of Chao*, 96.

82. This usage goes back to the late Han period, see Zhang Zhi's (d. 192) "Letter to the prefect" (Yu fujun shu), *Quan Hou Han wen* 64.4b (望遠懸想), trans. in Chung, "Study of the 'Shu'," 218. Other compounds include *xuangeng* 懸耿, *xuanyi* 懸悒, *xuannian* 懸念, *xuanzhi* 懸遲, *xuansong* 懸竦, *xuanyou* 懸憂, and *youxuan* 憂懸.

83. Wang Xizhi, "Zuxia ge ruchang tie," *Quan Jin wen* 26.2a.

84. Xi Yin, "Letter" (Tie), *Quan Jin wen* 109.12a.

85. Wang Xizhi, "Fu xiang an he tie," *Quan Jin wen* 24.11a.

86. Shen Jia, "Letter" (Shu), *Quan Jin wen* 143.9b.

87. Shi Huiyuan, "Letter to Sima Dezong [383–419, Emperor An of the Jin dynasty (r. 397–418)]" (Yu Jin Andi shu), *Quan Jin wen* 161.6b; trans. in Zürcher, *Buddhist Conquest*, 252.

88. Lu Yun, "Letter to Dai Jifu" (Yu Dai Jifu shu), no. 1, *Quan Jin wen* 103.1a.

89. Cao Pi, "Letter to Wu Zhi," *Wen xuan* 42.1895.

90. Wang Sengda (423–458), "Letter to Shen Pu" (Yu Shen Pu shu), *Quan Song wen* 19.12a.

91. While *xing shen xing shen* seems to have been a common formula in Han dynasty letters, it is rare in early medieval letters.

92. See the interpretation of the phrase in the letters found in Shuihudi by Yunmeng Shuihudi Qin mu bianxiezu, *Yunmeng Shuihudi Qin mu*, 25, as well as translations of the phrase by Burton Watson, "Cao Pi," 8, and by Erwin von Zach, *Die chinesische Anthologie*, 778, 797. Ying Shao's (ca. 140–ca. 204) *Comprehensive Meaning of Customs* (Fengsu tongyi) describes *wu yang* as a colloquial greeting exchanged conversationally and in letters. 無恙。俗說恙、病也。凡人相見, 及通書問, 皆曰無恙, *Fengsu tongyi* 11.20.152.

93. Koskenniemi, *Studien*, 130–32.

94. See the analysis of letters in the New Testament in Klauck, *Ancient Letters*, 33–36.

95. For an early mention of the friendship between the musician Bo Ya and Zhong Ziqi, who intuitively "understood his tone" (*zhi yin*), i.e., his music, see *Lüshi chunqiu* 14.2.71. Confucius is said to have refused minced meat because his disciple Zhong You (542–480 BCE) had been killed by being minced. See *Liji* 3.7.11; *Kongzi jiayu* 43.21.88.

96. An allusion to *Lunyu* 9.23 (後生可畏, 焉知來者之不如今也).

97. Cao Pi, "Further letter to Wu Zhi," no. 1, *Wen xuan* 42.1897–98.

98. See *Zhou yi* 66.83 and *Zuo zhuan* Xiang 8.7.240.

99. Sun Chu, "Letter on behalf of Shi Bao to Sun Hao" (*Wen xuan* 43.1931–39; *Quan Jin wen* 60.6a–7b; trans. in Zach, *Die chinesische Anthologie*, 789–94).

100. Dong Zhao (156–236), "Letter to Yuan Chunqing" (Yu Yuan Chunqing shu), *Quan Sanguo wen* 25.11a–b.

101. Shi Huiyuan, "Further letter to Kumārajīva" (Chong yu Jiumoluoshi shu), *Quan Jin wen* 161.2b–3a; trans. in Zürcher, *Buddhist Conquest*, 248.

102. Duke Huan of Qi (r. 685–643 BCE) was the first of the so-called Five Hegemons of the Warring States period.

103. *Zuo zhuan* Wen 18.7. 153–54.

104. This line alludes to the statement in *Lunyu* 14.17 that, owing to his adviser Guan Zhong, Duke Huan of Qi was able to assemble the feudal lords nine times (桓公九合諸侯, 不以兵車, 管仲之力也).

105. Ying Qu, "Memorandum recommending He Mo" (Jian He Lüze jian) (*Quan Sanguo wen* 30.1a–b). Other examples are Ying Qu's "Memorandum to Cao Cao, recommending Fei Lin" (Jian Fei Bowei jian) (*Quan Sanguo wen* 30.1b); Lu Ji's "Memorandum to Sima Lun, recommending Dai Yuan" (Yu Zhao wang Lun jian jian Dai Yuan) (*Quan Jin wen* 97.10a–b;

trans. in Mather, *Shih-shuo Hsin-yü*, 342–43); and Lu Yun's "Dispatch to the Grand Master of Ceremonies, recommending Zhang Zhan from his commandery" (Yishu Taichang jian tong jun Zhang Zhan) (*Jin shu* 54.1483–84, trans. in Wu Sujane, "The Biography of Lu Yun," 18–24).

106. Because Yang Hu appears to have had no sons (*Jin shu* 34.1024), Zhou Yiliang (*Wei Jin Nanbeichao shi*, 42) has suggested that the title of this letter, as it appears in *Yiwen leiju* 23.423 and then *Quan Jin wen* 41.7b, is corrupt and should read "Letter admonishing his nephews" (Jie xiong zi shu).

107. See Ma Yuan's "Letter admonishing his nephews Yan and Dun," *Quan Hou Han wen* 17.9a (吾欲汝曹聞人過失如聞父母之名耳, 可得聞而口不可得言也).

108. Yang Hu, "Letter admonishing his sons" (Jie zi shu), *Quan Jin wen* 41.7b.

109. *Wenxin diaolong zhu* 19.230.

110. Other strategies of intensifying reading are discussed in the "Letters as Substitutes for Face-to-Face Conversation" section of chapter 4.

111. On pre-Tang familial admonitory letters, see Richter, "Between Testament and Letter." See also Kroll, "Literary Criticism and Personal Character," 525–26, on admonitions in general and on Zheng Xuan's (127–200) "Letter admonishing his son Yi'en" (Jie zi Yi'en shu) in particular (*Quan Hou Han wen* 84.2b–3a; *Hou Han shu* 35.1209–10; *Yiwen leiju* 23.418; trans. in Chung, "Study of the 'Shu'," 503–10, 306–10).

112. *Lunyu* 7.11 (用之則行, 舍之則藏).

113. This could be an allusion to *Lunyu* 3.25.

114. *Zuo zhuan* Ai 1.6.434 (食不二味, 居不重席).

115. Wang Xizhi, "Further letter to Xie Wan" (You yi Xie Wan shu), *Quan Jin wen* 22.5b–6a. On the historical context, see *Shishuo xinyu jiaojian* 24.14.415–16, trans. in Mather, *Shih-shuo Hsin-yü*, 429–30.

116. 萬不能用, 果敗, *Jin shu* 80.2102–3.

117. Liu Chengzhi, "Letter to Shi Sengzhao," *Quan Jin wen* 142.5b–7a.

118. Ebrey, "T'ang Guides," 605. Andy Kirkpatrick ("Information Sequencing," 188) observed a similar arrangement in modern letters: "The letter[s] ranked the best or most polite . . . follow the schema: salutation—facework—reason—request." See also Kirkpatrick's follow-up article "The Arrangement of Letters."

119. When Shen Yue was twelve years old, his father, Shen Pu (416–453), was executed in connection with the turmoil following the assassination of Emperor Wen of the (Liu-)Song dynasty (420–79), i.e., Liu Yilong (407–453, r. 424–53).

120. The last phrase combines allusions to *Mao shi* 31 (死生契闊) and *Zhou yi* 3.5 (屯如邅如).

121. *Laozi* 44A.15 (知足不辱知止不殆).

122. I.e., Xiao Baojuan (483–501), last emperor, aka Marquis of Donghun (Donghun hou, r. 498–501), of the Qi dynasty (479–502).

123. I.e., Xu Xiaosi (453–499), director of the Department of State Affairs from 497 to 499.

124. If used as a unit of lenght, *fen* (part) refers to a tenth of a *cun* (inch). Since a change of "half a *fen*" (approximately 1.5 mm) is hardly detectable when grasping one's arm, we may assume that Shen Yue is speaking metaphorically.

125. Shen Yue, "Letter to Xu Mian" (Yu Xu Mian shu), *Quan Liang wen* 28.7b–8a. My translation largely follows Mather, *The Poet Shen Yüeh*, 132–34. For contextual information, see *Liang shu* 13.235–36.

126. See the dramatic description of the distress caused by the finiteness of every letter in Kafka's letter to Felice Bauer written on November 17, 1912 (Kafka, *Letters to Felice*, 46). See also Kafka, *Briefe an Felice*, 101.

127. This allusion to *Mao shi* 186 (毋金玉爾音而有遐心) is used in other letters as well.

128. *Zhou yi* 65.78.

129. *Mao shi* 196.

130. Zhao Zhi, "Letter to Xi Fan," *Wen xuan* 43.1942–43. The authorship of this letter is disputed. According to Li Shan's commentary on *Selections of Refined Literature* (*Wen xuan* 43.1940), Gan Bao (fl. 317–22) regarded the text as a letter written by Lü An (d. 263) to Xi Kang.

131. On the overlap between the roles of a friend with those of a teacher, see Vervoorn, "Friendship in Ancient China," 19.

132. Cynthia Chennault ("Representing the Uncommon," 198) described Wang Bao as "one of the Northern Zhou's most esteemed poets-in-captivity."

133. *Mao shi* 238 (金玉其相).

134. *Liji* 1.8.1 defines *jiyi* as a period of one hundred years.

135. The last two lines allude to an anecdote in *A New Account of Tales of the World* that tells of the close friendship between Sima Yu, Emperor Jianwen of the Jin dynasty, and the poet Xu Xun (fl. ca. 358). *Shishuo xinyu jiaojian* 8.144.128, trans. Mather, *Shih-shuo Hsin-yü*, 261–62.

136. Addressing his friend by his courtesy name (*zi*), the author associates their close relationship with that between Confucius and his favorite disciple, Yan Hui (521–481 BCE), whose courtesy name was also Ziyuan.

137. Zhou Hongrang, "Letter in reply to Wang Bao" (Da Wang Bao shu), *Quan Chen wen* 5.4b–5a. Emendation based on *Yiwen leiju* 30.536 and *Liuchao wenjie* 7.120–23.

138. Chung, "Study of the 'Shu,'" 204–5. In Xiao Yan's poem "In the Voice of Su Wu's Wife" (Dai Su Shuguo fu), the wild goose carries the letter in its beak. Lu, *Xian Qin Han Wei Jin Nanbeichao shi*, 1533–34. For earlier connotations of the image of the wild goose as a symbol of separation, see Shaughnessy, "Western Zhou History," 340.

139. Tsien, *Written on Bamboo and Silk*, 130.

140. This could be a loose allusion to *Mao shi* 9 (江之永矣、不可方思).

141. This line is an exact quotation from *Mao shi* 230. It had become widespread in letters, probably on account of Cao Pi's employment of the phrase in his famous "Letter to Wu Zhi" (*Wen xuan* 42.1896). See the translation in the "Lamenting Separation" section of chapter 4.

142. On the mythological Weak River (Ruo shui), see Knechtges, *Wen Xuan*, 2: 32.

143. This line alludes to the famous statement "Words are the means to get the idea where you want it; catch on to the idea and you forget about the words." 言者所以在意, 得意而忘言, *Zhuangzi* 26.79, trans. Graham, *Chuang-tzu*, 190.

144. Xiao Yi 蕭繹, "Letter to Liu Zhizang" (Yu Liu Zhizang shu), *Quan Liang wen* 17.5a–b.

145. See the description in *Shanhai jing* 12.58 and Suzanne Cahill's *Transcendence and Divine Passion*, 91–93.

146. *Baopuzi waipian jiaojian* 13.220.

147. See Ying Yang's "Letter in reply to Pang Huigong" (Bao Pang Huigong shu), *Quan Hou Han wen* 42.4b–5a, and Wang Lang's "Letter to Cao Pi" (Yu Wei taizi shu), *Quan Sanguo wen* 22.10b. For the medical properties of *xuancao*, see *Zhongyao dacidian*, no. 4900.

148. The phrase alludes to *Laozi* 72A.24 (聖人 . . . 自愛不自貴).

149. Wang Xizhi, "Bu de zhishou tie," *Quan Jin wen* 26.2b.

150. Wang Xianzhi, "Letter" (Tie), *Quan Jin wen* 27.7b.

151. Jiang Yan (444–505), "Letter in reply to Yuan Bing" (Bao Yuan Shuming shu), *Quan Liang wen* 38.6b–7a, trans. in Chang and Knechtges, "Jiang Yan: Letter in Response to Yuan Shuming."

152. Xu Jing (d. 222), "Letter to Cao Cao" (Yu Cao gong shu), *Quan Sanguo wen* 60.2a–3a.

153. Wang Rong 王融, "Letter on behalf of Xiao Ziliang to the recluse Liu Qiu," *Quan Qi wen* 12.9b–10b.

154. Sima Pi (341–365, Emperor Ai of the Jin dynasty [r. 361–65]), "Letter" (Shu), *Quan Jin wen* 11.2a.

155. Xiao Tong, "Letter in reply to Xiao Gang," *Quan Liang wen* 20.2a.

156. Wang Lang, "Letter to Xu Jing," no. 3, *Quan Sanguo wen* 22.12a–b.

157. Wang Xizhi, "Ge yi jiu tie," *Quan Jin wen* 23.8a.

158. Huan Xuan (369–404), "Letter to Wang Mi discussing whether monks need to revere the king" (Yu Wang Mi shu lun shamen ying zhi jing wang zhe), *Quan Jin wen* 119.5b.

159. Wang Xizhi, "Daochang tie," *Quan Jin wen* 22.8b.

160. Wang Qia (323–358), "Letter to Zhi Dun" (Yu Lin Fashi shu), *Quan Jin wen* 19.9a–b.

161. Wang Xianzhi, "Letter" (Tie), *Quan Jin wen* 27.6a.

162. Lu Yun, "Letter to Lu Dianshu," no. 1 (Yu Lu Dianshu shu), *Quan Jin wen* 103.3a–b.

163. Xiao Yi 蕭繹, "Letter by his own hand to Zhou Hongzheng" (Yu Zhou Hongzheng shou shu), *Quan Liang wen* 17.2a–b.

164. Xu Ling, "Further reply on behalf of Xiao Yuanming to Wang Sengbian," no. 2 (You wei Zhenyang hou da Wang taiwei shu), *Quan Chen wen* 8.9a.

165. Xiao Yan, "Letter to He Yin" (Yu He Yin shu), *Quan Liang wen* 6.1a–b.

166. Allusion to the correspondence between Yang Xiu, who was from Hongnong (near Huayin in modern-day Shaanxi), and Cao Zhi while he was stationed in Ye.

167. Alludes to the late Han letter writer Chen Zun from Henan.

168. Xiao Gang, "Letter to Xiao Ziyun," *Quan Liang wen* 11.2a. The wish to see a "Red Brilliance" poem (which is lexically and syntactically parallel to the letter sealed with "black clay") could be a seasonal reference, expressing the writer's wish to hear from Xiao Ziyun in the following summer. See the ritual hymn for summer of the same name in *Han shu* 22.1054–55. This letter's opening is translated in the "Lamenting Separation" section of chapter 4.

169. Xi Kang, "Letter to Shan Tao, severing their relationship," *Wen xuan* 43.1923–31.

170. Liu Ye (d. 234), "Letter to Lu Su" (Yi Lu Su shu), *Quan Sanguo wen* 27.1b.

171. Xiang Lang (186–247), "Words left to admonish his son" (Yi yan jie zi), *Quan Sanguo wen* 61.9a.

172. Ying Qu, "Letter to Cen Wenyu" (Yu Guangchuan zhang Cen Wenyu), *Wen xuan* 42.1916–18; *Quan Sanguo wen* 30.3b–4a. The phrasing alludes to *Lunyu* 3.8.

173. Wu Zhi, "Memorandum in reply to Cao Pi," *Wen xuan* 40.1827.

174. Huan Xuan, "Letter to Shi Huiyuan, in which he urges him to abandon monkhood" (Yu Shi Huiyuan shu quan ba dao), *Quan Jin wen* 119.4b–5a.

175. Bao Zhao, "Letter to his younger sister Bao Linghui about ascending the bank of Great Thunder Lake" (Deng Dalei an yu mei shu) (439), *Quan Song wen* 47.3a–4a; *Liuchao wenjie* 7.99–104; trans. in Su Jui-lung, "Bao Zhao."

176. Qiu Chi, "Letter to Chen Bozhi," *Wen xuan* 43.1943–49.

177. Liu Kun, "Letter in reply to Lu Chen," *Wen xuan* 25.1170.

178. An allusion to Qu Yuan's "Encountering Sorrow" (夕餐秋菊之落英, *Chu ci* 1.1.20).

179. Cao Pi, "Letter on the ninth to Zhong You," *Quan Sanguo wen* 7.3b–4a, emendation based on *Yiwen leiju* 4.84.

180. Cao Pi, "Further letter to Zhong You" (You yu Zhong You shu), *Quan Sanguo wen* 7.4b. For Cao Pi's fragmentarily transmitted "Rhapsody on a Jade Ring" (Yujue fu), see *Quan Sanguo wen* 4.6a.

181. Sima Yao (d. 396, Emperor Xiaowu of the Jin dynasty [r. 372–96]), "Letter to dharma-teacher Lang" (Yu Lang fashi shu), *Quan Jin wen* 11.10b–11a.

182. Wang Xizhi, "Da han tie," *Quan Jin wen* 23.12a.

183. Che Yong, "Letter in reply to Lu Yun," *Quan Jin wen* 109.4a.

184. Liu Chao (d. 328), "Letter" (Shu), *Quan Jin wen* 127.2a.

185. See Chao Yuen Ren's introductory article "Chinese Terms of Address" and Cao Xianghong's *Sociolinguistic Study.*

186. Ye Fan, *Shuxin guanyongyu cidian.* For Han dynasty letters, see Chung, "Study of the 'Shu'," 37–38, and Metelmann, "Schriftverkehr," 37–38.

187. The only pre-Tang text that deals with terms of address and self-designation in some detail, although not with particular regard to letter writing,

is the first part of chapter 6 of *Yanshi jiaxun* (*Yanshi jiaxun jijie* 6.69–99). See also Zhan, *Shishuo xinyu yufa*, 1–104, and Mather, "Translating Six Dynasties 'Colloquialisms'," 64–65.

188. See lines 59–60 in the translation of chapter 25 of *The Literary Mind* in chapter 2.

189. *Wo* (I, we) and *yu* 予 (I) usually appear only in literary allusions or quotations.

190. Although *mou* is common in official communication since the Han dynasty (Giele, *Imperial Decision-Making*, 130–35), it is rare in early medieval personal letters.

191. See *Song shu* 42.1308 on the instruction, issued between 454 and 456, to replace the self-designation *chen* by *xiaguan*.

192. *Shi ji* 6.236 and *Liji* 13.35.84.

193. See the famous repartee between Wang Rong 王戎 (234–305) and his wife about which personal pronouns to use between themselves. *Shishuo xinyu jiaojian* 35.6.492f., trans. in Mather, *Shih-shuo Hsin-yü*, 525.

194. Wang Yun, "Parting letter to Xiao Ye" (Yu Changsha wang bie shu), *Quan Liang wen* 65.2b–3a.

195. Wang Yun, "Letter to dharma-teacher Sheng from Dongyang" (Yu Dongyang Sheng fashi shu), *Quan Liang wen* 65.3a–b. I could not identify the addressee of this letter.

196. Neither *nü* (nosebleed) nor *beng* (landslide, demise of an emperor) need to be taken literally here.

197. Wang Yun, "Letter to Buddhist chief Yun" (Yu Yun sengzheng shu), *Quan Liang wen* 65.3b–4a.

198. Wang Xizhi, "Shiyi yue si ri tie," *Quan Jin wen* 24.8b.

199. Huan Qian (d. 410), "Letter in reply to Huan Xuan explaining why monks do not need to revere the king" (Da Huan Xuan shu ming shamen bu ying zhi jing wang zhe), *Quan Jin wen* 119.12a.

200. *Ling*, originally "(to issue) a command," had become an official title (director) in pre-imperial China, which is probably why it became an honorific. It could elevate not only persons but also objects related to the addressee, such as a letter. See Lu Yun's "Letter to Lu Dianshu," no. 10, *Quan Jin wen* 103.5a (每得令遠書).

201. There are five letters known that Cao Pi wrote to to Zhong You (*Quan Sanguo wen* 7.3b–5a) and three letters known that he wrote to Wu Zhi (*Quan Sanguo wen* 7.5a–6b).

202. Three of Zhong You's and four of Wu Zhi's letters to Cao Pi have been transmitted. See *Quan Sanguo wen* 24.8b and *Quan Sanguo wen* 30.8a–9b.

203. Cao Zhi, "Letter to Yang Xiu," *Quan Sanguo wen* 16.5b–6b.

204. Similar rules in Western letter writing are described in Meisner, *Archivalienkunde*, 177, 214–15; Goldberg, *Writing Matter*, 253; Chartier, *Correspondence*, 75–76.

205. Wang Xizhi, "Yimu tie," *Quan Jin wen* 26.6a, and "Heru tie" (*Quan Jin wen* 26.7a). See Liu Zhengcheng, *Zhongguo shufa quanji 18 & 19*, nos. 5, 14.

206. See Peng, "Chidu shufa," as well as the short explanations and illustrations in Bai, "Chinese Letters," 391–92, and Liu Heng, *Lidai chidu shufa*, 8. On *taitou* and various uses of leaving other blank spaces in Han dynasty manuscripts of mostly official communication, see Li and Liu, *Jiandu wenshu*, 101–6, 115–19.

CHAPTER 4. TOPOI

Epigraph: Melmoth, *Pliny*, I.XI, 38–39.

1. The best reference on literary topoi is still Ernst Robert Curtius, *European Literature and the Latin Middle Ages*, 79–105. Most studies of Western letter writing comment on epistolary topoi, e.g., Trapp, *Greek and Latin Letters*, 38–42; Klauck, *Ancient Letters*, 188–94.

2. Chartier, *Correspondence*, 19.

3. Friendship is a surprisingly understudied concept in Chinese studies. An excellent introduction is Aat Vervoorn's article "Friendship in Ancient China."

4. The friendships between Guan Zhong and Bao Shuya as well as Bo Ya and Zhong Ziqi are classical examples for the value of understanding or knowing (*zhi*) the other. See also Shields, "The Limits of Knowledge."

5. Jansen, "The Art of Severing Relationships," 348. For Confucius's discussion of beneficial and detrimental friendships, see *Lunyu* 16.4.

6. Vervoorn, "Friendship in Ancient China," 30.

7. *Quan Tang shi* 218.010, trans. by Eugene Eoyang, in Liu and Lo, *Sunflower Splendor*, 128.

8. 悲莫悲兮生別離, *Chu ci* 2.6.6, trans. in Hawkes, *Songs of the South*, 111.

9. P. Steven Sangren has suggested that "separations and reunions amount to a recurring cultural theme bordering upon obsession in China" ("Separations, Autonomy and Recognition," 53). See also Stafford, *Separation and Reunion in Modern China*.

10. Baron, *Always On*, 7. Writing about the changes brought about by the continuing virtual connectedness that is possible today, Naomi Baron also remarked that "if we are always together virtually, we may need to redefine the substance of meeting again face-to-face" (*Always On*, 8).

11. 聚散人理之常, Wang Xizhi, "Jia ye tie," *Quan Jin wen* 24.7a.

12. Violi, "Letters," 156.

13. Wang Yun, "Letter to dharma-teacher Sheng from Dongyang" (*Quan Liang wen* 65.3a); Wang Xizhi, "Ji xue ning han tie" (*Quan Jin wen* 22.6b); Ren Fang "Letter on behalf of Yu Gaozhi to the recluse Liu Qiu" (*Quan Liang wen* 43.9b).

14. Wang Lang, "Letter to Xu Jing," no. 3, *Quan Sanguo wen* 22.12a–b.

15. 一日不見如三月兮 . . . 如三秋兮. . . 如三歲兮, *Mao shi* 72. See also *Mao shi* 91 (一日不見。如三月兮). Although letters are not explicitly mentioned in the *Odes*, the women left behind or the men serving on the frontier who appear in these texts frequently express their hope for "good news" (*hao yin*, *Mao shi* 19, 30, 119, 149) and "messengers" (*shi*, *Mao shi* 167).

16. 數日不見。思子為勞, Cao Zhi, "Letter to Yang Xiu," *Quan Sanguo wen* 16.5b.

17. 遲面以日為歲, Wang Xizhi, "Wu qu ri jin tie," *Quan Jin wen* 22.12a. See also Wang's "Shu du tie" (aka "You mu tie"), *Quan Jin wen* 22.7a (遲此期, 真以日為歲).

18. 思君日積 . . . 一日當千載耳, Xie An, "Letter to Zhi Dun" (Yu Zhi Dun shu), *Quan Jin wen* 83.3b.

19. *Mao shi* 156 (零雨其濛).

20. *Mao shi* 253 (民亦勞止).

21. Xiao Gang, "Letter to Xiao Ziyun," *Quan Liang wen* 11.2a. Another example for a letter written immediately after the departure of the addressee would be Wang Xizhi's "Jia ye tie" (*Quan Jin wen* 24.7a).

22. Xiao Bing, "Letter in reply to his cousin Xiao Xiu" (Da congxiong Ancheng wang shu), *Quan Liang wen* 22.6a.

23. *Mao shi* 9 (江之永矣, 不可方思).

24. Xiao Gang, "Letter to Xiao Ziyun," *Quan Liang wen* 11.2a.

25. The phrase alludes to *Mao shi* 30 (願言則嚏 / 願言則懷) and 44 (願言思子).

26. On pellet chess (*danqi*), see Mather, *Shih-shuo Hsin-yü*, 390–91; on six sticks (*liubo*), see Andrew West's multipart study "The Lost Game of Liubo."

27. Both metaphors of death allude to early Han texts: *chang shi* to Sima Qian's "Letter in reply to Ren An" (*Wen xuan* 41.1855), *hua wei yiwu* to Jia Yi's (201–169 BCE) "Rhapsody on an Owl" (Funiao fu) (*Wen xuan* 13.607).

28. An exact quotation from *Mao shi* 230.

29. Cao Pi, "Letter to Wu Zhi," *Wen xuan* 42.1894–96; *Quan Sanguo wen* 7.5a–b; trans. in Zach, *Die chinesische Anthologie*, 778–79; Cutter, "Cao Zhi's Symposium Poems," 3–4; Watson, "Cao Pi," 8.

30. The quote can be traced back to a letter written by the thirty-year-old Liu Xiu (6 BCE–57 CE, Emperor Guangwu of the Eastern Han dynasty). *Dongguan Hanji* 23.16.170.

31. *Fayan* 2.5.

32. *Xinshu* 1.9.11. Both analogies refer to Cao Pi's father, Cao Cao.

33. An allusion to "Long Song Ballad" (Changge xing), *Wen xuan* 27.1279–80 (少壯不努力, 老大乃傷悲).

34. *Zhuangzi* 17.45 (年不可舉, 時不可止).

35. An allusion to the line "晝短苦夜長, 何不秉燭遊" in the fifteenth poem in "Nineteen Old Poems" (Gu shi shijiu shou) (*Wen xuan* 29.1349).

36. The term *cai shu* (to cut a piece of writing) first appears as referring to writing a letter with this text of Cao Pi and Wang Lang's roughly contemporary "Letter to Zhong You" (Yu Zhong You shu) (*Quan Sanguo wen* 22.12b). Further examples are Xi Zuochi's (d. ca. 384) "Letter to Shi Dao'an" (Yu Shi Daoan zhuan) (*Quan Jin wen* 134.3a), Wang Sengda's "Letter to Shen Pu" (*Quan Song wen* 19.12a), and Wang Sengru's "Letter to He Jiong" (*Quan Liang wen* 51.6a).

37. Cao Pi, "Further letter to Wu Zhi," no. 1, *Wen xuan* 42.1898.

38. To mention just one contemporaneous example, the twenty-four-year-old Cao Zhi explains his "Letter to Yang Xiu" (*Quan Sanguo wen* 16.6b) as the result of his maturity (lit., his "white head," *bai shou* 白首).

39. See line 64 in the translation of chapter 25 of *The Literary Mind* in chapter 2.

40. An allusion to Qu Yuan's "Encountering Sorrow" (夕餐秋菊之落英, *Chu ci* 1.1.20).

41. Literally, "when our ears will be smooth" (*er shun*), a quality that Confucius, in his famous autobiographical sketch in *Lunyu* 2.4, attributed to his sixtieth year.

42. Lu Yun, "Letter to Yang Yanming" (Yu Yang Yanming shu), no. 2, *Quan Jin wen* 103.2b.

43. Wang Xizhi, "Congmei jia ye tie," *Quan Jin wen* 25.5a.

44. Wang Xizhi, "Ci duan bu jian zuxia tie," *Quan Jin wen* 23.2a.

45. Xie Fa, "Letter" (Shu), *Quan Jin wen* 143.10b.

46. Ying Qu, "Letter to his cousins Junmiao and Junzhou" (Yu congdi Junmiao Junzhou shu), *Wen xuan* 42.1921; *Quan Sanguo wen* 30.3b.

47. Wang Xizhi, "Kuobie tie," *Quan Jin wen* 25.7b.

48. The phrase *pi xin fu* (to cut open heart and belly) quotes a famous Han dynasty communication, Zou Yang's (ca. 206–129 BCE) "Memorial of self-explanation written in prison" (Yuzhong shangshu ziming), *Quan Han wen* 19.10a; trans. in Chung, "Study of the 'Shu'," 451. Another famous letter writer used a variation of the phrase that became popular as well; see Ruan Yu's fragmentarily transmitted "Letter written on behalf of Cao Cao to Liu Bei" (Wei Cao gong yu Liu Bei shu), *Quan Hou Han wen* 93.4a (披懷解帶).

49. Xiao Yi 蕭繹, "Letter to Xiao Yi 蕭挹" (Yu Xiao Yi shu), *Quan Liang wen* 17.2.

50. See Kieschnick, *The Impact of Buddhism*, 222–49.

51. Lu Yun, "Letter to Lu Dianshu," no. 7, *Quan Jin wen* 103.4b.

52. Wang Xizhi, "Fu xiang qinghe tie," *Quan Jin wen* 26.1a.

53. Wang Xizhi, "Qun xiong tie," *Quan Jin wen* 26.4b.

54. Lu Yun "Letter" (Shu), *Quan Jin wen* 103.7a.

55. Xie Lingyun, "Letter in reply to the two dharma-teachers Gang and Lin" (Da Gang Lin er fashi shu), *Quan Song wen* 32.4b.

56. See also Liu Chengzhi's "Letter to Shi Sengzhao," quoted in chapter 3.

57. Franklin, *The Poems of Emily Dickinson*, no. 983.

58. See line 27 in the translation of chapter 25 of *The Literary Mind* in chapter 2.

59. 江南諺云。尺牘書疏千里面目也, *Yanshi jiaxun jijie* 19.507.

60. Koskenniemi, *Studien*, 38–42, 172–80; Klauck, *Ancient Letters*, 191–93.

61. 相見無期。惟是筆跡。可以當面, Cai Yong, "Letter" (Shu), *Quan Hou Han wen* 73.5b.

62. Wang Xizhi, "Letter to Xie Wan" (Yu Xie Wan shu), *Quan Jin wen* 22.5b.

63. He Chengtian, "Letter in reply to Zong Bing" (Da Zong jushi shu), no. 2, *Quan Song wen* 23.4a.

64. An allusion to Zhao Zhi's "Letter to Xi Fan," *Wen xuan* 43.1942 (去矣嵇生).

65. Wang Sengru, "Letter to He Jiong," *Quan Liang wen* 51.6a.

66. Cao Zhi, "Letter to Wu Zhi," *Wen xuan* 42.1906.

67. Du Yu, "Letter" (Shu), no. 2, *Quan Jin wen* 42.10a. The late Han scholar Ma Rong (79–166) in his "Letter to Dou Boxiang" (Yu Dou Boxiang shu) (*Quan Hou Han wen* 18.9a) used a similar phrase: "seeing your handwriting made me so happy, it was almost like being face-to-face with you" (見手跡。歡喜何量。次于面也). This wording is also found in *Yiwen leiju* and *Taiping yulan*, but in *Hou Han shu* (23.821 n. 1) the last part of the phrase appears as "it was like seeing you face-to-face" (見於面也).

68. Shi Sengzhao, "Letter in reply to Liu Chengzhi," *Quan Jin wen* 164.1a, trans. in Liebenthal, *Book of Chao*, 96.

69. The term *fu shi* describes various techniques that aim at "nourishing life" (*yang sheng*) by ingesting medicines, certain foods, or talismans. In Wang Xizhi's letters, it is usually interpreted as referring to the practice of taking cold-food powder (*hanshi san*), a composite drug popular during the medieval period that owes its name to the fact that one needed to eat cold food in order to balance the heating up of the body that was one of the drug's side effects. See Yu Jiaxi, "Han shi san kao"; Wang Yao, *Zhonggu wenren shenghuo*, 1–43; Wagner, "Lebensstil und Drogen"; and Satō, "Ō Gishi to goseki san."

70. The *tertium comparationis* in this sentence is ambiguous. Apart from his age group, as suggested in my translation, it could also be the past year: "But on the whole, compared with the past years, I am fairly well."

71. Wang Xizhi, "Ji xue ning han tie," *Quan Jin wen* 22.6b–7a.

72. 雖書疏往返。未足解其勞結, Cao Pi, "Further letter to Wu Zhi," no. 1, *Wen xuan* 42.1896. See the translation in chapter 3.

73. Suo Jing (239–303), "Letter" (Shu), *Quan Jin wen* 84.8a.

74. 相見亦不勝讀此書也, Wang Wei, "Letter to his cousin Wang Sengchuo" (Yu congdi Sengchuo shu), *Quan Song wen* 19.5a.

75. This was already pointed out by Demetrius, who in *On Style* modified Artemon's equation of letters with dialogues, writing that "the letter should be a little more formal than the dialogue, since the latter imitates improvised conversation, while the former is written and sent as a kind of gift." Klauck, *Ancient Letters*, 185. See also Guillén, "Notes," 78.

76. See the discussion of reasons to prefer cover letters instead of face-to-face meetings in Ditter, "Genre and the Transformation of Writing," 104–5.

77. *Ad Familiares* V.12 (Bailey, *Cicero*, 77). Many other letter writers have expressed this sentiment. Addressing his brother's wife, John Keats wrote, "If you were here, my dear Sister, I could not pronounce the words which I can write to you from a distance" (letter to George and Georgiana Keats, October 14, 1818) (Rollins, *Letters of John Keats*, 1: 392).

78. *Hou Han shu* 57.1839.

79. See also Chartier, *Correspondence*, 132–34.

80. See the "Proem" section of chapter 3.

81. See also Che Yong's "Letter in reply to Lu Yun," mentioned in chapter 3.

82. Yang Xiu, "Memorandum in reply to Cao Zhi," *Wen xuan* 40.1818.

83. Chen Lin, "Letter on behalf of Cao Hong to Cao Pi" (Wei Cao Hong yu Wei taizi shu), *Wen xuan* 41:1880; *Quan Hou Han wen* 92.4a.

84. Lu Yun, "Letter to Lu Dianshu," no. 1, *Quan Jin wen* 103.3a.

85. Liu Kun, "Letter in reply to Lu Chen," *Wen xuan* 25.1169.

86. Wang Xizhi, "Qu dong zai Dongmao tie," *Quan Jin wen* 23.8a.

87. Shi Daogao, "In reply to Li Miao who had questioned whether the Buddha does appear [on earth]" (Da Li Jiaozhou Miao nan Fo bu jian xing), *Quan Song wen* 63.12a.

88. Xiao Tong, "Letter in reply to Xiao Gang," *Quan Liang wen* 20.1b–2a. The last sentence alludes to a passage in Chen Lin's "Memorandum in reply to Cao Zhi" that describes the author's response to Cao Zhi's writing (載懽載笑。欲罷不能。謹韞櫝玩耽。以為吟頌, *Wen xuan* 40.1824), which again quotes *Lunyu* 9.11 (欲罷不能).

89. Cavallo and Chartier, *A History of Reading*, 2.

90. This treatment of writings as tangible material objects was not restricted to letters, as proved by, e.g., Pan Yue's (247–300) "Dirge for Yang Zhongwu" (Yang Zhongwu lei) (執玩周復。想見其人。紙勞于手。涕沾于巾, *Quan Jin wen* 92.8b). See the translation and analysis in Cutter, "Saying Goodbye," 126–27.

91. See also Lowry, "Personal Letters," 159.

92. See also Tian, *Beacon Fire*, 198–99, and, on the connotations of the word *wan* during the Ming dynasty, Clunas, *Superfluous Things*, 84–85.

93. *Zhou yi* 65.77.

94. 夜光之珠。何得專玩於隨掌, Liu Kun, "Letter in reply to Lu Chen," *Wen xuan* 25.1169.

95. See *Yanzi chunqiu* 5.23 (君子贈人以軒不如贈人以言) and *Xunzi* 5.19 (贈人以言重於金石珠玉).

96. We find the idea in ancient Greece as well. See Koskenniemi, *Studien*, 35.

97. Lu Jing, "Letter to his elder brother Lu Yan," no. 2, *Quan Sanguo wen* 70.1a–b.

98. Violi, "Letters," 160.

99. Gay, *The Naked Heart*, 318.

100. Egan, "Su Shih's 'Notes'," 587.

101. 書不盡言, 言不盡意, *Zhou yi* 65.80.

102. See *Guanzhui bian* 453–59, trans. in Egan, *Limited Views*, 297–303; James Liu, "The Paradox of Poetics," 49–70; Lynn, "Wang Bi."

103. Lu Chen, "Zeng Liu Kun bing shu," *Wen xuan* 25.1177.

104. Cao Zhi, "Letter to Yang Xiu," *Quan Sanguo wen* 16.6b.

105. Lu Yun, "Letter to Lu Dianshu," no. 6, *Quan Jin wen* 103.4b.

106. Wang Xizhi, "Yimin tie," *Quan Jin wen* 22.6b.

107. Wang Xizhi, "Zuxia ci ju tie," *Quan Jin wen* 24.1b.

108. Yuan Qiao (ca. 312–ca. 347), "Letter to Chu Bao, severing their relationship" (Yu Zuojun Chu Bao jiejiao shu), *Quan Jin wen* 56.2b.

109. Xiao Yi 蕭繹, "Further letter to Xiao Ji" (You yu Wuling wang Ji shu), *Quan Liang wen* 17.4b.

110. Shi Daogao, "Da Li Jiaozhou Miao nan Fo bu jian xing," *Quan Song wen* 63.12a.

111. Koskenniemi, *Studien*, 23–28; Guillén, "Notes," 76. The notion that a short letter is more difficult to accomplish than a long one has been expressed frequently. Among the more common quotes is the sixteenth letter in Blaise Pascal's (1623–1662) *Les Lettres Provinciales* (1656–57), in which he says that "the present letter is a very long one, simply because I had no leisure to make it shorter" (Stewart, *"Les Lettres Provinciales" de Blaise Pascal*, 210). In China, the famous Han dynasty calligrapher Zhang Zhi is credited with expressing a similar idea on the level of handwriting: "I am in a hurry and do not have the leisure to write in draft cursive script" (匆匆不暇草書). *Hou Han shu* 80.2144; *Jin shu* 36.1065.

112. Wang Xizhi, "Yimu tie," *Quan Jin wen* 26.6a.

113. Wang Shao, "Letter" (Shu), *Quan Jin wen* 19.10a.

114. Zhong You, "Letter" (Tie), *Quan Sanguo wen* 24.10a.

115. Mao Xi, "Letter to Shi Zhikai" (Yu Shi Zhikai shu), *Quan Chen wen* 15.5b.

116. Cao Zhi, "Letter to Wu Zhi," *Wen xuan* 42.1907.

117. Wang Xianzhi, "Letter" (Tie), *Quan Jin wen* 27.10a.

118. Wang Xizhi, "Jin fu zhui fu qi tie," *Quan Jin wen* 24.11b.

119. Xie An, "Letter to someone" (Yu mou shu), no. 1, *Quan Jin wen* 83.3b.

120. Wang Xianzhi, "Letter" (Tie), *Quan Jin wen* 27.8b.

121. Xu Ling, "Further letter on behalf of Xiao Yuanming to Wang Sengbian" (Wei Liang Zhenyang hou chong yu Wang Taiwei shu), *Quan Chen wen* 8.8b.

122. Lu Yun, "Letter to his elder brother Lu Ji," no. 27, *Quan Jin wen* 102.9a.

123. Wang Qia, "Letter" (Shu), no. 2, *Quan Jin wen* 19.9a.

124. Wang Hong (379–432), "Letter to Xie Lingyun asking about the meaning of his *Disquisition on Distinguishing What Is Essential*" (Yu Xie Lingyun shu wen *Bianzonglun* yi), *Quan Song wen* 18.7a.

125. Lu Yun, "Letter of condolence for Chen Yongzhang," no. 3 (Diao Chen Yongzhang shu), *Quan Jin wen* 103.6a.

126. Wei Zhangxian, "Further letter to an old friend" (Fu qinggu shu), *Quan Bei Qi wen* 4.14a.

127. Sima Cheng (264–322), "Letter in reply to Gan Zhuo" (Da Annan jiangjun Gan Zhuo shu), *Quan Jin wen* 15.5b.

128. 得之於手而應於心, 口不能言, *Zhuangzi* 13.37.

CHAPTER 5. NORMATIVITY AND AUTHENTICITY

Epigraph: Dickens, *David Copperfield*, 544.

1. While model letters go back as far as around 1800 BCE (Wente and Meltzer, *Letters from Ancient Egypt*, no. 78), an instructional text about letter writing dates from around 1100 BCE (Lichtheim, *Ancient Egyptian Literature*, 2:167–75). The oldest Greek letter-writing guide, *Epistolary Types*

(Typoi Epistolikoi) (2nd century BCE to 3rd century CE?), was penned in Egypt, too. It contains models for twenty-one types of letters and is also falsely attributed to Demetrius, the author of *On Style.* For the sake of differentiation, the author of *Epistolary Types* is usually called Pseudo-Demetrius. See Klauck, *Ancient Letters*, 194–205. On the history of letter-writing guides in Europe, see Nickisch's entry "Briefsteller" in *Historisches Wörterbuch der Rhetorik*, 2: 76–86; Nickisch, *Brief*, 76–92; Chartier, *Correspondence*; Poster and Mitchell, *Letter-Writing Manuals.*

2. See the ninety-page classified bibliography in Poster and Mitchell, *Letter-Writing Manuals.*

3. *Sui shu* 33.971, *Jiu Tang shu* 46.2008–9; *Xin Tang shu* 58.1490–93.

4. On the Dunhuang letter-writing guides, see Ebrey, "T'ang Guides"; Zhao Heping, *Dunhuang xieben shuyi yanjiu*; Zhou and Zhao, *Tang Wudai shuyi yanjiu*; Zhang Xiaoyan, *Dunhuang shuyi yuyan yanjiu.*

5. The best-known among them are Sima Guang's (1019–1086) *Mr. Sima's Letter-Writing Etiquette* (Sima shi shuyi) and Sun Di's (1081–1169) model-letter collection *Inner Letters* (Neijian chidu).

6. See Lowry, "Personal Letters"; Bai, "Chinese Letters," 390–94; and two partial translations of two popular Qing dynasty model-letter collections: von Zach's "Auszüge aus einem chinesischen Briefsteller," a translation of Xu Simei's early nineteenth-century *Letters from Autumn Floods Studio* (Qiushuixuan chidu) and Kádár's *Model Letters in Late Imperial China*, a translation of Gong Weizhai's (1738–1811) *Letters from Snow Swan Studio* (Xuehongxuan chidu).

7. Western guides of this kind are legion. A representative American example would be Thomas E. Hill's (1832–1915) once enormously popular *Hill's Manual of Social & Business Forms.*

8. Chartier, *Correspondence*, 5.

9. See Suo Jing's biography in *Jin shu* 60.1648–50.

10. See the chapter "Monthly Commands" (Yueling) in *Liji* (6.38–50) and the first sections of the twelve chapters in the "Ji" section in *Lüshi chunqiu* (1.1–12.62).

11. Similarly structured letter-writing manuals were also found among the Dunhuang manuscripts. Zhou and Zhao, *Tang Wudai shuyi yanjiu*, 3. A Tang dynasty letter-writing guide for each month, *Letters between Friends for the Twelve Months* (Shi'er yue pengyou xiang wen shu), is kept in the Palace Museum in Taipei.

12. Zhao Heping, *Dunhuang xieben shuyi yanjiu*, 9; Zhou and Zhao, *Tang Wudai shuyi yanjiu*, 105 n. 1; Liu Heng, *Lidai chidu shufa*, 4; Bai, "Chinese Letters," 389–90.

13. See also Qian Zhongshu's remarks on this use of *jun* in *Guanzhui bian* 1159–61.

14. *Dacu*, the third of the twelve notes of the chromatic scale (*shi'er lü*), is correlated with the first month of spring, i.e., the first month of the lunar year (*Lüshi chunqiu* 1.1.1; *Liji* 6.1.38). *Bu qi* (lit., "spreading *qi*") refers to the rise of atmospheric or climatic *yang qi* and is correlated with spring.

15. "Aplenty" (*biaobiao*) alludes to *Mao shi* 79.

16. The "four hoaries" (*si hao*) are famous recluses who escaped the turmoil of the Qin-Han transition by retreating to the mountains. *Shi ji* 55.2044–47.

17. The fifteenth day (*san wu*) and sixteenth day (*er ba*) of the month in the traditional lunar calendar represent the full moon.

18. The "bright pearl" (*ming zhu*) appears not only as an omen of good government (*Dongguan Hanji* 2.2.15) but also as a symbol of loyal subjects. See Liu Xiang's (79–8 BCE) "Sorrow and bitterness" (Youku) (*Chuci* 16.141–42). An alternative translation would thus be "a lofty meeting in the luster of loyal subjects."

19. The legendary birds *luan* and *huang* are also among the auspicious omina (*Dongguan Hanji* 2.2.15).

20. *Quan Jin wen* 84.8b.

21. *Yingzhong*, the last of the twelve notes of the chromatic scale, is correlated with the first month of winter, i.e., the tenth month of the lunar year. *Lüshi chunqiu* 10.1.47; *Liji* 6.97.47.

22. My translation of the last four lines is tentative; I am not sure what they refer to.

23. *Quan Jin wen* 84.9b–10a.

24. See the discussion of Wu Zhi's "Memorandum in reply to Cao Pi" in the "Proem" section of chapter 3.

25 *Quan Jin wen* 84.10a.

26. Jansen, "The Art of Severing Relationships," 361.

27. Ebrey, "T'ang Guides," 611–12.

28. See lines 9–10 in the translation of chapter 25 of *The Literary Mind* in chapter 2.

29. A piece that is similar in tone and explicitly mentions a death is Lu Yun's letter to Yang Yanming, "Yongyao is already buried and far away in the netherworld. Whenever I think of him, pain is cutting through my liver and heart. What can I do? What can I do? . . . " (永耀已葬。冥冥遠矣。存想其人。痛切肝懷。奈何奈何 . . .). "Letter to Yang Yanming," no. 7, *Quan Jin wen* 103.3a.

30. Yang Xin, "Letter" (Shu), *Quan Song wen* 22.1a.

31. In Choderlos de Laclos' (1741–1803) exceptional epistolary novel *Les Liaisons dangereuses* (1782), the vicomte de Valmont explains that this, like any other aesthetic effect, can be produced intentionally, remarking, "I took great pains with my letter and attempted to reproduce in it that disorder which alone can portray feeling" (150).

32. Thraede, *Grundzüge*, 1–3.

33. Constable, *Letters and Letter Collections*, 11–12.

34. 別人以為他這回是赤條條的上場了罷, 他其實還是穿著肉色緊身小衫褲, 甚至於用了平常决不應用的奶罩, Lu Xun, "Preface to Kong Lingjing's *Letters of Contemporary Poets*," in *Lu Xun quanji* 6, 409.

35. Samuel Johnson, letter to Mrs. Thrale, October 27, 1777 (Chapman, *The Letters of Samuel Johnson*, no. 559).

36. See lines 59–60 in the translation of chapter 25 of *The Literary Mind* in chapter 2.

CONCLUSION

1. On this issue, see Baron, *Always On*, 198–99.

2. Peter Steiner in the caption of his now most famous *New Yorker* cartoon, published as early as 1993, summarized this new situation as "On the Internet, nobody knows you're a dog."

3. To mention just one article that voices ethical concerns about this development, see the media critic Roger Silverstone's "Complicity and Collusion in the Mediation of Everyday Life."

4. From W. H. Auden's 1950 poem "Their Lonely Betters," in Mendelson, *Auden*, 583.

BIBLIOGRAPHY

Altman, Janet Gurkin. *Epistolarity: Approaches to a Form*. Columbus: Ohio State University Press, 1982.

Aristotle. *On Poetics*. Translated by Seth Benardete and Michael Davis. South Bend, IN: St. Augustine's Press, 2002.

Bagnall, Roger S., and Raffaella Cribiore, eds. *Women's Letters from Ancient Egypt, 300 BC–AD 800*. Ann Arbor: University of Michigan Press, 2006.

Bai Qianshen. "Chinese Letters: Private Words Made Public." In *The Embodied Image: Chinese Calligraphy from the John B. Elliott Collection*, edited by Robert E. Harrist and Wen C. Fong, 380–99. Princeton: The Art Museum, Princeton University, 1999.

Bailey, David Roy Shakleton. *Cicero: Epistulae ad Familiares*. Cambridge: Cambridge University Press, 1977.

Baopuzi waipian jiaojian 抱樸子外篇校箋. Compiled by Ge Hong 葛洪 (283–343), commentary by Yang Mingzhao 楊明照. Beijing: Zhonghua shuju, 1996.

Baron, Naomi S. *Always On: Language in an Online and Mobile World*. London: Oxford University Press, 2008.

Bauer, Wolfgang. *Das Antlitz Chinas: Autobiographische Selbstdarstellungen in der chinesischen Literatur von ihren Anfängen bis heute*. Munich: Hanser, 1990.

Beebee, Thomas O. *Epistolary Fiction in Europe: 1500–1850*. Cambridge: Cambridge University Press, 1999.

Behr, Wolfgang. "Language Change in Premodern China: Notes on Its Perception and Impact on the Idea of a 'Constant Way'." In *Historical Truth, Historical Criticism, and Ideology: Chinese Historiography and Historical Culture from a New Comparative Perspective*, edited by Helwig Schmidt-Glintzer, Achim Mittag, and Jörn Rüsen, 13–51. Leiden: Brill, 2005.

Behr, Wolfgang, and Bernhard Führer. "Einführende Notizen zum Lesen in China mit besonderer Berücksichtigung der Frühzeit." In *Aspekte des Lesens in China in Vergangenheit und Gegenwart: Referate der Jahrestagung 2001 der Deutschen Vereinigung für Chinastudien (DVCS)*, edited by Bernhard Führer, 1–42. Bochum, Germany: Projekt, 2005.

Belke, Horst. *Literarische Gebrauchsformen*. Düsseldorf, Germany: Bertelsmann, 1973.

Benjamin, Walter, ed. *Deutsche Menschen: Eine Folge von Briefen*. Frankfurt, Germany: Suhrkamp, 1962. Originally published under the pseudonym Detlef Holz by Vita Nova, 1936.

Birch, Cyril, ed. *Anthology of Chinese Literature*. New York: Grove, 1965.

Bloom, Allan, trans. *"The Republic" of Plato*. New York: Basic Books, 1991.

Branner, David, and Li Feng, ed. *Writing and Literacy in Early China: Studies from the Columbia Early China Seminar*. Seattle: University of Washington Press, 2011.

Brook, Timothy. "Communications and Commerce." In *The Cambridge History of China*. Vol. 13, *The Ming Dynasty, Part 2*, edited by Denis Twitchett and Frederick W. Mote, 579–707. Cambridge: Cambridge University Press, 1998.

———. *The Confusions of Pleasure: Commerce and Culture in Ming China*. Berkeley: University of California Press, 1998.

Brown, John L. "Whatever Happened to Mme de Sévigné? Reflections on the Fate of the Epistolary Art in a Media Age." *World Literature Today* 64.2 (1990): 215–20.

Bürgel, Peter. *Literarische Kleinprosa: Eine Einführung*. Tübingen, Germany: Narr, 1983.

Cahill, Suzanne E. *Transcendence and Divine Passion: The Queen Mother of the West in Medieval China*. Stanford: Stanford University Press, 1993.

Camargo, Martin. *Ars dictaminis, ars dictandi*. Typologie des sources du moyen âge occidental 60. Turnhout, Belgium: Brepols, 1991.

Campbell, Duncan. "The Epistolary World of a Reluctant 17th Century Magistrate: Yuan Hongdao in Suzhou." *New Zealand Journal of Asian Studies* 4.1 (2002): 159–93.

Cao Damin 曹大民 and Cao Zhizhan 曹之瞻. *Wang Xizhi shiqi tie jiexi* 王羲之十七帖解析. Shanghai: Shanghai guji chubanshe, 2005.

Cao Xianghong 曹湘洪. *A Sociolinguistic Study of Addressing, Openings and Closings in Contemporary Personal Letters*. Beijing: Kexue chubanshe, 2008.

Cavallo, Guglielmo, and Roger Chartier, eds. *A History of Reading in the West*. Translated by Lydia G. Cochrane. Amherst: University of Massachusetts Press, 1999.

Chang Ch'ung-ho and Hans H. Frankel, trans. *Two Chinese Treatises on Calligraphy*. New Haven: Yale University Press, 1995.

Chang, Taiping, and David R. Knechtges, trans. "Jiang Yan: Letter in Response to Yuan Shuming." *Renditions* 41–42 (1994): 25–31.

Chao Yuen Ren. "Chinese Terms of Address." *Languange* 32.1 (1956): 217–44.

Chapa, Juan. *Letters of Condolence in Greek Papyri*. Papyrologica Florentina 29. Florence, Italy: Edizioni Gonnelli, 1998.

Chapman, R. W., ed. *The Letters of Samuel Johnson with Mrs. Thrale's Genuine Letters to Him*. Oxford: Clarendon, 1952.

Chartier, Roger, Alain Boureau, and Cécile Dauphin, eds. *Correspondence: Models of Letter-Writing from the Middle Ages to the Nineteenth Century*. Translated by Christopher Woodall. Princeton: Princeton University Press, 1997.

Chen Jing 陳靜. "'Biezhi' kaoshi" 別紙考釋. *Dunhuangxue jikan* 敦煌學輯刊 35.1 (1999): 105–14.

Chen Lanlan 陳蘭蘭. "Handai jiandu zhong de siwenshu fazhan tezheng yanjiu" 漢代簡牘中的私文書發展特徵研究. *Sichuan wenwu* 四川文物 4 (2005): 57–63.

Chen Pan 陳槃. *Han Jin yijian shi xiao qi zhong* 漢晉遺簡識小七種. Shanghai: Guji chubanshe, 2009.

Chen Wuyun 陳五雲, ed. *Shuxin daquan* 書信大全. Shanghai: Jiaoyu chubanshe, 1991.

Cheng Daode 程道德 and Fang Jixiao 方繼孝. *Zizi zhenzang: Mingren xinzha de shouzang yu jianshang* 字字珍藏: 名人信札的收藏與鑑賞. Beijing: Beijing tushuguan chubanshe, 2004.

Cheng Ying-wan. *Postal Communication in China and Its Modernization, 1860–1896*. Harvard East Asian Monographs 34. Cambridge, MA: Harvard University Press, 1970.

Chennault, Cynthia L. "Representing the Uncommon: Temple-Visit Lyrics from the Liang to Song Dynasties." In *Interpretation and Literature in Early Medieval China*, edited by Alan K. L. Chan and Yuet-keung Lo, 189–222. SUNY Series in Chinese Philosophy and Culture. Albany: State University of New York Press, 2010.

Chu ci 楚辭. See Lau and Ching, *A Concordance to the "Chuci."*

Chu Hui-liang 朱惠良. "Songdai ceye zhong de chidu shufa" 宋代冊頁中的尺牘書法. In *Songdai shuhua ceye mingpin tezhan* 宋代書畫冊頁名品特展, edited by Guoli Gugong bowuyuan bianji weiyuanhui 國立故宮博物院編輯委員會, 10–20. Taipei: Guoli Gugong bowuyuan, 1995.

Chung, Eva Yuen-wah. "A Study of the 'Shu' (Letters) of the Han Dynasty (206 B.C.–A.D. 220)." PhD diss., University of Washington, 1982.

Cimeddorji, Jaqa. *Die Briefe des K'ang-Hsi-Kaisers aus den Jahren 1696–97 an den Kronprinzen Yin-ch'eng aus mandschurischen Geheimdokumenten: Ein Beitrag zum ersten Dsungarenkrieg der Ch'ing 1690–1697.* Asiatische Forschungen 113. Wiesbaden, Germany: Harrassowitz, 1991.

Clunas, Craig. *Superfluous Things: Material Culture and Social Status in Early Modern China.* Cambridge: Polity Press, 1991.

Constable, Giles. *Letters and Letter Collections.* Typologie des sources du moyen âge occidental 17. Turnhout, Belgium: Brepols, 1976.

Crystal, David. *Txtng: The Gr8 Db8.* Oxford: Oxford University Press, 2002.

Cui Xuelu 崔學路. *Chidu baifa* 尺牘白法. Beijing: Zhongguo shudian, 2008.

Curtius, Ernst Robert. *European Literature and the Latin Middle Ages.* Translated by Willard R. Trask. Princeton: Princeton University Press, 1990.

Cutter, Robert Joe. "Cao Zhi's Symposium Poems." *Chinese Literature: Essays, Articles, Reviews* 6 (1984): 1–32.

———. "Personal Crisis and Communication in the Life of Cao Zhi." In *Rhetoric and the Discourses of Power in Court Culture: China, Europe and Japan*, edited by David R. Knechtges and Eugene Vance, 149–68. Seattle: University of Washington Press, 2005.

———. "Saying Goodbye: The Transformation of the Dirge in Early Medieval China." *Early Medieval China* 10–11 (2004): 67–130.

———. "To the Manner Born? Nature and Nurture in Early Medieval Chinese Literary Thought." In *Culture and Power in the Reconstitution of the Chinese Realm, 200–600*, edited by Scott Pearce, Audrey G. Spiro, and Patricia Buckley Ebrey, 53–71. Cambridge, MA: Harvard University Press, 2001.

Davis, A. R. "The Double Ninth Festival in Chinese Poetry: A Study of Variations upon a Theme." In *Wen-lin: Studies in the Chinese Humanities*, edited by Chow Tse-tsung, 45–64. Madison: University of Wisconsin Press, 1968.

Day, Robert Adams. *Told in Letters: Epistolary Fiction before Richardson.* Ann Arbor: University of Michigan Press, 1966.

Derrida, Jacques. *The Post Card: From Sokrates to Freud and Beyond.* Translated by Alan Bass. Chicago: University of Chicago Press, 1987.

Dickens, Charles. *David Copperfield.* New York: Bantam, 1981.

Dien, Albert E. "A Sixth Century Father's Advice on Literature: Comments on Chapter Nine of *Yanshi jiaxun*." *Asia Major* 13.1 (2000): 67–82.

———. "The Stirrup and Its Effect on Chinese Military History." *Ars Orientalis* 16 (1986): 33–56.

Dietz, Siglinde. *Die buddhistische Briefliteratur Indiens: Nach dem tibetischen Tanjur.* Asiatische Forschungen 84. Wiesbaden, Germany: Harrassowitz, 1984.

Ditter, Alexei Kamran. "Genre and the Transformation of Writing in Tang Dynasty China (618–907)." PhD diss., Princeton University, 2009.

Dongguan Hanji 東觀漢記. See Lau and Ching, *A Concordance to the "Dongguan Hanji."*

Dubrow, Heather. *Genre.* The Critical Idiom 42. London: Methuen, 1982.

Durrant, Stephen W. "Self as the Intersection of Traditions: The Autobiographical Writings of Ssu-ma Ch'ien." *Journal of the American Oriental Society* 106.1 (1986): 33–40.

Ebrey, Patricia. "T'ang Guides to Verbal Etiquette." *Harvard Journal of Asiatic Studies* 45.2 (1985): 581–613.

Edwards, E. D. "A Classified Guide to the Thirteen Classes of Chinese Prose." *Bulletin of the School of Oriental and African Studies* 12.3–4 (1948): 770–88.

Egan, Ronald C. *Limited Views: Essays on Ideas and Letters by Qian Zhongshu.* Cambridge, MA: Harvard University Press, 1998.

———. "Su Shih's 'Notes' as a Historical and Literary Source." *Harvard Journal of Asiatic Studies* 50.2 (1990): 561–88.

Eriksen, Thomas H. *Tyranny of the Moment: Fast and Slow Time in the Information Age.* London: Pluto, 2001.

Evans, Trevor V. "Orality, Greek Literacy, and Early Ptolemaic Papyri." In *Oral Performance and Its Context*, edited by C. J. Mackie, 195–208. Orality and Literacy in Ancient Greece 5. Leiden: Brill, 2004.

Fang, Achilles. "Rhymeprose on Literature: The *Wen-fu* of Lu Chi (A.D. 261–303)." *Harvard Journal of Asiatic Studies* 14 (1951): 527–66.

Fayan 法言. See Lau and Ching, *A Concordance to the "Fayan, Taixuanjing."*

Fengsu tongyi 風俗通義. See Lau and Ching, *A Concordance to the "Fengsu tongyi."*

Findeisen, Raoul David. "From Literature to Love: Glory and Decline of the Love-Letter Genre." In *The Literary Field in Twentieth-Century China*, edited by Michael Hockx, 79–112. London: Curzon, 1999.

Forster, E. M. *Goldsworthy Lowes Dickinson.* London: E. Arnold, 1962.

Franke, Herbert, and Denis Twitchett. *The Cambridge History of China.* Vol. 6, *Alien Regimes and Border States, 907–1368.* Cambridge: Cambridge University Press, 1994.

Frankel, Hans H., trans. "Ma Yuan: Letter to His Nephews Ma Yan and Ma Dun." *Renditions* 41–42 (1994): 4–6.

Franklin, R. W., ed. *The Poems of Emily Dickinson: Variorum Edition.* Cambridge, MA: Belknap Press of Harvard University Press, 1998.

Fu Gang 傅剛. "'Wen gui qingsheng' shuo de shidai yiyi: Lüe tan Lu Yun 'Yu xiong Pingyuan shu'" "文貴清省"說的時代意義: 略談陸雲〈與兄平原書〉. *Wenyi lilun yanjiu* 文藝理論研究 2 (1984): 93–99.

Fuehrer, Bernhard. "The Court Scribe's *Eikon Psyches*: A Note on Sima Qian and His Letter to Ren An." *Asian and African Studies* 6.2 (1997): 170–83.

Gansu sheng wenwu kaogu yanjiusuo 甘肅省文物考古研究所. "Gansu Dunhuang Handai Xuanquan zhi yizhi fajue jianbao" 甘肅敦煌漢代懸泉置遺址發掘簡報. *Wenwu* 文物 528.5 (2000): 4–20.

Gay, Peter. *The Naked Heart: The Bourgeois Experience, Victoria to Freud.* London: Norton, 1995.

Genette, Gérard. *Paratexts: Thresholds of Interpretation.* Cambridge: Cambridge University Press, 1997.

Giele, Enno. *Imperial Decision-Making and Communication in Early China: A Study of Cai Yong's* Duduan. Opera Sinologica 20. Wiesbaden, Germany: Harrassowitz, 2006.

Goitein, Friedrich. *Letters of Medieval Jewish Traders.* Princeton: Princeton University Press, 1973.

Goldberg, Jonathan. *Writing Matter: From the Hands of the English Renaissance.* Stanford: Stanford University Press, 1990.

Goodman, Bryna. "'Words of Blood and Tears': Petty Urbanites Write Emotion." *Nan Nü* 9 (2007): 270–301.

Graham, A. C., trans. *Chuang-tzu: The Seven Inner Chapters and Other Writings from the Book Chuang-tzu.* London: Allen & Unwin, 1981.

———. *Yin-Yang and the Nature of Correlative Thinking.* IEAP Occasional Paper and Monograph Series 6. Singapore: Institute of East Asian Philosophies, 1986.

Grünbart, Michael. *Formen der Anrede im byzantinischen Brief vom 6. bis zum 12. Jahrhundert.* Wiener Byzantinische Studien 25. Vienna: Österreichische Akademie der Wissenschaften, 2005.

Gu Yin Hai 顧音海. *Ming Qing chidu* 明清尺牘. Taipei: Dujia chubanshe, 1995.

Guillén, Claudio. 1986. "Notes towards the Study of the Renaissance Letter." In *Renaissance Genres: Essays on Theory, History, and Interpretation.* Edited by Barbara Kiefer Lewalski. Cambridge, MA: Harvard University Press, 70–101.

Guwenci leizuan 古文辭類纂. Compiled by Yao Nai 姚鼐 (1732–1815). Shanghai: Shanghai guji chubanshe, 1998.

Han shu 漢書. Compiled by Ban Gu 班固 (32–92). Beijing: Zhonghua shuju, 1962.

Han Wei Liuchao baisan mingjia ji 漢魏六朝百三名家集. Compiled by Zhang Pu 張溥 (1602–1641). Nanjing: Jiangsu guji chubanshe, 2002.

"Hand Scroll Copy of Ancient Chinese Calligrapher Sold for 308 Mln Yuan." 2010. http://arts.cultural-china.com/en/63Arts10054.html (accessed June 2, 2012)

Hanfeizi 韓非子. See Zhou Zhongling et al., *Hanfeizi suoyin.*

Hanna, Martha. *Your Death Would Be Mine: Paul and Marie Pireaud in the Great War.* Cambridge, MA: Harvard University Press, 2006.

Harrist, Robert E. "Copies, All the Way Down: Notes on the Early Transmission of Calligraphy by Wang Xizhi." *East Asian Library Journal* 10 (2001): 176–96.

———. "A Letter from Wang Hsi-chih and the Culture of Chinese Calligraphy." In *The Embodied Image: Chinese Calligraphy from the John B. Elliott Collection*, edited by Robert E. Harrist and Wen C. Fong, 240–59. Princeton: The Art Museum, Princeton University, 1999.

———. "Reading Chinese Calligraphy." In *The Embodied Image: Chinese Calligraphy from the John B. Elliott Collection*, edited by Robert E. Harrist and Wen C. Fong, 3–27. Princeton: The Art Museum, Princeton University, 1999.

———. "Replication and Deception in Calligraphy of the Six Dynasties Period." In *Chinese Aesthetics: The Ordering of Literature, the Arts, and the Universe in the Six Dynasties*, edited by Cai Zong-qi, 31–59. Honolulu: University of Hawai'i Press, 2004.

Harrist, Robert E., and Wen C. Fong, eds. *The Embodied Image: Chinese Calligraphy from the John B. Elliott Collection.* Princeton: The Art Museum, Princeton University, 1999.

Hawkes, David, trans. *Ch'u Tz'u: The Songs of the South.* Harmondsworth, Middlesex: Penguin, 1985.

Hay, John. "The Human Body as a Microcosmic Source of Macrocosmic Values in Calligraphy." In *Theories of the Arts in China*, edited by Susan Bush and Christian Murck, 74–102. Princeton: Princeton University Press, 1983.

Halliwell, Stephen. *Aristotle's "Poetics."* Chapel Hill: University of North Carolina Press, 1986.

Hightower, James R. "Some Characteristics of Parallel Prose." In *Studies in Chinese Literature*, edited by John L. Bishop, 108–39. Cambridge, MA: Harvard University Press, 1965.

———. "The *Wen Hsüan* and Genre Theory." *Harvard Journal of Asiatic Studies* 20 (1957): 512–33.

———, trans. "Tao Qian: Letter to His Sons." *Renditions* 41–42 (1994): 16–17.

Hill, Thomas E. *Hill's Manual of Social & Business Forms: A Guide to Correct Writing.* Chicago: Moses Warren & Co., 1875.

Ho, Richard M. W., trans. "Cao Zhi: Letter to Yang Dezu." *Renditions* 41–42 (1994): 12–14.

Holzman, Donald. "Confucius and Ancient Chinese Literary Criticism." In *Chinese Approaches to Literature from Confucius to Liang Ch'i-ch'ao*, edited by Adele Rickett, 21–41. Princeton: Princeton University Press, 1978.

———. "Literary Criticism in China in the Early Third Century A.D." *Asiatische Studien / Études Asiatiques* (1974) 28.2: 113–49.

———. "Liu Hsieh, *The Literary Mind and the Carving of Dragons.*" *Artibus Asiae* 23 (1960): 136–39.

———. *Poetry and Politics: The Life and Works of Juan Chi (A.D. 210–263)*. Cambridge: Cambridge University Press, 1976.

Hou Han shu 後漢書. Compiled by Fan Ye 范曄 (398–446). Beijing: Zhonghua shuju, 1965.

Hu Chuanhai 胡傳海. *Chidu shi jiang* 尺牘十講. Shanghai: Shuhua chubanshe, 2003.

Hu Pingsheng 胡平生 and Zhang Defang 張德芳. *Dunhuang Xuanquan Han jian shicui* 敦煌懸泉漢簡釋粹. Shanghai: Shanghai guji chubanshe, 2001.

Huainanzi 淮南子. See Lau and Ching, *A Concordance to the "Huainanzi."*

Hucker, Charles O. *A Dictionary of Official Titles in Imperial China*. Stanford: Stanford University Press, 1985.

Hughes, E. R. *The Art of Letters: Lu Chi's "Wen Fu," A.D. 302, a Translation and Comparative Study*. Princeton: Princeton University Press, 1951.

Institut für Textkritik, ed. "BRIEFkasten: Bibliographie zur Briefforschung." 2005. http://www.textkritik.de/briefkasten/bkprojekt.htm (accessed June 2, 2012).

Jansen, Thomas. "The Art of Severing Relationships (*juejiao*) in Early Medieval China." *Journal of the American Oriental Society* 126.3 (2006): 347–65.

———. *Höfische Öffentlichkeit im frühmittelalterlichen China: Debatten im Salon des Prinzen Xiao Ziliang*. Freiburg, Germany: Rombach, 2000.

Jin shu 晉書. Compiled by Fang Xuanling 房玄齡 (578–648). Beijing: Zhonghua shuju, 1974.

Jiu Tang shu 舊唐書. Compiled by Liu Xu 劉煦 (887–946). Beijing: Zhonghua shuju, 1975.

Kádár, Dániel Z. *Historical Chinese Letter Writing*. London: Continuum, 2010.

———, trans. *Model Letters in Late Imperial China: 60 Selected Epistles from "Letters from Snow Swan Retreat."* Munich: Lincom, 2009.

Kafka, Franz. *Briefe an Felice and andere Korrespondenz aus der*

Verlobungszeit. Edited by Erich Heller and Jürgen Born. Frankfurt, Germany: Fischer, 1976.

———. *Briefe an Milena*. Edited by Willy Haas. Frankfurt, Germany: Fischer, 1965.

———. *Letters to Felice*. Translated by James Stern and Elisabeth Duckworth. New York: Schocken, 1973.

———. *Letters to Milena*. Translated by Philip Boehm. New York: Schocken, 1990.

Kauffman, Linda S. *Special Delivery: Epistolary Modes in Modern Fiction*. Women in Culture and Society. Chicago: University of Chicago Press, 1992.

Kern, Martin. "'Persuasion' or 'Treatise'? The Prose Genres *Shui* and *Shuo* 說 in the Light of the *Guwenci leizuan* of 1779." In *Ad Seres et Tungusos: Festschrift für Martin Gimm zu seinem 65. Geburtstag am 25. Mai 1995*, edited by Lutz Bieg, Erling von Mende, and Martina Siebert, 221–43. Wiesbaden, Germany: Harrassowitz, 2000.

Kieschnick, John. *The Impact of Buddhism on Chinese Material Culture*. Princeton: Princeton University Press, 2003.

Kirkpatrick, Andy. "The Arrangement of Letters: Hierarchy or Culture? From Cicero to China." *Journal of Asian Pacific Communication* 17.2 (2007): 245–58.

———. "Information Sequencing in Mandarin Letters of Request." *Anthropological Linguistics* 33.2 (1991): 183–203.

Klauck, Hans J. *Ancient Letters and the New Testament: A Guide to Context and Exegesis*. Waco, TX: Baylor University Press, 2006.

Knechtges, David R. "'Key Words,' Authorial Intent, and Interpretation: Sima Qian's Letter to Ren An." *Chinese Literature: Essays, Articles, Reviews* 30 (2008): 75–84.

———. "The Liu Hsin/Yang Hsiung Correspondence on the *Fang Yen*." *Monumenta Serica* 33 (1977/78): 309–25.

———. "Liu Kun, Lu Chen, and Their Writings in the Transition to the Eastern Jin." *Chinese Literature: Essays, Articles, Reviews* 28 (2006): 1–66.

———, trans. *Wen Xuan or Selections of Refined Literature*. 3 vols. Princeton: Princeton University Press, 1982, 1987, 1996.

Kongcongzi 孔叢子 See Lau and Ching, *A Concordance to the "Kongcongzi," "Dengxizi," "Yinwenzi," "Gongsun Longzi."*

Kongzi jiayu 孔子家語. See Lau and Ching, *A Concordance to the "Kongzi jiayu."*

Koskenniemi, Heikki. *Studien zur Idee und Phraseologie des griechischen Briefes bis 400 n.Chr.* Annales Academiae Scientiarum Fenniciae B 102.2. Helsinki: Suomalainen Tiedeakatemia, 1956.

Kroll, Paul W. "Literary Criticism and Personal Character in Poetry, ca. 100–300 CE." In *China's Early Empires*, edited by Michael Nylan and Michael Loewe, 517–33. Cambridge: Cambridge University Press, 2010.

Laclos, Choderlos de. *Dangerous Liaisons*. Translated by P. W. K. Stone. London: Penguin, 2009.

Laozi 老子. See Lau and Ching, *A Concordance to the "Laozi."*

Lau, D. C., and Chen Fong Ching, eds. *A Concordance to the "Chuci."* Hong Kong: Commercial Press, 2000.

———, eds. *A Concordance to the "Dongguan Hanji."* Hong Kong: Commercial Press, 1994.

———, eds. *A Concordance to the "Fayan, Taixuanjing."* Hong Kong: Commercial Press, 1995.

———, eds. *A Concordance to the "Fengsu tongyi."* Hong Kong: Commercial Press, 1996.

———, eds. *A Concordance to the "Huainanzi."* Hong Kong: Commercial Press, 1992.

———, eds. *A Concordance to the "Jia Yi Xinshu."* Hong Kong: Commercial Press, 1994.

———, eds. *A Concordance to the "Kongcongzi, Dengxizi, Yinwenzi, Gongsun Longzi."* Hong Kong: Commercial Press, 1998.

———, eds. *A Concordance to the "Kongzi jiayu."* Hong Kong: Commercial Press, 1992.

———, eds. *A Concordance to the "Laozi."* Hong Kong: Commercial Press, 1996.

———, eds. *A Concordance to the "Liji."* Hong Kong: Commercial Press, 1992.

———, eds. *A Concordance to the "Liutao, Yuzi."* Hong Kong: Commercial Press, 1997.

———, eds. *A Concordance to the "Lunyu."* Hong Kong: Commercial Press, 1995.

———, eds. *A Concordance to the "Lüshi chunqiu."* Hong Kong: Commercial Press, 1994.

———, eds. *A Concordance to the "Maoshi."* Hong Kong: Commercial Press, 1995.

———, eds. *A Concordance to the "Mengzi."* Hong Kong: Commercial Press, 1995.

———, eds. *A Concordance to the "Shangshu."* Hong Kong: Commercial Press, 1995.

———, eds. *Concordances to the "Shanhai jing," "Mutianzi zhuan," "Yandan zi."* Hong Kong: Commercial Press, 1994.

———, eds. *A Concordance to the "Xunzi."* Hong Kong: Commercial Press, 1996.

———, eds. *A Concordance to the "Yanzi chunqiu."* Hong Kong: Commercial Press, 1993.

———, eds. *A Concordance to the "Zhouyi."* Hong Kong: Commercial Press, 1995.

———, eds. *A Concordance to the "Zhuangzi."* Hong Kong: Commercial Press, 2000.

———, eds. *A Concordance to the "Zuo zhuan."* Hong Kong: Commercial Press, 1995.

Le Faye, Deirdre, ed. *Jane Austen's Letters*. London: The Folio Society, 2003.

Ledderose, Lothar. *Mi Fu and the Classical Tradition in Chinese Calligraphy*. Princeton: Princeton University Press, 1979.

Li Junming 李均明 and Liu Jun 劉軍. *Jiandu wenshu xue* 簡牘文書學. Nanning: Guangxi jiaoyu chubanshe, 1999.

Liang shu 梁書. Compiled by Yao Cha 姚察 (533–606) and Yao Silian 姚思廉 (d. 637). Beijing: Zhonghua shuju, 1973.

Lichtheim, Miriam. *Ancient Egyptian Literature: A Book of Readings*. Volume 2, *The New Kingdom*. Berkeley: University of California Press, 1976.

Liebenthal, Walter, trans. *The Book of Chao*. Monumenta Serica Monograph 13. Peking: The Catholic University Press, 1948.

Liji 禮記. See Lau and Ching, *A Concordance to the "Liji."*

Lin, Pauline. "Rediscovering Ying Qu and His Poetic Relationship to Tao Qian." *Harvard Journal of Asiatic Studies* 69.1 (2009): 37–74.

Liu Guangsheng 劉廣生 and Zhao Meizhuang 趙梅莊. *Zhongguo gudai youyi shi: Xiuding ban* 中國古代郵驛史: 修訂版. Beijing: Renmin youdian chubanshe, 1999.

Liu Heng 劉恒. *Lidai chidu shufa* 歷代尺牘書法. Beijing: Zhishi chubanshe, 1992.

Liu Shipei 劉師培. *Zhongguo zhonggu wenxue shi jiangyi* 中國中古文學史講義. Shanghai: Shanghai guji chubanshe, 2000.

Liu tao 六韜. See Lau and Ching, *A Concordance to the "Liutao, Yuzi."*

Liu Tao 劉濤 and Wang Su 王素, eds. *Changsha Dongpailou Dong Han jiandu shufa yishu* 長沙東牌樓東漢簡牘書法藝術. Beijing: Wenwu chubanshe, 2010.

Liu Wu-chi and Irving Yucheng Lo, eds. *Sunflower Splendor: Three Thousand Years of Chinese Poetry*. Bloomington: Indiana University Press, 1975.

Liu Yeqiu 劉葉秋. "Lüetan gudai shuxin de geshi" 略談古代書信的格式. *Wenshi zhishi* 文史知識 43.1 (1985): 117–22.

Liu Zhengcheng 劉正成, ed. *Zhongguo shufa quanji 18 & 19: Sanguo Liang Jin Nanbeichao Wang Xizhi Wang Xianzhi juan* 中國書法全集: 三國兩晉南北朝王羲之王獻之卷. Beijing: Rongbaozhai chubanshe, 1991.

———, ed. *Zhongguo shufa quanji 20: Wei Jin Nanchao ming jia juan* 中國書法全集: 魏晉南朝名家卷. Beijing: Rongbaozhai chubanshe, 1996.

Liu, James J. Y. "The Paradox of Poetics and the Poetics of Paradox." In *The Vitality of the Lyric Voice: Shih Poetry from the Late Han to the T'ang*, edited by Lin Shuen-fu and Stephen Owen, 49–70. Princeton: Princeton University Press, 1986.

Liuchao wenjie jianzhu 六朝文絜箋注 (1888). Compiled by Xu Lian 許槤, commentary by Li Jinggao 黎經誥. Shanghai: Shanghai guji chubanshe, 1982.

Lowry, Kathryn. "Personal Letters in Seventeenth-Century Epistolary Guides." In *Under Confucian Eyes: Writings on Gender in Chinese History*, edited by Susan Mann and Yu-yin Cheng, 154–67. Berkeley: University of California Press, 2001.

Lu Qinli 逯欽立, ed. *Xian Qin Han Wei Jin Nanbeichao shi* 先秦漢魏晉南北朝詩. Beijing: Zhonghua shuju, 1983.

Lu Xun quanji 魯迅全集. Beijing: Renmin wenxue chubanshe, 1973.

Lunheng jiaoshi 論衡校釋. Compiled by Wang Chong 王充 (27–ca. 100), commentary by Huang Hui 黃暉. Beijing: Zhonghua shuju, 1990.

Lunyu 論語. See Lau and Ching, *A Concordance to the "Lunyu."*

Luo Zhenyu 羅振玉. "Jiandu yiwen kaoshi: Liusha zhuijian 3" 簡牘遺文考釋: 流沙墜簡三. In *Liusha zhuijian* 流沙墜簡, edited by Luo Zhenyu 羅振玉 and Wang Guowei 王國維, 215–47, 65–74. Beijing: Zhonghua shuju, 1993.

Lüshi chunqiu 呂氏春秋. See Lau and Ching, *A Concordance to the "Lüshi chunqiu."*

Lynn, Richard John. "Wang Bi and Liu Xie's *Wenxin diaolong*." In *A Chinese Literary Mind: Culture, Creativity, and Rhetoric in "Wenxin diaolong,"* edited by Cai Zong-qi, 83–98. Stanford: Stanford University Press, 2001.

MacLean, Gerald. "Re-siting the Subject." In *Epistolary Histories: Letters, Fiction, Culture*, edited by Amanda Gilroy and W. M. Verhoeven, 176–97. Charlottesville: University Press of Virginia, 2000.

Malherbe, A. J. *Ancient Epistolary Theorists*. Atlanta, GA: Scholars Press, 1988.

Malmqvist, Göran, trans. "Letters between Qin Jian and His Wife Xu Shu." *Renditions* 41–42 (1994): 1–3.

Mao shi 毛詩. See Lau and Ching, *A Concordance to the "Maoshi."*

Marney, John. *Liang Chien-wen Ti*. Boston: Twayne, 1976.

Mather, Richard B. *The Poet Shen Yüeh (441–513): The Reticent Marquis*. Princeton: Princeton University Press, 1988.

———, trans. *Shih-shuo Hsin-yü: A New Account of Tales of the World*. Michigan Monographs in Chinese Studies 95. Ann Arbor: Center for Chinese Studies, University of Michigan, 2002.

———. "Translating Six Dynasties 'Colloquialisms' into English: The *Shih-shuo hsin-yü*." In *Translating Chinese Literature*, edited by Eugene Eoyang and Lin Yao-fu, 57–66. Bloomington: Indiana University Press, 1995.

McClatchy, J. D., ed. *The Whole Difference: Selected Writings of Hugo von Hofmannsthal*. Princeton: Princeton University Press, 2008.

McDougall, Bonnie S. *Love-Letters and Privacy in Modern China: The Intimate Lives of Lu Xun and Xu Guangping*. Studies on Contemporary China. Oxford: Oxford University Press, 2002.

McNair, Amy. "Engraved Calligraphy in China: Recension and Reception." *The Art Bulletin* 77.1 (1995): 106–14.

———. "The Engraved Model-Letters Compendia of the Song Dynasty." *Journal of the American Oriental Society* 114.2 (1994): 209–25.

Meisner, Heinrich Otto. *Archivalienkunde vom 16. Jahrhundert bis 1918*. Göttingen, Germany: Vandenhoeck & Ruprecht, 1969.

Melmoth, William, trans. *Pliny: Letters*. London: Heinemann, 1915.

Mendelson, Edward, ed. *W. H. Auden: Collected Poems*. New York: Vintage, 1991.

Mengzi 孟子. See Lau and Ching, *A Concordance to the "Mengzi."*

Metelmann, Carsten. "Schriftverkehr der Han-Zeit." PhD diss., Universität Hamburg, 2001.

Minford, John, and Joseph S. M. Lau, eds. *Classical Chinese Literature: An Anthology of Translations*. Vol. 1, *From Antiquity to the Tang Dynasty*. New York: Columbia University Press, 2000.

Mittleman, Leslie B. "The Twentieth-Century English Letter: A Dying Art?" *World Literature Today* 64.2 (1990): 221–26.

Miyasaka Yūsho 宮坂宥勝, ed. *Kōbō Daishi Kūkai zenshū* 弘法大師空海全集. 8 vols. Tokyo: Chikuma Shobō, 1983–85.

Morino Shigeo 森野繁夫 and Satō Toshiyuki 佐藤利行. *Ō Gishi zen shokan* 王羲之全書翰. Tokyo: Hakuteisha, 1996.

Muir, John. *Life and Letters in the Ancient Greek World*. London: Routledge, 2009.

Müller, Wolfgang G. "Der Brief." In *Prosakunst ohne Erzählen: Die Gattungen der nicht-fiktionalen Kunstprosa*, edited by Klaus Weissenberger, 67–87. Tübingen, Germany: Niemeyer, 1985.

———. "Der Brief als Spiegel der Seele: Zur Geschichte eines Topos der Epistolartheorie von der Antike bis Samuel Richardson." *Antike und Abendland* 26 (1980): 138–57.

Nan Qi shu 南齊書. Compiled by Xiao Zixian 蕭子顯 (489–537). Beijing: Zhonghua shuju, 1972.

Needham, Joseph, Wang Ling, and Lu Gwei-djen, eds. *Science and Civilisation in China*. Vol. 4, part 3, *Physics and Physical Technology: Civil Engineering and Nautics*. Cambridge: Cambridge University Press, 1971.

Ng, Daisy Sheung-yuen. "Li Ang's Experiments with the Epistolary Form." *Modern Chinese Literature* 3.1–2 (1987): 91–106.

Nickisch, Reinhard M. G. *Brief*. Sammlung Metzler 260. Stuttgart, Germany: Metzler, 1991.

———. "Der Brief und andere Textsorten im Grenzbereich der Literatur." In *Grundzüge der Literaturwissenschaft*, edited by Heinz-Ludwig Arnold and Heinrich Detering, 357–64. Munich: dtv, 1996.

Nishibayashi Shōichi 西林昭一 and Chen Songchang 陳松長, eds. *Xin Zhongguo chutu shuji* 新中國出土書蹟. Beijing: Wenwu chubanshe, 2009.

Nylan, Michael. "Calligraphy, the Sacred Text and Test of Culture." In *Character and Context in Chinese Calligraphy*, edited by Cary Y. Liu, Dora C. Y. Ching, and Judith G. Smith, 16–77. Princeton: The Art Museum, Princeton University, 1999.

Oppenheim, A. Leo. *Letters from Mesopotamia: Official, Business, and Private Letters on Clay Tablets from Two Millennia*. Chicago: The University of Chicago Press, 1967.

Owen, Stephen, trans. *An Anthology of Chinese Literature: Beginnings to 1911*. New York: Norton, 1996.

———. *Readings in Chinese Literary Thought*. Cambridge, MA: Harvard University Press, 1992.

Pattinson, David John. "The *Chidu* in Late Ming and Early Qing China." PhD diss., Australian National University, 1997.

———. "Privacy and Letter Writing in Han and Six Dynasties." In *Chinese Concepts of Privacy*, edited by Bonnie S. McDougall and Anders Hansson, 97–118. Leiden: Brill, 2002.

Peng Lizhi 彭礪志. "Chidu shufa suojian pingque xingzhi yanjiu" 尺牘書法所見平闕形制研究. In *Quanguo di liu jie shu xue taolun hui lunwen ji* 中國第六屆書學討論會論文集, edited by Zhongguo shuxie xueshu weiyuanhui 中國書協學術委員會, 95–112. Zhengzhou: Henan meishu chubanshe, 2004.

Pollard, David. "*Ch'i* in Chinese Literary Theory." In *Chinese Approaches to Literature from Confucius to Liang Ch'i-ch'ao*, edited by Adele Rickett, 43–66. Princeton: Princeton University Press, 1978.

Poster, Carol, and Linda C. Mitchell, eds. *Letter-Writing Manuals and Instruction from Antiquity to the Present: Historical and Bibliographic Studies*. Columbia: University of South Carolina Press, 2007.

Pregadio, Fabrizio, ed. 2008. *The Encyclopedia of Taoism*. 2 vols. London: Routledge.

Puett, Michael. "The Temptations of Sagehood, or: The Rise and Decline of Sagely Writing in Early China." In *Books in Numbers: Conference Papers in Celebration of the Seventy-Fifth Anniversary of the Harvard-Yenching Library*, edited by Wilt L. Idema, 23–47. Hong Kong: University of Hong Kong Press, 2007.

Pulleyblank, Edwin G. *Lexicon of Reconstructed Pronunciation in Early Middle Chinese, Late Middle Chinese, and Early Mandarin*. Vancouver: University of British Columbia Press, 1991.

Qi Xiaochun 祁小春. *Mai shi zhi feng: You guan Wang Xizhi ziliao yu renwu de zonghe yanjiu* 邁世之風: 有關王羲之資料與人物的綜合研究. Taipei: Shitou chuban, 2007.

Qian Nanxiu. *Spirit and Self in Medieval China: The "Shih-shuo hsin-yü" and Its Legacy*. Honolulu: University of Hawai'i Press, 2001.

Qian Zhongshu 錢鍾書. *Guanzhui bian* 管錐編. Beijing: Zhonghua shuju, 1986.

Quan Chen wen 全陳文. In *Quan shanggu Sandai Qin Han Sanguo Liuchao wen* 全上古三代秦漢三國六朝文, compiled by Yan Kejun 嚴可均 (1762–1843). Beijing: Zhonghua shuju, 1958.

Quan Hou Han wen 全後漢文. In *Quan shanggu Sandai Qin Han Sanguo Liuchao wen*.

Quan Hou Zhou wen 全後周文. In *Quan shanggu Sandai Qin Han Sanguo Liuchao wen*.

Quan Han wen 全漢文. In *Quan shanggu Sandai Qin Han Sanguo Liuchao wen*.

Quan Jin wen 全晉文. In *Quan shanggu Sandai Qin Han Sanguo Liuchao wen*.

Quan Liang wen 全梁文. In *Quan shanggu Sandai Qin Han Sanguo Liuchao wen*.

Quan Qi wen 全齊文. In *Quan shanggu Sandai Qin Han Sanguo Liuchao wen*.

Quan Sanguo wen 全三國文. In *Quan shanggu Sandai Qin Han Sanguo Liuchao wen*.

Quan Song wen 全宋文. In *Quan shanggu Sandai Qin Han Sanguo Liuchao wen*.

Rawski, Evelyn Sakakida. *Education and Popular Literacy in Ch'ing China*. Ann Arbor: University of Michigan Press, 1979.

Richter, Antje. "Between Testament and Letter: Letters of Familial Admonition in Han and Six Dynasties China." In *Handbook of Chinese Epistolary Literature and Culture*, edited by Antje Richter. Leiden: Brill, forthcoming.

———. "Beyond Calligraphy: Reading Wang Xizhi's Letters." *T'oung Pao* 96 (2011): 370–407.

———. "Empty Dreams and Other Omissions: Liu Xie's *Wenxin diaolong* Preface." *Asia Major* 25.1 (2012): 83–110.

———. "Letters and Letter Writing in Early Medieval China." *Early Medieval China* 12 (2006): 1–29.

———. "Notions of Epistolarity in Liu Xie's *Wenxin diaolong*." *Journal of the American Oriental Society* 127.2 (2007): 143–60.

———. "Table of Non-official Letters from Early Medieval China." 2004–11. http://spot.colorado.edu/~richtea/table.pdf (accessed June 2, 2012).

Richter, Antje, and Charles Chace. "Writing about Maladies and Moods: Reading Wang Xizhi's Letters as Medical Narratives." Unpublished manuscript.

Rollins, Hyder Edward, ed. *The Letters of John Keats, 1814–1821*. 2 vols. Cambridge, MA: Harvard University Press, 1958.

Rosenmeyer, Patricia A. *Ancient Epistolary Fictions: The Letter in Greek Literature*. Cambridge: Cambridge University Press, 2001.

———, trans. *Ancient Greek Literary Letters: Selections in Translation*. London: Routledge, 2006.

Sangren, P. Steven. "Separations, Autonomy and Recognition in the Production of Gender Differences: Reflections from Considerations of Myths and Laments." In *Living with Separation in China: Anthropological Accounts*, edited by Charles Stafford, 53–84. London: RoutledgeCurzon, 2003.

Sanguo zhi 三國志. Compiled by Chen Shou 陳壽 (233–97), commentary by Pei Songzhi 裴松之 (372–451). Beijing: Zhonghua shuju, 1959.

Satō Toshiyuki 佐藤利行. "Ō Gishi to goseki san" 王羲之と五石散. *The Hiroshima University Studies, Graduate School of Letters* 65 (2005): 1–13.

———. *Riku Un kenkyū* 陸雲研究. Tokyo: Hakuteisha, 1990.

Schaberg, David. *A Patterned Past: Form and Thought in Early Chinese Historiography*. Cambridge, MA: Harvard University Press, 2001.

Schafer, Edward H. "The *Yeh Chung Chi*." *T'oung Pao* 76 (1990): 147–207.

Schmidt-Glintzer, Helwig. *Das "Hung-ming chi" und die Aufnahme des Buddhismus in China*. Münchener Ostasiatische Studien 12. Wiesbaden, Germany: Steiner, 1976.

Schnider, Franz, and Werner Stenger. *Studien zum neutestamentlichen Briefformular.* New Testament Tools and Studies 11. Leiden: Brill, 1987.

Schuessler, Axel. *ABC Etymological Dictionary of Old Chinese.* Honolulu: University of Hawai'i Press, 2007.

Shangshu 尚書. See Lau and Ching, *A Concordance to the "Shangshu."*

Shanhai jing 山海經. See Lau and Ching, *Concordances to the "Shanhai jing," "Mutianzi zhuan," "Yandan zi."*

Shaughnessy, Edward L. "Military Histories of Early China." *Early China* 21 (1996): 159–82.

———. "Western Zhou History." In *The Cambridge History of Ancient China: From the Origins of Civilization to 221 B.C.*, edited by Michael Loewe and Edward L. Shaughnessy, 292–351. Cambridge: Cambridge University Press, 1999.

Shi ji 史記. Compiled by Sima Qian 司馬遷 (?145–?86 BCE). Beijing: Zhonghua shuju, 1959.

Shields, Anna M. "The Limits of Knowledge: Three Han Yu Letters to Friends, 799–802." *T'ang Studies* 22 (2004): 41–80.

Shih, Vincent Yu-chung, trans. *The Literary Mind and the Carving of Dragons: A Study of Thought and Pattern in Chinese Literature.* Hong Kong: Chinese University Press, 1983.

Shisanjing zhushu 十三經注疏. Compiled by Ruan Yuan 阮元 (1764–1849). Beijing: Zhonghua shuju, 1980.

Shishuo xinyu jiaojian 世說新語校箋. Compiled by Liu Yiqing 劉義慶 (403–44), commentary by Xu Zhen'e 徐震堮. Beijing: Zhonghua shuju, 1984.

Shuihudi Qin mu zhujian zhengli xiaozu 睡虎地秦墓竹簡整理小組, ed. *Shuihudi Qin mu zhujian* 睡虎地秦墓竹簡. Beijing: Wenwu chubanshe, 1990.

Shuowen jiezi 說文解字. See *Shuowen jiezi zhu.*

Shuowen jiezi zhu 說文解字注. Compiled by Xu Shen 許慎 (ca. 55–ca. 149), commentary by Duan Yucai 段玉裁 (1735–1815). Shanghai: Guji chubanshe, 1981.

Silverstein, Adam J. *Postal Systems in the Pre-modern Islamic World.* Cambridge: Cambridge University Press, 2007.

Silverstone, Roger. "Complicity and Collusion in the Mediation of Everyday Life." *New Literary History* 33.4 (2002): 761–80.

Sivin, Nathan. *Traditional Medicine in Contemporary China: A Partial Translation of "Revised Outline of Chinese Medicine" (1972) with an Introductory Study on Change in Present-Day and Early Medicine.* Ann Arbor: Centre for Chinese Studies, University of Michigan, 1987.

Song shu 宋書. Compiled by Shen Yue 沈約 (441–513). Beijing: Zhonghua shuju, 1974.

Soothill, William Edward, and Lewis Hodous, eds. *A Dictionary of Chinese Buddhist Terms*. London: Kegan Paul, 1937.

Stafford, Charles. *Separation and Reunion in Modern China*. Cambridge: Cambridge University Press, 2000.

Steinhausen, Georg. *Geschichte des deutschen Briefes: Zur Kulturgeschichte des deutschen Volkes*. Berlin: Gaertner, 1889–91; reprint, Dublin: Weidmann 1968.

Stewart, H. D., ed. *"Les Lettres Provinciales" de Blaise Pascale*. Manchester: Manchester University Press, 1920.

Su Jui-lung, trans. "Bao Zhao: Letter to My Younger Sister upon Ascending the Bank of Thunder Lake." *Renditions* 41–42 (1994): 18–25.

Sui shu 隋書. Compiled by Wei Zheng 魏徵 (580–643). Beijing: Zhonghua shuju, 1973.

Sun Zhiping 孫志平. "Yi you chuan qing de minjian tongxin" 以郵傳情的民間通信. In *Zhongguo gudai youyi shi: Xiuding ban* 中國古代郵驛史: 修訂版, edited by Liu Guangsheng 劉廣生 and Zhao Meizhuang 趙梅莊, 598–632. Beijing: Renmin youdian chubanshe, 1999.

Takakusu Junjirō 高楠順次郎 and Watanabe Kaigyoku 渡邊海旭, eds. *Taishō shinshū Daizōkyō* 大正新修大藏經. 85 vols. Tokyo: Taishō issaikyō kankōkai, 1924–29.

Theiss, Janet. "Love in a Confucian Climate: The Perils of Intimacy in Eighteenth-Century China." *Nan Nü* 11 (2009): 197–233.

Thraede, Klaus. *Grundzüge griechisch-römischer Brieftopik*. Zetemata 48. Munich: Beck, 1970.

Tian Xiaofei. *Beacon Fire and Shooting Star: The Literati Culture of the Liang (502–557)*. Cambridge, MA: Harvard University Press, 2007.

———. "The Twilight of the Masters: Masters Literature (*zishu*) in Early Medieval China." *Journal of the American Oriental Society* 126.4 (2006): 465–86.

Toynbee, Paget, ed. *Dantis Alagherii epistolae: The Letters of Dante*. Oxford: Clarendon, 1920.

Trapp, Michael, ed. *Greek and Latin Letters: An Anthology, with Translation*. Cambridge: Cambridge University Press, 2003.

Tsien Tsuen-hsuin 錢存訓. "Paper and Printing." In *Science and Civilisation in China*. Vol. 5, part 1, *Chemistry and Chemical Technology*. Cambridge: Cambridge University Press, 1985.

———. *Written on Bamboo and Silk: The Beginnings of Chinese Books and Inscriptions, Second Edition*. Chicago: University of Chicago Press, 2004.

———. "Zhi de qiyuan xinzheng: Shilun Zhanguo Qin jian zhong de zhi zi"

紙的起源信證: 試論戰國秦簡中的紙字. *Wenxian jikan* 文獻季刊 1 (2002): 4–11.

Trunz, Erich, and Hans Joachim Schrimpf, eds. *Goethes Werke: Hamburger Ausgabe in 14 Bänden*. Munich: Beck, 1981.

Vervoorn, Aat. "Friendship in Ancient China." *East Asian History* 27 (2004): 1–32.

Violi, Patrizia. "Letters." In *Discourse and Literature*, edited by Teun A. van Dijk, 149–68. Amsterdam: John Benjamins, 1985.

Wagner, Rudolf G. "Lebensstil und Drogen im Chinesischen Mittelalter." *T'oung Pao* 59 (1973): 79–178.

———. "The Original Structure of the Correspondence between Shih Hui-yuan and Kumārajīva." *Harvard Journal of Asiatic Studies* 31 (1971): 28–48.

Wang Ping. *The Age of Courtly Writing: "Wen xuan" Compiler Xiao Tong (501–531) and His Circle*. Leiden: Brill, 2012.

Wang Yao 王瑤. *Zhonggu wenren shenghuo* 中古文人生活. Shanghai: Tangdi chubanshe, 1953.

Wang Yunxi 王運熙 and Yang Ming 楊明. *Wei Jin Nanbeichao wenxue piping shi* 魏晉南北朝文學批評史. Shanghai: Shanghai guji chubanshe, 1989.

Wang Zhenping. "Speaking with a Forked Tongue: Diplomatic Correspondence between China and Japan, 238–608 A.D." *Journal of the American Oriental Society* 114.1 (1994): 23–32.

Watson, Burton, trans. "Cao Pi: Two Letters to Wu Zhi, Magistrate of Zhaoge." *Renditions* 41–42 (1994): 9–11.

Wen xuan 文選. Compiled by Xiao Tong 蕭統 (501–531). Shanghai: Shanghai guji chubanshe, 1986.

Wente, Edward, and Edmund S. Meltzer. *Letters from Ancient Egypt*. Atlanta, GA: Scholars Press, 1990.

Wenti mingbian xushuo 文體明辨序說 (1570). Compiled by Xu Shizeng 徐師曾 (1517–1580). Beijing: Renmin wenxue, 1962.

Wenxin diaolong zhu 文心雕龍註. Compiled by Fan Wenlan 范文瀾 (1891–1969). Beijing: Renmin wenxue chubanshe, 1958.

Wenzhang bianti xushuo 文章辨體序說 (1464). Compiled by Wu Na 吳訥 (1372–1457). Beijing: Renmin wenxue, 1962.

West, Andrew. "The Lost Game of Liubo." 2009–11. http://babelstone.blogspot.com/2009/05/lost-game-of-liubo-part-1-funerary.html (accessed June 2, 2012).

Whitaker, Ki P. K. "Some Notes on the Authorship of the Lii Ling / Su Wuu Letters." *Bulletin of the School of Oriental and African Studies* 15 (1953): 113–37, 566–87.

White, Peter. *Cicero in Letters: Epistolary Relations of the Late Republic.* Oxford: Oxford University Press, 2010.

Wong Siu-kit. *Early Chinese Literary Criticism.* Hong Kong: Joint Publishing, 1983.

Wong Siu-kit, Allan Chung-hang Lo, and Lam Kwong-tai, trans. *The Book of Literary Design.* Hong Kong: Hong Kong University Press, 1999.

Wright, Suzanne Elaine. "Visual Communication and Social Identity in Woodblock-Printed Letter Papers of the Late Ming Dynasty." PhD diss., Stanford University, 1999.

Wu Guangxing 吳光興. *Xiao Gang Xiao Yi nianpu* 蕭綱蕭繹年譜. Beijing: Shehui kexue wenxian chubanshe, 2006.

Wu Sujane. "The Biography of Lu Yun (262–303) in *Jin shu* 54." *Early Medieval China* 7 (2001): 1–38.

———. "Clarity, Brevity, and Naturalness: Lu Yun and His Works." PhD diss., University of Wisconsin–Madison, 2001.

Xinshu 新書. See Lau and Ching, *A Concordance to the "Jia Yi Xinshu."*

Xin Tang shu 新唐書. Compiled by Ouyang Xiu 歐陽修 (1007–1072) and Song Qi 宋祁 (998–1061). Beijing: Zhonghua shuju, 1975.

Xunzi 荀子. See Lau and Ching, *A Concordance to the "Xunzi."*

Yang Guobin and Zhou Zhenfu, trans. *Wenxin Diaolong: Dragon-Carving and the Literary Mind.* Beijing: Foreign Language Teaching and Research Press, 2003.

Yanshi jiaxun jijie 顏氏家訓集解. Compiled by Yan Zhitui 顏之推 (531–ca. 591), commentary by Wang Liqi 王利器. Beijing: Zhonghua shuju, 1993.

Yanzi chunqiu 晏子春秋. See Lau and Ching, *A Concordance to the "Yanzi chunqiu."*

Ye Fan 葉帆, Zhang Wu 張武, and Hua Hailin 華海林, eds. *Shuxin guanyongyu cidian* 書信慣用語詞典. Wuhan: Hubei cishu chubanshe, 1989.

Ye Youming 葉幼明, Bei Yuanchen 貝遠晨, and Huang Jun 黃鈞, eds. *Lidai shuxin xuan* 歷代書信選. Changsha: Renmin chubanshe, 1980.

Ye zhong ji 鄴中記. In *Congshu jicheng* 叢書集成. Shanghai: Shangwu chubanshe, 1937.

Yip, Terry Siu-han. "The Reception of *Werther* and the Rise of the Epistolary Novel in China." *Tamkang Review* 22.1–4 (1991–92): 287–304.

Yiwen leiju 藝文類聚. Compiled by Ouyang Xun 歐陽詢 (557–641). Shanghai: Shanghai guji chubanshe, 1965.

Yoshikawa Tadao 吉川忠夫 and Mugitani Kunio 麥谷邦夫, eds. *Zhengao jiaozhu* 真告校註. Translated by Zhu Yueli 朱越利. Beijing: Zhongguo shehui kexue chubanshe, 2006.

Yu Jiaxi 余嘉錫. "Han shi san kao" 寒食散考. In *Yu Jiaxi lunxue zazhu* 余嘉錫論學雜著, 181–226. Taipei: He Luo tushu chubanshe, 1976.

Yu Li. "A History of Reading in Late Imperial China, 1000–1800." PhD diss., The Ohio State University, 2003. http://etd.ohiolink.edu/send-pdf.cgi?osu1054655134 (accessed June 2, 2012).

Yu, Pauline. "Formal Distinctions in Chinese Literary Theory." In *Theories of the Arts in China*, edited by Susan Bush and Christian Murck, 28–53. Princeton: Princeton University Press, 1983.

Yu Shiling 俞士玲. "Lu Yun 'Yu xiong Pingyuan shu' zhaji yize" 陸雲〈與兄平原書〉札記一則. *Guji zhengli yanjiu xuekan* 古籍整理研究學刊 3 (1996): 47–48.

Yuefu shiji 樂府詩集. Compiled by Guo Maoqian 郭茂倩 (fl. 1264–69). Beijing: Zhonghua shuju, 1979.

Yunmeng Shuihudi Qin mu bianxiezu 雲夢睡虎地秦墓編寫組, ed. *Yunmeng Shuihudi Qin mu* 雲夢睡虎地秦墓. Beijing: Wenwu chubanshe, 1981.

Yutai xinyong jianzhu 玉臺新詠箋注. Compiled by Xu Ling 徐陵 (507–83), commentary by Wu Zhaoyi 吳兆宜 and Cheng Yanshan 程琰刪. Beijing: Zhonghua shuju, 1985.

Zach, Erwin von, trans. "Auszüge aus einem chinesischen Briefsteller." *Mitteilungen der Deutschen Gesellschaft für Natur- und Völkerkunde Ostasiens* 14.1 (1911): 27–72.

———, trans. *Die chinesische Anthologie: Übersetzungen aus dem "Wen hsüan."* Harvard-Yenching Institute Studies 18. Cambridge, MA: Harvard University Press, 1958.

———, trans. "Ein Briefwechsel in Versen: Zwei Gedichte von Po Chü-i und Yuan Chen." *Mitteilungen der Deutschen Gesellschaft für Natur- und Völkerkunde Ostasiens* 14.3 (1913): 197–227.

Zeng Li. "The Past Revisited: Popular Memory of the Cultural Revolution in Contemporary China." PhD diss., Northwestern University, 2008.

Zhan Xiuhui 詹秀惠. *Shishuo xinyu yufa tanjiu* 世說新語語法探究. Taipei: Taiwan xuesheng shuju, 1974.

Zhang Defang 張德芳. "Xuanquan Han jian zhong de 'Zhuanxin jian' kaoshi" 懸泉漢簡中的〈傳信簡〉考述. In *Chutu wenxian yanjiu 7* 出土文獻研究 第七輯, edited by Zhongguo wenwu yanjiusuo 中國文物研究所, 65–81. Shanghai: Shanghai guji chubanshe, 2005.

Zhang Mengxin 張夢新. *Zhongguo sanwen fazhan shi* 中國散文發展史. Hangzhou: Zhejiang daxue chubanshe, 1996.

Zhang Shaokang 張少康. *Wenxin diaolong yanjiu shi* 文心雕龍研究史. Beijing: Beijing daxue chubanshe, 2001.

Zhang Xiaoyan 張小豔. *Dunhuang shuyi yuyan yanjiu* 敦煌書儀語言研究. Beijing: Shangwu chubanshe, 2007.

Zhao Heping 趙和平. *Dunhuang xieben shuyi yanjiu* 敦煌寫本書儀研究. Taipei: Xinwenfeng chuban gongsi, 1993.

Zhao Shugong 趙樹功. *Zhongguo chidu wenxue shi* 中國尺牘文學史. Shijiazhuang: Hebei renmin chubanshe, 1999.

Zhongyao dacidian 中藥大辭典. Edited by Jiangsu xinyi xueyuan 江蘇新醫學院. Shanghai: Shanghai kexue jishu chubanshe, 1977.

Zhou yi 周易. See Lau and Ching, *A Concordance to the "Zhouyi."*

Zhou Yiliang 周一良. *Wei Jin Nanbeichao shi zhaji* 魏晉南北朝史札記. Beijing: Zhonghua shuju, 1985.

Zhou Yiliang and Zhao Heping 趙和平. *Tang Wudai shuyi yanjiu* 唐五代書儀研究. Beijing: Zhongguo shehui kexue chubanshe, 1996.

Zhou Zhongling 周鍾靈, Shi Xiaoshi 施孝適, and Xu Weixian 許惟賢, eds. *Hanfeizi suoyin* 韓非子索引. Beijing: Zhonghua shuju, 1982.

Zhou Zuoren 周作人. *Zhou Zuoren shuxin* 周作人書信. Hong Kong: Shiyong shuju, 1967.

———. *Zhou Zuoren wen leibian* 周作人文類編. Changsha: Hunan wenyi chubanshe, 1998.

Zhu Guangqian 朱光潛. "Du shu du" 讀書牘. *Yiwen zatan* 藝文雜談 (1981): 161–74.

Zhuangzi 莊子. See Lau and Ching, *A Concordance to the "Zhuangzi."*

Zott, Regine. "Die unzeitgemäßen Hundsposttage . . . : Fragen nach einer Brieftheorie." In *Wissenschaftliche Briefeditionen und ihre Probleme: Editionswissenschaftliches Symposion*, edited by Hans-Gert Roloff, 43–72. Berlin: Weidler, 1998.

Zou Zhenhuan 鄒振環. "Qingdai shuzha wenxian de fenlei yu shiliao jiazhi" 清代書札文獻的分類與史料價值. *Shilin* 史林 5 (2006): 175–84.

Zuo zhuan 左傳. See Lau and Ching, *A Concordance to the "Zuo zhuan."*

Zürcher, Erik. *The Buddhist Conquest of China: The Spread and Adaptation of Buddhism in Early Medieval China*. Leiden: Brill, 1959.

GLOSSARY-INDEX

References to individual letters, their writers, and addressees indicate the pages of the main text that quote or discuss this letter. In some cases the indexed term itself does not occur in the main text but in the corresponding endnote.

www.ingramcontent.com/pod-product-compliance
Lightning Source LLC
LaVergne TN
LVHW040158080826
844660LV00001B/22

* 9 7 8 0 2 9 5 9 9 2 7 7 8 *